Petrochemical Planet

Petrochemical Planet

Multiscalar Battles of

Industrial Transformation

ALICE MAH

DUKE UNIVERSITY PRESS
Durham and London
2023

© 2023 DUKE UNIVERSITY PRESS
This work is licensed under a Creative Commons Attribution-NonCommercial-NoDerivatives 4.0 International License, available at https://creativecommons.org/licenses/by-nc-nd/4.0/.
Printed in the United States of America on acid-free paper ∞
Project Editor: Michael Trudeau
Designed by A. Mattson Gallagher
Typeset in Untitled Serif and Univers LT Std
by Westchester Publishing Services

Library of Congress Cataloging-in-Publication Data
Names: Mah, Alice, [date] author.
Title: Petrochemical planet : multiscalar battles of industrial transformation / Alice Mah.
Description: Durham : Duke University Press, 2023. |
Includes bibliographical references and index.
Identifiers: LCCN 2023003693 (print)
LCCN 2023003694 (ebook)
ISBN 9781478025122 (paperback)
ISBN 9781478020141 (hardcover)
ISBN 9781478027126 (ebook)
ISBN 9781478093671 (ebook other)
Subjects: LCSH: Petroleum chemicals industry—Environmental aspects. | Environmental justice. | Environmental protection—International cooperation. | BISAC: NATURE / Environmental Conservation & Protection | SOCIAL SCIENCE / Anthropology / Cultural & Social
Classification: LCC TD195.P39 M34 2023 (print) | LCC TD195.P39 (ebook) | DDC 363.7—DC23/ENG/20230307
LC record available at https://lccn.loc.gov/2023003693
LC ebook record available at https://lccn.loc.gov/2023003694

Cover art: (*Front*) Flare from an oil platform off the coast of Angola, October 14, 2003. Photo by MARTIN BUREAU/AFP via Getty Images. (*Back*) Open sea. Photo by Righteous Anchor via Unsplash.

This title is freely available in an open access edition made possible by a generous contribution from the Leverhulme Trust. This project has received funding from the European Research Council (ERC) under the European Union's Horizon 2020 research and innovation program (Grant Agreement No. 639583), with additional funding from the Philip Leverhulme Prize.

CONTENTS

Abbreviations	vii
Preface	ix
Acknowledgments	xvii

	Introduction	1
1	**The Petrochemical Game of War**	25
2	**Enduring Toxic Injustice and Fenceline Mobilizations**	53
3	**Multiscalar Activism and Petrochemical Proliferation**	71
4	**The Competing Stakes of the Planetary Petrochemical Crisis**	95
5	**Petrochemical Degrowth, Decarbonization, and Just Transformations**	119
6	**Toward an Alternative Planetary Petrochemical Politics**	141

Notes	153
Bibliography	185
Index	207

ABBREVIATIONS

2-BE	2-Butoxyethanol
BP	British Petroleum
BPA	bisphenol A
BSR	Business for Social Responsibility
BTEX	benzene, toluene, ethylbenzene, and xylene
BTX	benzene, toluene, and xylene
CCS	carbon capture and storage
CDP	Carbon Disclosure Project
CEFIC	European Chemical Industry Council
CIEL	Center for International Environmental Law
CNOOC	China National Offshore Oil Corporation
COP21	United Nations Climate Change Conference (Paris, 2015)
COP26	United Nations Climate Change Conference (Glasgow, 2021)
COP27	United Nations Climate Change Conference (Sharm el-Sheikh, 2022)
COTC	crude-oil-to-chemicals
DDT	dichlorodiphenyltrichloroethane

EPCA	European Petrochemical Association
ESG	environmental, social, and governance
GAIA	Global Alliance for Incinerator Alternatives
GMO	genetically modified organisms
ICI	Imperial Chemical Industries
IEA	International Energy Agency
ILO	International Labour Organization
IP Week	International Petrochemical Week
IPCC	Intergovernmental Panel on Climate Change
LNG	liquified natural gas
MTBE	methyl tertiary butyl ether
NPRA	National Petroleum Refiners Association (United States)
OCAW	Oil, Chemical, and Atomic Workers (United States)
OECD	Organisation for Economic Co-operation and Development
PCB	polychlorinated biphenyls
PESTEL	political, economic, social, technological, ecological, and legal
PFAS	per- and polyfluoroalkyl substances
PFOA	perfluorooctanoic acid
PPE	personal protective equipment
PVC	polyvinyl chloride
PX	paraxylene
SABIC	Saudi Basic Industries Corporation
TEK	traditional ecological knowledge
VUCA	volatility, uncertainty, complexity, and ambiguity
WBCSD	World Business Council for Sustainable Development

PREFACE

While plastics are highly visible in everyday life, the petrochemicals that comprise them are less visible. Derived primarily from fossil fuels, petrochemicals are the building blocks of polymers, found in thousands of consumer products, from phones, cars, and computers to windows, food packaging, and medical equipment. Many petrochemicals are toxic.

Petrochemicals sound dirty, but they are also technical and confusing. Not many people know what they are exactly, or how they relate to oil, other kinds of chemicals, or plastics. A full understanding would take advanced knowledge of polymer science. An industry spokesperson once told me, with a sense of frustration: "You will not believe how many people I meet that say, 'Wah, petrochemicals, that must be the dirty stuff that makes the feathers of the ducks blue, the BP Deepwater Horizon thing.' We say, 'No, it's not, first of all, and secondly, did you know your iPhone contains petrochemicals and the windmill blades?'"[1] She failed to mention that the petrochemical 2-Butoxyethanol (or 2-BE for short) was an additive in the oil dispersant that was used in the 2010 Deepwater Horizon oil spill, and particularly toxic to aquatic life.[2]

The first time I saw a petrochemical plant up close was in April 2013. I was in New Orleans, doing research on labor struggles in the port, driving with a longshoreman to a crawfish boil at a seafarers' center along the Mississippi

River. We drove past fields, churches, and old plantations. Then, seemingly out of nowhere, we came across a massive petrochemical plant, metallic and looming. It felt like a scene out of a dystopian novel.

I was struck by how alive the plant was. For years, I had been researching the impacts of industrial decline and postindustrial change, including the toxic legacies of the abandoned chemical industry in Niagara Falls. But I had only ever tackled the ruins and embers of manufacturing.

As I soon learned, this was just one of 150 petrochemical plants clustered along an 85 mile stretch along the Mississippi River between New Orleans and Baton Rouge, infamously known as "Cancer Alley." The plants are located on former slave plantation land, which was sold to oil and chemical companies in the early and mid-twentieth century, attracted by cheap natural resources and low taxes. Since the 1980s, Cancer Alley has been at the forefront of environmental justice battles over high levels of toxic pollution in rural Black communities on the fenceline of industry. Yet for all these efforts, the toxic industrial landscape remains.

My introduction to Cancer Alley sparked the beginning of a new journey. Months later, I noticed similar petrochemical complexes, from a distance, along the maritime fringes of other port cities: Marseille, Liverpool, Antwerp. Most large petrochemical facilities are located in coastal regions, near to ports, for access to shipping lines. Tightly enclosed behind security gates, they resemble cities with tall towers and giant cylindrical storage tanks. Many have their own hospitals, fire brigades, and contractor villages. They flare and steam and crackle.

How do these petrochemical plants relate to the ports? How do they work? How are they regulated? And what drives their operations? Who are the main global corporate players? Who are the biggest polluters? How do the environmental justice movements in Cancer Alley compare with activism in different petrochemical communities around the world? These questions informed my next research project, "Toxic Expertise: Environmental Justice and the Global Petrochemical Industry," which ran from 2015 to 2020 and was funded by the European Research Council. It was a five-year multi-sited sociological study of the global petrochemical industry in relation to corporate social responsibility and environmental justice. This book is an attempt to bring together and to extend the myriad findings of the research, which spanned high-level industry meetings, petrochemical plant tours, and polluted communities in the United States, China, and Europe—the top three petrochemical-producing regions in the world.

Engaging with questions of environmental justice requires a recognition of the ground that you stand on and your relations with land, people, histories, and multispecies worlds. So too does ethnography as a practice. In this book, I draw on both traditions, albeit unconventionally, across multiple sites, scales, and perspectives. It is difficult to describe the ground that I stand on in relation to a complex, vast, and extensive global industry, but I will try. The only way I can find is circuitous.

I am a third-generation, mixed-race Chinese Canadian, and I grew up in a small forest-dependent town called Smithers in northern British Columbia on the unceded land of the Wet'suwet'en people. I am also a naturalized British citizen and have lived in Coventry, once known as the United Kingdom's "motor city," for the past decade. Despite my training as a sociologist, I have often felt uncomfortable about personal questions of identity. When I was a doctoral student at the London School of Economics and Political Science, researching the industrial decline of shipyards in Newcastle-upon-Tyne, chemical factories in Niagara Falls, and textile factories in Ivanovo in Russia, a professor once asked me what my "real story" was. He was trying to identify some aspect of my personal history that could explain my research interests. I resisted this line of questioning, responding that I had no personal ties to any of these places, and that my research was motivated by questions about the uneven geography of capitalist development. I cannot remember how the conversation ended, just the impression that I had provided an unsatisfactory answer. Since then, I have come to realize that the professor was right. The personal connection was not to specific places, as such, but to working-class experiences of deindustrialization. My maternal grandfather, of Irish-settler descent, was a millworker, and my mother spent her childhood moving from one mill town to another across Canada. They eventually settled in Mackenzie, a sawmill town in northern BC. Mackenzie went through decades of decline as a one-job town tied to the fortunes of the mill. When I visited my grandparents, aunts, uncles, and cousins in Mackenzie as a child, I found it depressing, infused with the smell of pulp and cigarettes. Somehow it was too close to look at directly.

This is just one story, though, a journey from the mill towns of northern BC to the abandoned chemical factories of Niagara Falls to the petrochemical plants of Cancer Alley. Perhaps it is a little too neat. There is another, more troubling personal story, which is perhaps more telling. Early in 2019, I was in my office at the University of Warwick, reading through Toxic Expertise researcher Thom Davies's field notes about resistance mobilizations over the construction of the Bayou Bridge oil pipeline in Cancer Alley.[3] As I searched for media articles about the pipeline, a related news story caught my attention: the Wet'suwet'en people in northern BC were demonstrating over the construction of the Coastal GasLink Pipeline, designed to cross 190 kilometers of their lands, including my hometown. The natural gas pipeline would carry fracked gas from northeast BC to the northwest coast for export to petrochemical markets in Asia. The Wet'suwet'en land defenders set up a blockade to prevent the pipeline construction and were forcibly removed from their territory by armed Canadian police officers, sparking solidarity protests from Indigenous groups and climate activists around the country. A rally was held in Smithers in January 2019 in support of the Wet'suwet'en people. It was a strange feeling to see photos of my hometown on the international news, embroiled in fierce battles over environmental justice, with the familiar snow-covered mountain in the background.

After reading about the Wet'suwet'en pipeline resistance movement, I started digging. I discovered a book called *Shared Histories* written by the geographer Tyler McCreary, who was in my brother's class at school, about the history of Wet'suwet'en and settler relations in Smithers.[4] I learned some disturbing things about the history of my hometown. I knew that the town was on Wet'suwet'en territory, but I knew little else. I found out that the house that I grew up in was part of a planned modernist subdivision built in the 1970s, which had displaced the Wet'suwet'en settlement known as "Indiantown" in Smithers. In all my years, I had never heard of Indiantown. It was a settlement that had grown on the fringes of Smithers since the 1920s, the only place where the town authorities permitted Wet'suwet'en people to live, and had high levels of poverty due to systemic discrimination, including a lack of access to basic public services such as waste collection. Indiantown was completely destroyed by town development between the 1960s and 1970s. The adjacent local elementary school that I attended was also part of this planned displacement, along with a companion Christian school, a senior citizen's home, and leafy cul-de-sacs, all designed to foster a middle-class sense of community and public safety. I actually felt sick reading about my childhood landscape in McCreary's book, as if the ground beneath me had sunk.

Smithers has an idyllic quality, nestled in a valley surrounded by mountains, glaciers, forests, canyons, lakes, and rivers, a thirteen-hour drive northeast from Vancouver. It was founded in 1913 as the divisional headquarters of the Grand Trunk Pacific Railway and incorporated as a town in 1967. My parents moved to Smithers in 1975, attracted by the idea of starting a family in a small town. My father came from suburban Toronto, venturing west, contrary to the expectations of his Chinese Canadian family, and he met my mother during a summer job in Mackenzie. They married young, and my father joined an accountancy firm in Smithers, while my mother stayed home to raise four children before finding work in the primary school. It was in this forest-valley town built on a swamp, teeming with folk and country music, where I gained a strong sense of place. I can still trace the contours of the valley in my mind, the way the snow crept down the mountain as winter approached, the winding dirt backroads and forest trails. But I also wanted to escape.

Smithers is a majority white town with a population of 5,300. It is located on Highway 16 between Prince George and Prince Rupert, a 725-kilometer corridor known as the "Highway of Tears" because dozens of Indigenous women have gone missing and been murdered along its length since the 1970s. Growing up, I often felt a sense of unease. There were so many judgments and assumptions in the public spaces of the town, and violence was never far from the surface. I did not encounter many incidents of explicit racism, despite being half Chinese, or at least I did not recognize them as such as the time. There were occasional barbed comments, but mostly I managed to ignore them. More often, I faced racist attitudes due to being mistaken for an Indigenous person. I will not recount these experiences here, as they never felt like my own stories to tell. They did give me some insights, though, into racism.

Despite the rhetoric of multiculturalism that was taught in the schools, there was tacit racism in the white settler community toward Indigenous people, and tensions between Smithers and the nearby Wet'suwet'en village, which was located on the reserve. One time, when I was about fifteen, a Wet'suwet'en feast was held in my high school, led by an Indigenous leader, a rare occasion for cultural exchange. The leader's opening speech was full of accusations against the white settler community, in ways of speaking that I had not heard before. I do not recall any of my classmates or teachers talking about it afterward; they just shared the food and went on with their day. Looking back, I wish I had asked more questions. It is clear to me now that the whole history of the settlement of the town, like many other communities across Canada and around the world, is one of environmental injustice.

This book asks difficult questions about entanglement and complicity in the fraught relationships between petrochemicals, toxicity, injustice, and our planet. The violence of settler colonialism, systemic racism, and dispossession runs deep through the reckless global expansion of toxic and wasteful petrochemicals and the unfolding climate catastrophe. As the chapters in this book will detail, this violence is founded on willful ignorance, half-truths, and detached justifications. Confronting these questions has compelled me to move into further uncomfortable ground, through "studying up" and examining corporate petrochemical worldviews and logics, with the aim of identifying levers for change. It has not been an easy journey to home in on the sources of injury and destruction, only to find that they are even worse than I had imagined, deeply rooted in a calculated war mentality.

Throughout the waves of the COVID-19 pandemic, I have sometimes felt as though a snake was encircling my head, slowly tightening its grip. This book has been an ordeal to write, getting under my skin and giving me nightmares. It has caused me to question long-held beliefs about human nature. I like to believe in the possibilities for transcendence, in a Buddhist sense, and do not believe in the idea of "evil" in this world. It has been a difficult position to sustain. Yet this book is not only about conflict and injustice; it is also about the possibilities for repair through interconnection, across multiple sites and scales, from the personal to the planetary, and from the human to the forests and mountains.

My search for interconnection through this project led me beyond North America and Europe to China. Over the past two decades, China has emerged as the largest petrochemical producer and consumer in the world, and it has also faced tremendous problems with toxic pollution. When I first designed the Toxic Expertise project in 2014, anti-PX (paraxylene) protests were dominating the news headlines in China, peaceful mass "strolls" across cities and regions throughout the country, with people protesting the development of petrochemical projects. In subsequent years, the anti-PX protests subsided, under the tighter societal controls of Xi Jinping, and the research brought us instead to heavily polluted but less controversial petrochemical peri-urban areas in Nanjing and Guangzhou. There were many differences between these petrochemical areas in China and Cancer Alley in Louisiana, but there were also striking parallels, as this book will discuss. There was also a more personal connection. The city of Guangzhou in south China, a major petrochemical hub, is located only a few hours' drive away from the village where my grandfather's family came from, a place I had never been before.

In March 2018, I accompanied Toxic Expertise researcher Loretta Lou on a trip to Guangzhou. We walked along the dirt roads of the petrochemical villages on the outskirts of the city, talking with local migrant workers, food vendors, and villagers. As Lou has evocatively described, the villagers took pains to "unnotice" the pollution in their everyday lives, faced with few other choices.[5] The air was so noxious that I lost my sense of smell for weeks. On our travels from Guangzhou to another petrochemical city in the region, we stopped to visit my family's ancestral village. Although I had no living relatives there, remarkably this rice-producing village was still inhabited by the Mah clan. There was something profoundly restorative about that journey of return. It was weirdly familiar, with a veneer of tranquility overlaying a century of trauma and rupture, echoing the unease that I once felt in my hometown.

The notion of return brings me back to the present moment, in my adopted city of Coventry, a place of incredible diversity and hidden gems, which has often been stigmatized in the national public imagination as a concrete cityscape marked by social deprivation. Since the start of the pandemic, like many other people, I have come to appreciate the parks, community spaces, and uncrowded streets of the city, but I have also been saddened to observe the devastating local impacts of the global health crisis on gender-based violence, food and fuel poverty, social inequalities, unemployment, and mental health.

The ground that we stand on is constantly shifting. This is a lesson of contingency, which opens up possible worlds. What started off as a book about global environmental injustice and the toxic impacts of the petrochemical industry has slowly expanded into a meditation on the wider stakes of ecological crisis, including the climate implications of doing research. The urgency of the task has propelled me to swing between registers of despair and hope, writing during the pandemic, which has magnified existing social and environmental inequalities. Within the context of profound ecological crisis, this book examines the possibilities of radical and just industrial transformations, despite the many barriers. This involves recognizing obligations to past, present, and future generations, and the consequences of the stories that we tell ourselves.

ACKNOWLEDGMENTS

This book is the result of several years of research into the global petrochemical industry, environmental justice, and what I have come to call the "planetary petrochemical crisis." It would not have been possible without the support of numerous people.

First, I would like to thank the Toxic Expertise team for contributing to the research that informs this book and for many rewarding collaborations: David Brown, Thom Davies, Lorenzo Feltrin, Patricio Flores Silva, India Holme, Calvin Jephcote, Alexandra Kviat, Loretta Lou, Thomas Verbeek, Chris Waite, and Xinhong Wang. I also extend thanks to the Toxic Expertise international advisory board for offering valuable advice about fieldwork, ethics, methodology, and intellectual framing: Carol Adams, Barbara Allen, Shaun Breslin, Ben Boer, Phil Brown, Robert Bullard, Hong Dayong, Scott Frickel, Jennifer Gabrys, Christelle Gramalgia, Jennifer Holdaway, Hannah Jones, Peter C. Little, Miguel Ángel López-Navarro, Anna Lora-Wainwright, Goldie Osuri, Gwen Ottinger, Peter Phillimore, Bryan Tilt, and Gordon Walker.

Many thanks are due to all the research participants who shared their experiences and perspectives and helped to shape my understandings of diverse contexts, issues, and struggles. I would also like to acknowledge the inspiring multiscalar activism of individuals and movements around the world who are fighting for environmental justice.

Chapter 5 is a revised version of work that was originally published in my article "Ecological Crisis, Decarbonisation, and Degrowth: The Dilemmas of Just Petrochemical Transformations," *Stato e Mercato*, no. 121 (2021): 51–78. Some of the arguments in the book extend on work that was originally published in my article "Future-Proofing Capitalism: The Paradox of the Circular Economy for Plastics," *Global Environmental Politics* 21, no. 2 (2021): 121–42.

I am grateful to Gisela Fosado at Duke University Press for unwavering support and enthusiasm for this project, and to Alejandra Mejía for helpful editorial assistance. Many thanks to two anonymous readers of the book, who provided valuable and insightful comments, which improved the manuscript greatly.

Several of the key ideas for this book were first presented at conferences and workshops, most notably in the following invited talks: the Environmental Justice: Looking Back, Looking Forward conference, University of Sydney, 2017; the Science in Public Annual Conference, Cardiff, 2018; the "Chemical" Workshop, University College London, 2019; the Living in a Plastic Age lecture series, Goethe University, Frankfurt, 2019; the virtual British Sociological Association Annual Conference, 2021; the "Profiting while the Planet Burns" Independent Social Research Foundation workshop, City University, London, 2022; the Society for the Advancement of Socio-Economics Annual Conference, Amsterdam, 2022; and the Deindustrialization and the Politics of Our Time annual conference, Bochum, Germany, 2022. I would like to thank all the academics and students who have engaged with my work and helped to develop my thinking.

Thank you to Claire Blencowe and Akwugo Emejulu for being early close readers and for encouraging me to delve deeper into themes of war and racial capitalism. Thanks to many academics, colleagues, and friends who gave helpful feedback and support at different stages of the research: Gurminder Bhambra, Philippe Blanchard, Nerea Calvillo, Nickie Charles, Amy Clarke, Agnes Czajka, Sandra Eckert, Steve Fuller, Manuela Galetto, Nick Gane, Amy Hinterberger, Virinder Kalra, Mouzayian Khalil-Babatunde, Ulf Liebe, Noortje Marres, Linsey McGoey, Maria do Mar Pereira, Lynne Pettinger, Nirmal Puwar, Brigit Ramsingh, Leon Sealey-Huggins, Sanjay Sharma, Alex Smith, John Solomos, Celine Tan, Nathaniel Tkacz, George Ttoouli, and Noel Whiteside.

Thanks so much to my parents, Eric and Kathy Mah, and to my siblings Alex, Erica, and Jennifer Mah, for your love, care, and generosity. To Colin Stephen and Lucian Stephen-Mah, thanks for your "infinity and beyondest" love and support, for your faith in the power of books, and for joining me on this ecological journey.

    I gratefully acknowledge that the research leading to this book received funding from the European Research Council (ERC) under the European Union's Horizon 2020 research and innovation program (Grant Agreement No. 639583) and the Leverhulme Trust (Philip Leverhulme Prize).

Introduction

The global petrochemical industry is at a crossroads. As an essential modern industry but also a major polluter, it faces threats to its core business. Petrochemicals surround us in thousands of everyday products, yet they pose health and climate risks across every stage of their lifecycle. On the eve of the COVID-19 pandemic, the petrochemical industry was facing mounting public pressure to address issues of climate crisis, plastic waste, and toxic pollution. The coronavirus pandemic and the historic crude oil crash of 2020 turned the industry upside down, temporarily casting sustainability issues to the sidelines. If the industry had been preparing for a fossil fuel endgame scenario already, what would the future after the pandemic look like in the global "Race to Zero"?[1] This book argues that a profound planetary industrial transformation is underway, challenging the reigning age of plastics and fossil fuels, and opening new but tenuous possibilities for ecological alternatives. Century-old corporate and state alliances are being shaken as oil and chemical giants fight battles on multiple fronts to retain their power.

Drawing on multi-sited research on the global petrochemical industry between 2015 and 2022, this book examines multiscalar battles over the stakes of transforming a toxic yet essential industry. The petrochemical industry has long viewed the world in terms of militaristic corporate strategies: to conquer markets across its value chain, deny responsibility for harm, and mitigate risk. In response, polluted communities living adjacent to industrial facilities, known as "fenceline communities," have fought numerous battles with companies for recognition and redress.[2] One of the key battles has been over the issue of social and ecological "expendability": Whose voices and lives matter?[3] Following global patterns of environmental injustice, the burdens of toxic petrochemical pollution are unequally distributed, heavily concentrated in low-income, working-class, and minority ethnic communities living on the fenceline of industry.[4] For the past half century of environmental justice struggles, we have witnessed a "double movement," Polanyi's concept underlying the "great transformation" of the Industrial Revolution, between the destructive forces of capitalism and the salving counterforces of society.[5]

David and Goliath metaphors of capitalist conflict abound, but they have taken us only so far. Despite decades of struggle, fenceline disputes over petrochemical pollution have rarely posed fundamental threats to industry. Yet the pressure for industrial transformation is intensifying, coming not only from activists and regulators but also from investors and shifting geopolitical interests. Across our petrochemical planet, we face existential questions about societal and ecological values: What is "essential" or "expendable"? What is harmful or healthy? What is just and what are the alternatives? This book grapples with these important questions, building on debates in environmental justice, corporate sustainability, just transitions, degrowth, and anti-colonial ecologies.

A key contribution of this book is the concept of "multiscalar activism," a form of collective resistance that makes connections across diverse issues, sites, and scales of political struggle. Multiscalar activism against the hegemonic power of the global oil, petrochemical, and plastics complex spans interconnected issues of environmental justice, climate, pollution, health, extractivism, land rights, workers' rights, systemic racism, and toxic colonialism—across local, urban, regional, national, and planetary sites and scales. It has the capacity to raise the public visibility of separate campaigns, but it can also pose political risks. The idea of multiscalar activism draws on Antonio Gramsci's account of "wars of position" to describe cultural struggles between hegemonic and counter-hegemonic groups, and Stuart Hall's related analysis of "articulation," the process of making connections between different elements to form a "unity," with the strategic aim of shaping political interventions in particular social formations.[6]

This book examines the obstacles as well as the openings for critical interventions in the complex, adaptive, and destructive petrochemical industry. Corporate executives routinely rally their troops in "a war to stay in the game," amid perceived threats from environmental regulators and activists.[7] Industrial transformation toward a more just and sustainable planet is necessary, but it will not happen without a battle.

Petrochemical Planet

When I think of planets, I think of a visit to the Science Museum in London with my son when he was five years old, just before the start of the coronavirus pandemic, and his delight in watching the giant holograms of planets in the space exhibit and glimpsing the Earth from the International Space Station at the IMAX theater. Until recently, as an adult going about my everyday life, researching sociology rather than geology or archaeology or astronomy, I rarely reflected on the planetary facts that my son now finds so fascinating: the Earth is 4.54 billion years old; there have been five mass extinctions; the modern human species is about 300,000 years old; and humans began to make permanent settlements only around 10,000 years ago. Deep time scales are difficult to grasp and have an air of unreality about them. Yet at the start of a sixth mass extinction, in the face of melting ice caps, raging forest fires, deadly toxic pollution, and climate breakdown, it is becoming clear that deep-time thinking should not be just an abstraction. On the contrary, it speaks to urgent questions about planetary survival.

Over the past few years, there has been a turn toward planetary thinking in the environmental humanities and social sciences. Postcolonial scholar Gayatri Chakravorty Spivak makes a distinction between the globe and the planet, in the context of rapidly accelerating globalization. For Spivak, the globe is an "abstract ball covered in latitudes and longitudes," which is "in our computers" and "the logo of the World Bank."[8] By contrast, "the planet is in the species of alterity, belonging to another system; and yet we inhabit it, indeed are it." In this context, Spivak proposes that we use "the planet to overwrite the globe."[9] Historian Dipesh Chakrabarty makes a similar comparison between the global and the planetary, but more in relation to deep time.[10] For Chakrabarty, the global relates to capitalism: to ideas of humanity linked to modernity, progress, equality, democracy, and freedom; and to the boundaries of recorded human history. The idea of the planetary challenges the global narrative of capitalist modernity by recognizing the role of humans as geological agents in the cumulative history of the Earth. Chakrabarty's framing of the planetary engages with political theorist William Connelly's influential work on planetary processes of change in complex nonhuman systems, and how understanding these processes could provide insights for changing capitalist systems.[11]

This book draws attention to the material basis of the petrochemical planet and to the societal, political, economic, colonial, and ecological implications of pollution. In *Pollution Is Colonialism*, Max Liboiron proposes the concept of "plastics as Land" to underscore how multiple species live inextricably alongside plastics, as part of the entangled fabric of modern ecosystems, rather than thinking of plastics as only doing harm.[12] Many organisms in the ocean form synergistic relationships with microplastics, they note, and human lives have been saved with endocrine-disrupting plastic blood bags and medical tubes.[13] This poignant reflection highlights the complex dilemmas of living in a toxic and interdependent world. But despite the problem of entanglement, and with careful attention to the ethical challenges, I do want to focus on petrochemical harm, both as a systemic problem of capitalism, colonialism, and environmental injustice, and as a call for radical industrial transformation.

My analysis of the petrochemical planet combines the dynamics of global capitalism and toxic colonialism with planetary deep time: the planet enmeshed in petrochemicals, which are quintessential fossil fuel creations of the modern industrial era; and the existential threat of escalating petrochemical expansion to multispecies life on Earth. Petrochemicals are ubiquitous, forming the building blocks of 95 percent of all manufactured goods, including plastics, rubbers, solvents, fertilizers, and other synthetic materials.[14] Petrochemicals are also toxic, accumulate in bodies and ecosystems, and pose a significant threat to the climate.[15] Toxic petrochemical exposures are associated with a range of health problems, including cancer, neurological damage, reproductive disorders, and other diseases. The petrochemical industry is the largest industrial consumer of fossil fuels, the third largest industrial emitter of greenhouse gases, and one of the top four "hard-to-abate" industrial sectors (alongside iron/steel, cement, and aluminum). It has considerable "carbon lock-in" due to its long investment cycles, embedded infrastructure, and societal dependence.[16] Some 99 percent of petrochemicals are derived from fossil fuels.[17]

Petrochemicals are produced through an industrial process called "cracking": using extreme heat and pressure to break down heavy hydrocarbons into lighter hydrocarbons. Originally a satellite of the oil, gas, and chemical industries, the petrochemical industry emerged as a powerful industry in its own right during the Second World War, fueled by unprecedented wartime demand for synthetic rubber and polymerized high-octane gasoline.[18] Since then, the industry has expanded to nearly every corner of the globe in its insatiable quest to create and dominate new petrochemical markets. Many petrochemical products have become "essential" to modern life and are found in medical equipment, computers, building insulation, and household appliances, but the biggest petrochemical market is for plastics (80 percent), particularly the most wasteful kind: plastic packaging, which accounts for 40 percent of global plastics production by volume.[19]

Unsustainable growth in petrochemical production shows no signs of abating (see figure I.1), despite the global momentum to address plastic pollution and climate change. According to the International Energy Agency (IEA), petrochemicals will be the main driver of oil demand during the energy transition, predicted to rise from 14 percent today to 45 percent by 2050.[20] Analysts from the IEA expect continual petrochemical growth due to rising global plastics demand and new markets for green technologies.[21] However, IEA market forecasts are skewed to overestimate future oil demand, thus perpetuating fossil fuel investments.[22] Indeed, anticipating these trends, many oil majors have started to branch further into petrochemicals.[23] In the business-as-usual scenario of global petrochemical growth, the amount of plastic entering the ocean each year is predicted to rise from 11 million metric tons per year in 2020 to 29 million annually by 2040.[24] Meanwhile, the levels of chemical and plastic pollution have already exceeded planetary boundaries.[25] We are facing a planetary petrochemical crisis, which is underpinned by two opposing dynamics: the escalating threat of the petrochemical industry to planetary life, and the threat of ecological crisis for the future of petro-capitalism.

In a guide to long-term thinking about how nuclear engineers envision the far-off future of the Earth, anthropologist Vincent Ialenti asks: How could we signal to future species that nuclear waste is dangerous? What recognizable signs, outside language, could create such a warning?[26] An analogy could be made with petrochemicals, which are toxic, bioaccumulate,

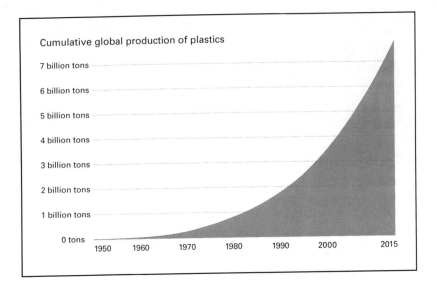

Figure I.1. Cumulative global plastics production, 1950 to 2015. Plastics production refers to the production of polymer resin and fibers. Source: Geyer, Jambeck, and Law, "Production, Use, and Fate of All Plastics."

and persist in the environment, seemingly forever, at least in human timescales.[27] The problem is not one of singular concentration, but precisely one of entanglement and proliferation across the materiality of the planet itself. Plastics will break down eventually, and so too will nuclear waste, beyond the wreckage of the sixth mass extinction. Some find planetary deep-time thinking terrifying, but I find it oddly grounding. Confronting existential questions about the future of life on the planet puts the present moment of ecological crisis into sharp relief.

The planetary petrochemical crisis raises profound ethical questions about responsibility, complicity, and resistance within unjust systems. London's Science Museum, for example, has come under scrutiny from climate activists for taking funding from fossil fuel companies.[28] From a global vantage point, the edifice of the petrochemical planet seems unbreakable, built on the entrenched beliefs and complex systems of capitalism, colonialism, and modern science and technology. There are many different words to describe the nature of this edifice: racial capitalism; fossil capitalism; petrocapitalism; carbon capitalism; extractivism; toxic colonialism; and waste colonialism—to name a few, which together convey the intimate connections between capitalism, colonialism, racism, and fossil fuel dependence. The petrochemical industry is a paradigmatic example of capitalism and colonialism in their most parasitic forms, constantly expanding to create more capacity and demand for toxic and wasteful products, inflicting harm on vulnerable communities and ecosystems. It is sustained through the exponential proliferation of petrochemicals around the planet, driven by the global imperatives of perpetual economic growth and consumer capitalism. From a planetary perspective, however, the petrochemical edifice is unstable, and despite appearances, it is showing signs of rupture.

Corporate Petrochemical Worldviews

When you enter the corporate world of the petrochemical industry, one of the first things that you encounter is a flowchart of the petrochemical value chain. "Petrochemicals make things happen" is the title of one of the most widely circulated flowcharts, produced by Petrochemicals Europe, an industry sector of the European Chemical Industry Council (CEFIC).[29] At the bottom are the raw material feedstocks: crude oil and natural gas. Stacked above are the refined gases and the petrochemical building blocks, divided into two main categories: olefins and aromatics. From these sprout branches of refined chemicals and polymers, culminating in stylized images of consumer end products along the top: smartphones, paints, bicycles, balloons.

Some petrochemical flowcharts include different details, such as the alternative feedstocks of coal and biomass. Others invert the perspective, with the upstream fossil fuels on top. But by and large, each flowchart follows the same script. Another popular petrochemical flowchart, produced by a market analytics company, highlights the "vital" role of petrochemicals, inviting viewers to "discover the chain that the goods we consume follow."[30] For corporate representatives, the flowchart serves as a reminder of their dominant place in the complex system. For everyone else, it conveys a key political message: petrochemicals are essential for everyday life.

The petrochemical flowchart is a process map. Like other maps, it is based on the politics of knowledge and power. According to Timothy Mitchell, the map "signifies the massive production of knowledge, the accuracy of calculation, and the entire politics based upon a knowledge of population and territory that Foucault characterizes as governmentality, the characteristic power of the modern state."[31] This resonates with James Scott's argument that modern statecraft produced "maps that, when allied with state power, would enable much of the reality that they depicted to be remade."[32]

At first, I puzzled over the petrochemical flowchart, daunted by its intricate webs and unfamiliar chemical names. Then, slowly, it dawned on me: the petrochemical flowchart offered a useful guide to the terrain of petrochemical profit-making, both through what it included and through what it left out. Yes, it was complex, but it was not indecipherable. And not all the petrochemicals it covered were essential for everyday life.

As I followed the petrochemical value chain across its different sites and controversies, I started to highlight particularly toxic parts on the flowchart with sticky notes. First, there were the toxic gases: phosgene, so deadly that it has extremely high corporate barriers to entry, used in the production of foams and as a chemical weapon during World War I; and hydrogen cyanide, used in nylon, nail polish, gold mining, and by the Nazis in the gas chambers. Second, there were the BTX (benzene, toluene, and xylene) compounds, derivatives, and applications—the kind of things people use every day, such as polystyrene, polyester, and bisphenol A (BPA), variously linked to cancer, reproductive illnesses, and numerous other health impacts. Third, there were the flexible plastics including phthalates and other plasticizers, used in flexible polyvinyl chloride (PVC), found in pipes, flooring, and construction; these are linked to endocrine disruption and are legally banned in the United States and Europe in children's toys. This was just the beginning.

Glancing at a petrochemical flowchart on my office wall, a visiting chemist commented that it was in fact a highly idealized representation. It was missing some of the most toxic parts, such as the heaviest crude oil residue, which never makes it into the refining process. He drew me a diagram of its typical molecular structure. I added another sticky note labeled "heavy, heavy crude" to the bottom of the flowchart.

Through simplified flowcharts highlighting the essential role of petrochemicals in everyday life, the industry conceals the destructiveness of its real-world operations. The relentless expansion of the petrochemical industry is systemically linked to the violence of human and ecological plunder. Sometimes the violence is overt: murders of environmental activists in resource frontiers; deadly explosions at chemical factories; repression of protests over petrochemical pollution; and devastation of wildlife and ecosystems. More often, petrochemical violence manifests in the everyday "slow violence" of toxic pollution, "a violence of delayed destruction that is dispersed across time and space, an attritional violence that is typically not viewed as violence at all."[33]

My analysis of corporate petrochemical worldviews takes inspiration from the work of James Scott on "seeing like a state" and James Ferguson on "seeing like an oil company."[34] Scott's study of the logics of modern statecraft in utopian state social-engineering schemes examined why these schemes failed in practice when confronted with the complexities of "real, functioning social order."[35] According to Scott, these reductive logics applied equally to global capitalism. Ferguson countered this claim with the example of capital investment patterns in African mineral resource extraction, particularly oil, which frequently bypassed national grids of legibility and concentrated in highly risky countries with political instability. My research follows Scott by juxtaposing the logics of the petrochemical industry with their messy social consequences, and it follows Ferguson by focusing on dynamics within global capitalism that contradict societal expectations.

The petrochemical industry is a slippery object of study, located at the intersection of the upstream oil and gas industry and the downstream refining, chemicals, and plastics industries. The major players work across different parts of the value chain; some are vertically integrated oil companies like ExxonMobil and Chinese state-owned Sinopec, while others are multinational chemical companies, like BASF and Dow. The industry is dominated by a small number of powerful firms with a history of anticompetitive practices and lack of transparency.[36] It relies on complex global supply chains, which are rooted in histories of military and colonial supply lines.[37] Deborah Cowen details how the invention of the global supply chain was based on the old art of military logistics, as a "banal management science—a science that was born of war—in the recasting of the economies of life and death."[38] The global petrochemical industry and its ways of seeing were also born of war, legacies that endure. The operational logic of the industry is militaristic, guided by efforts to gain geopolitical advantage, navigate risk and complexity, and annihilate opposition. Toxicity is deftly hidden behind arsenals of multiscale expertise, from the geopolitical to the molecular, and within multiple frameworks, from technological to financial and legal. Corporate responsibility is avoided at all costs.

Both value and supply chains are vital for understanding the way the petrochemical industry works. These chains overlap, with subtle differences. Value chains include all the activities that add value in the lifecycle of a product. They are fundamentally processes for profit maximization. By contrast, supply chains are networks of production and distribution between a company and its suppliers. The petrochemical industry uses supply chains to transport its materials and to offload its waste.

INTRODUCTION

When confronted with public criticism, the petrochemical industry often deflects attention downstream along its supply chain. As one industry representative remarked on a public tour of the Fawley ExxonMobil petrochemical plant in the UK: "If you see a sulfur tanker sometimes dripping a bit of yellow stuff behind it, which is totally harmless but unsightly, it's come from us, but it's the sulfuric acid industry."[39] In other words, the sulfuric acid industry bears responsibility for the petrochemical industry's waste. Another corporate executive at a plastics conference in Antwerp blamed transporters for the heaps of tiny plastic pellets known as "nurdles" that wash up on industrial port shorelines.[40]

Yet the petrochemical industry is protective of its value chain, with a long history of concealing and denying the harms of its toxic products. At the training workshops I attended on petrochemical markets, industry representatives lamented the decline of profitable toxic plastic markets, such as polystyrene and BPA, due to bans, regulations, and public controversies.[41] I also observed how the industry protects its value chain through continually reinventing itself, seeking new technological solutions to its own problems, from "innovative" circular economy projects to green chemistry and sustainable packaging. A corporate executive at a petrochemical industry conference in 2016 reflected: "There are critical issues that we are facing as an industry. We became the bad guys; we became the non-sexy industry. We are not fashionable nowadays. But if well-addressed and properly debated, we can find potentially alternative solutions."[42]

The idea of industry proposing technological solutions to its own environmental problems is based on the modern belief in the power of technological innovation. It exemplifies what philosophy of science scholar Isabelle Stengers called the "techno-industrial capitalist path" to describe how the chemical company Monsanto promoted genetically modified organisms (GMO) in the 1990s as an innovative and risk-free "solution" to world hunger.[43] Industry leaders concealed industry-backed scientific studies about the risks of GMO crops to pesticide resistance in insects. Their true motivations were to profit through commodifying agriculture.[44] Stengers's critique of the techno-industrial capitalist path echoes Ulrich Beck's observations about the failure of techno-scientific rationality within what he calls "risk society." Beck argued that "the sciences are entirely incapable of reacting adequately to civilizational risks, since they are prominently involved in the origin and growth of those very risks."[45]

Driven by the endless pursuit of profit, the global petrochemical industry has an imperialist logic of continual expansion and speculation, akin to other extractive industries within global capitalism. The industry also holds a deep-rooted belief in the power of science and technology to generate profit as well as to fix problems, which it shares with other modern, technology-based industries.[46] However, the petrochemical industry is also distinctive, poised between upstream and downstream players, ubiquitous yet hidden across complex global value and supply chains, and at the nexus of overlapping social and ecological crises.

Petrochemical industry plans for perpetual toxic expansion have not yet failed, unlike Scott's state social-engineering schemes. However, like Scott's "state simplifications," corporate petrochemical logics are also simplifications, despite their basis in navigating complex systems. In the real world, the petrochemical industry interacts with multiple other complex social, political, economic, and ecological systems. While the ecological crisis intensifies, the industry is facing existential threats to its future survival. As Ferguson observes, "New times bring new dangers, and new dangers require new tools for critical analysis."[47]

The Resonance of Environmental Justice

This book examines the oil, petrochemical, and plastics complex in terms of a multiscalar, planetary battle for environmental justice, with various points of articulation and struggle. It draws inspiration from a diverse range of scholarship and activism within environmental justice studies, particularly critical environmental justice studies and Indigenous and anti-colonial environmental justice studies.[48] Julie Sze writes that the "expanding resonance of the environmental justice movement framework is a concrete response to intensifying and interconnected conditions of pollution and inequality.... That perspective matters now more than ever, as communities face hydra-headed assaults."[49] In the spirit of expanding resonance, this book explores themes of interconnection across different movements, while recognizing the importance of diverse local and national contexts and struggles. It adopts a critical environmental justice studies perspective by focusing on enduring issues of systemic toxic injustice, rooted in long histories of racial capitalism and colonialism, but it also seeks to find pragmatic possibilities for ecological alternatives.

The petrochemical industry has a key role within the wider history of the environmental justice movement in the United States, which emerged in the 1980s in response to disproportionate toxic waste dumping and environmental hazards in predominantly low-income Black communities. Many of the first major environmental justice cases in the United States relate to the environmental health impacts of the petrochemical industry, from the protests over the PBC (polychlorinated biphenyls) landfill site in Warren County, North Carolina, in 1982, to the contamination of water with DDT (dichlorodiphenyltrichloroethane) in Triana, Alabama, in the 1980s, to the grassroots struggles over toxic petrochemical pollution in the region nicknamed Cancer Alley in Louisiana, which began in the 1980s and continue to this day.[50]

The problem of petrochemical pollution was also a defining issue in the mainstream US environmental movement of the 1960s and 1970s. Rachel Carson's publication of *Silent Spring* in 1962 brought international attention to the toxic implications of pesticides on ecosystems and public health.[51] In 1978, the discovery of a toxic chemical dump buried in the residential community of Love Canal, New York, was a pivotal disaster that shaped environmental policy in the United States, leading to the creation of the Superfund Act of 1980, national legislation that taxed corporations to clean up hazardous waste sites.[52] Arguably, the significance of the petrochemical industry as a serious perceived public threat to environmental health and safety was surpassed only by the threat of the nuclear industry at the height of the Cold War.[53] Public concern over these risks has changed over the past half century, with periods of outrage and alarm following disasters as well as with periods of relative calm. With rising concerns about the plastic, toxic, and climate crises in recent years, the petrochemical industry has come under scrutiny again.

This book situates the environmental injustices of the global petrochemical industry within a multiscalar approach, including a wider temporal perspective than it is typically framed by, within the context of five hundred years of colonialism, and in relation to planetary deep time. This may sound odd, given that the first petrochemical plants were developed only a century ago, built in order to find uses for the waste by-products of oil refining, and given that petrochemicals rose to become a major global industry only after the Second World War.[54] Even the use of fossil fuels as the engine of industrial growth is a modern capitalist phenomenon. Yet there are two reasons why a deeper temporal perspective on petrochemical injustice is warranted, one which relates to history, and another which relates to the future.

First, as many Indigenous scholars and activists contend, environmental injustice did not begin with the discovery of fossil fuels; rather, it can be traced to first contact throughout five hundred years of colonialism.[55] Indigenous scholar and activist Dina Gilio-Whitaker argues that settler colonialism is itself a structure of environmental injustice, and she criticizes dominant environmental justice approaches for failing to address issues of decolonization. According to Gilio-Whitaker, environmental justice for Indigenous peoples "must be capable of a political scale beyond the homogenizing, assimilationist, capitalist State. It must conform to a model that can frame issues in terms of their colonial condition and can affirm decolonization as a potential framework within which environmental justice can be made available to them."[56] This relates to the insightful observations by Kathryn Yusoff and Myles Lennon that energy transitions debates focus too narrowly on the history of fossil capitalism without acknowledging that the fossil fuel transition was made possible by first using human labor as a form of energy under slavery.[57]

David Pellow's framework of critical environmental justice studies also highlights the limitations of dominant environmental justice approaches that seek paths to justice through the state, particularly in the US context of state-sanctioned racial violence. The critical environmental justice studies framework is based on the idea of "indispensability," which builds on the work of critical race and ethnic studies scholar John Marquez on "racial expendability" to argue that, within a white-dominated society, people of color are typically viewed as expendable. Furthermore, it is an intersectional approach that "recognizes that social inequality and oppression in all forms intersect, and that actors in the more-than-human world are subjects of oppression and frequently agents of social change."[58] The role of scale in the production and possible resolution of environmental injustices is also central, not only in terms of size and space but also in terms of historical time, taking into consideration the European conquest of Indigenous lands and the enslavement of people of African descent.[59] Within this perspective, "environmental injustice is a form of violence created through systems of racial capitalism, settler colonialism, and enslavement that are sustained by the state."[60]

The second reason to consider a long temporal perspective relates to the future. Many environmental justice struggles are based on deep connections to land and ecosystems, which challenge destructive ways of thinking while offering hope for the future of multispecies relations on the planet. These struggles include Indigenous resistance mobilizations and other place-based ecological movements in defense of territory, particularly those with nondualistic perspectives, which emphasize interdependent relationships between humans and the natural world.[61] Arturo Escobar calls these struggles instances of "pluriversal politics," encompassing efforts to move toward an alternative world, "a world where many worlds fit."[62] The "pluriverse" is a response to interrelated crises of development, modernity, and dualistic thinking, which underlie capitalist and colonial systems. As Escobar writes, "Faced with crisis of our modes of existence in the world, we can credibly constitute the conjuncture as a struggle over a new reality, what might be called the pluriverse, and over the designs of the pluriverse."[63]

While there is a great deal of resonance between these perspectives, there are also some key differences. Aimee Carrillo Rowe and Eve Tuck argue for an "ethic of incommensurability" in the context of settler colonialism, rejecting the idea that all social rights and justice projects can be aligned with Indigenous land rights struggles.[64] On the theme of incommensurability, this book will discuss the importance of examining contexts of environmental injustice in which the concept of environmental justice is not an established discourse among environmental activists—for instance, in the case of China. Environmental groups in China tend to avoid the language of rights or justice, instead using more pragmatic and subtle modes of "embedded activism" within the constraints of an authoritarian state.[65]

On the scale of the interconnected mesh of the petrochemical planet, this book extends the discussion of environmental injustice to the interconnected concepts of "waste colonialism" and "ecologically unequal exchange," which relate to the petrochemical value chain, particularly its downstream consumption and waste streams. Many scholars, activists, and politicians have used the concept of "waste colonialism" since the 1980s, as well as the related terms "garbage imperialism" and "toxic colonialism," to describe the unjust transnational export of hazardous waste from high-income to low- and middle-income countries.[66] Waste colonialism has renewed relevance today in debates about the transnational trade (and illegal transnational dumping) of hazardous plastic waste.[67] According to Liboiron, waste colonialism is based on the "assumed entitlement to use Land as a sink, no matter where it is," and it extends beyond exporting the problem of waste itself to exporting waste management "solutions."[68]

The related concept of "ecologically unequal exchange" highlights how the structures of international trade and consumption shape the uneven global distribution of environmental harms, including deforestation, biodiversity loss, greenhouse-gas emissions, and pollution.[69] The mass overconsumption of plastics on a global level, particularly single-use plastics, is a major yet under-examined form of ecologically unequal exchange.[70] The later chapters in this book discuss the problem of mass overconsumption of petrochemical products, which is driven by the industry's tireless project of manufacturing demand in new markets.

Petrochemical degrowth is crucial for transforming the industry: dramatically reducing the production of toxic, wasteful, and carbon-intensive petrochemical products. Just transition policies are also vital to assist displaced workers and communities and to ensure that low-carbon transitions do not have unequal benefits and harms.[71] The wider imperative for both "degrowth" and "just transitions"—across the global capitalist system—is embraced in the environmental justice call for "just sustainabilities," which Julian Agyeman, Robert Bullard, and Bob Evans define as "the need to ensure a better quality of life for all, now and into the future, in a just and equitable manner, whilst living within the limits of supporting ecosystems."[72] However, radical proposals for just and sustainable transformations of the petrochemical industry—involving deep decarbonization, decolonization, detoxication, and downscaling—have yet to gain traction in policy or practice. Many workers and residents rely on the petrochemical industry for their livelihoods, whether directly or indirectly.[73] Moreover, people around the world depend on the petrochemical industry and on its complex supply chains and interconnected industries for their food, transport, health, connectivity, housing, and consumer lifestyles.[74]

This book addresses the dilemmas of deep industrial transformation. How can we tackle the complex "wicked problem" of a powerful, dirty, yet "essential" industry?[75] Unpicking dominant capitalist narratives and their power is one place to start. Another is through stepping up the level of resistance.

Multiscalar Battles of Industrial Transformation

Long-standing battles over the necessary transformation of the petrochemical industry are intensifying across multiple fronts, sites, and scales. By engaging not only with environmental justice movements but also with corporate worldviews, this book identifies some of the mechanisms of power and resistance for transforming planetary petrochemical politics.

My analysis of industrial transformation expands upon and brings together insights from two perspectives: first, critical political economy perspectives on global capitalism, racial capitalism, fossil capitalism, and historical transformation; and second, anti-colonial and de-colonial perspectives on environmental justice and alternative ecologies of "degrowth," "indispensability," "just transitions," and the "pluriverse" in dialogue with a wide range of scholars. Both sets of critical perspectives are relevant for navigating the stakes and dilemmas of industrial transformation—on the one hand recognizing the barriers of embedded state-sanctioned racial violence and the power of capitalist adaptation and cultural hegemony; while on the other hand recognizing the capacities for resistance and alternative ways of thinking, being, and living.

This book shows how the petrochemical industry engages in deceptive campaigns to avoid responsibility for toxic harms as well as in proactive "wars of position" in response to public concerns over the ecological crisis, through positioning itself as part of the solution within green transitions. Writing on the challenges of energy transitions in societies dependent on fossil fuels, Peter Newell draws on insights from Gramsci on the distinction between "trasformismo" and "transformation" in wars of position over hegemonic green capitalist ideas.[76] Gramsci's concept of "trasformismo" describes a process of co-optation that "serves as a strategy for assimilating and domesticating potentially dangerous ideas by adjusting them to the policies of the dominant coalition and [which] can thereby obstruct the formation of organized opposition to established social and political power."[77] The petrochemical industry deploys strategies of co-optation through highlighting its role in producing green technologies and aligning its discourse with sustainability policy buzzwords, including the "circular economy" and "net zero."[78]

This book also examines escalating forms of resistance to the petrochemical industry, on multiple fronts and levels. It draws attention to examples of multiscalar activism against the dominant oil, petrochemical, and plastics regime, a form of collective resistance that is articulated across separate but interconnected issues, sites, and scales.[79] Some fenceline petrochemical communities have aligned their struggles with broader campaigns over plastics pollution, climate justice, and Indigenous land rights, which pose increasingly existential threats to industry. While multiscalar activism can increase political visibility and solidarity across movements, there are often setbacks—and in many cases, toxic petrochemical pollution and proliferation continue. My analysis of multiscalar activism extends not only to scaling up resistance but also to "scaling wide," across diverse networks, as well as to scaling down to less visible modes of activism.[80]

In *The Mushroom at the End of the World*, Anna Lowenhaupt Tsing reflects on the problem with ideas of scalability for diverse practices. The "art of noticing," of paying attention to specific local ecologies, does not scale up. This problem relates to scientific knowledge, but it also extends to modernity and capitalist expansion: "Progress itself has often been defined by its ability to make projects expand without changing their framing assumptions. This quality is 'scalability.'" In order to make projects scalable, Tsing argues, they need to be able to change frames smoothly, to "be oblivious to the indeterminacies of encounter; that's how they allow smooth expansion. Thus, too, scalability banishes meaningful diversity, that is, diversity that might change things."[81] Yet Tsing notes that both scalable and non-scalable projects can be either destructive or benign, pointing to the example of unregulated loggers as more ecologically harmful than scientific foresters. The main distinction between scalable and non-scalable projects, she suggests, is that the latter are more diverse.

Max Liboiron and Josh Lepawsky make a related intervention about the importance of scale. They argue that scale is "a way of understanding the relationships that *matter* to defining an issue, and thus of locating where and how interventions might best take place."[82] The problem with scale emerges from dominant and exclusive approaches to knowledge, which produce "'scalar mismatch,' where one instance is taken to be the whole phenomenon, or where one perspective is assumed to work in all cases."[83] Scale is relational: "think of how gravity matters to elephants but doesn't matter nearly as much to viruses, whose local movements are more influenced by the capillary action of their host liquids." Nor is scale a continuum. Many things cannot "scale up"—"a skin cell cannot 'scale up' to become an arm"—because there are "disjunctures in scale when things *change*."[84] There are practical implications of understanding scale as "relationships that matter within a situated context" for the kinds of multiscalar interventions to be taken in addressing social and environmental problems.

Multiscalar battles involve clashes over toxic injustices, including over diverse ways of seeing and constructing the world. There are deep conflicts, tensions, and sticking points in battles over green transformations, including powerful vested interests in fossil fuel-based economic growth; complex, interdependent systems with significant path dependencies and fossil fuel lock-in; and incommensurable values between different social groups. The clash between different values and ways of seeing the world is one of the most pivotal challenges for transforming the petrochemical industry.

Methodology

This book examines diverse perspectives, struggles, and sites across the petrochemical planet, focusing on major petrochemical-producing regions in the United States, China, and Europe. The book draws primarily on a selection of material from a wide body of research that was collected collaboratively for the project "Toxic Expertise: Environmental Justice and the Global Petrochemical

Industry" (2015–20), for which I was the principal investigator. The Toxic Expertise project examined debates about the environmental and health impacts of the petrochemical industry from multiple perspectives, including those of corporations and of communities and other stakeholders.[85]

The research was undertaken in different stages by the project's research team, with each researcher focusing on different questions across global, regional, and local levels. At first, I gravitated toward the global corporate ethnographic side of the project, which expanded to become the inspiration for this book. The corporate research was the least familiar, the most frustrating, and the most intriguing. It pushed me outside my comfort zone, and it involved many puzzles and unexpected turns. The findings propelled me to extend my study of the industry beyond the original scope of the project, tracing it through the first two years of the pandemic and the ever-intensifying plastics and climate crises.

Methodologically, my research on the petrochemical industry was influenced by studies on the material politics of oil in relation to global capitalism.[86] Within a global historical context, Timothy Mitchell's work on "carbon democracy" follows the "oil itself," including its material qualities and its locations of extraction and refining. Through exploring these connections, we discover "how a peculiar set of relations was engineered among oil, violence, finance, expertise and democracy."[87] Tracing the emergence of disputes about the BP Baku-Tbilisi-Ceyhan oil pipeline, Andrew Barry's *Material Politics* reveals how the implementation of corporate transparency, contrary to corporate expectations, fostered new forms of contestation.[88] Another insightful ethnographic study, Hannah Appel's *The Licit Life of Capitalism*, examines how the US oil industry creates forms of legality and legitimacy within local contexts in Equatorial Guinea, and the complex entanglements of local populations who work and live in the vicinity of the industry.[89] The material politics of petrochemicals are intimately connected to oil, but they are more extensive yet elusive, at the intersection of complex supply chains and ecological crises.

Most research studies about toxic exposures in the petrochemical industry focus on single case studies of environmental injustice or movements in polluted fenceline communities. The few existing studies of the global petrochemical industry, in comparative perspective, are corporate and business histories.[90] This book aims to present a systematic sociological analysis of the global petrochemical industry in relation to debates about corporate responsibility and environmental justice. With such an extensive subject, the book is necessarily partial and selective, aiming to offer insights into the complex struggles over petrochemical lifeworlds and transformations across multiple sites and scales. It approaches the question of scale from contrasting spatial and temporal viewpoints, juxtaposing the corporate imperative for expanding production with the importance of place-based contexts in environmental justice movements, and situating the question of industrial transformation within long planetary histories and futures. Multiscalar forms of activism present possibilities for traversing scales—finding points of convergence and solidarity, as well as tension, across environmental struggles.

Building on methods of comparative case-study research, which I explored in previous work, my research aimed to span micro and macro connections.[91] Overall, the Toxic Expertise research project included 160 interviews with a range of different people in the United States, Europe, and China, including corporate representatives, policymakers, NGO representatives, environmental activists, lawyers, scientists, trade union representatives, petrochemical workers and managers, and community residents. In addition, the research included analysis of corporate reports, documents, trade magazines, and websites. The corporate ethnographic research involved participant observation at industry conferences, training events, official petrochemical plant tours, and multiple stakeholder events, conducted between 2015 and 2019 in locations in the United States, Europe, and China.[92] Between 2020 and 2022, I conducted follow-up research to track rapidly changing petrochemical industry and fenceline community developments during the pandemic, attending virtual industry conferences and examining a wide range of reports, documents, and secondary literature.

Between 2016 and 2019, our research team conducted in-depth case studies in petrochemical residential areas in St. James Parish in Louisiana; Nanjing and Guangzhou in China; Grangemouth and Fawley in the United Kingdom; Antwerp in Belgium; and Porto Marghera in Italy.[93] Across these diverse petrochemical fenceline communities, we explored how people made sense of living with risk and pollution in everyday life; how people took action in response to social and environmental injustices; and how people perceived environmental threats, hazards, and politics. We also conducted studies of broader industry dynamics and environmental health impacts, including a corporate social and spatial network analysis of the global petrochemical industry; a regional analysis of pollution and health data related to the European petrochemical industry; and a meta-analysis of lung cancer incidence for residents living in close proximity to petrochemical facilities.[94] Finally, our research team compiled seventy-five qualitative case studies of petrochemical sites and controversies around the world, triangulated with corporate network and emissions data, to create a public, collaborative online global petrochemical map.[95]

Researching and writing this book has inspired many reflections about my own position and practice, through conducting research in diverse contexts of environmental injustice and through "studying up" to critically examine powerful corporations.[96] It has been a journey of continual learning, challenging some of my own assumptions, particularly in terms of recognizing embedded dualistic thinking, including within sociology. As I discussed in the preface, engaging with questions of environmental justice has required me to reflect on "where I stand," including a closer examination of my relationship to the settler colonial history of my hometown in Canada. Working in collaboration with researchers and activists on a large project with many different parts, it took a long time before I felt that I had my own story to tell about the research. Initially, I thought it was far too complex to even try. Gradually, my own story came into focus, involving studying up but also across, connecting debates about toxic pollution, corporate responsibility, and environmental justice to existential questions about deep industrial transformations.

I should note that my research is critical of the petrochemical industry but on a systemic rather than an individual level. Many corporate representatives whom I spoke with seemed genuinely concerned about climate change and plastic waste, and exhibited cognitive dissonance between personal and organizational values. The corporate justification of plunder—of land, lives, and communities—lies in the detachment of responsibility across a complex system.

Complex Systems

Now we reach the crux of the "wicked problem" that the petrochemical industry presents: its complexity as a system. The problem of complex systems is methodological, concerning the nature of the object of study and the question of how to study the object. The problem is also political, concerning the challenge of how to critically intervene in complex systems.

The theme of complex systems emerged at the beginning of my research. From my first industry conference to my first visit to a petrochemical plant, to my first interview with a corporate executive, I was overwhelmed by the sheer complexity of the industry. The networks of the petrochemical industry include thousands of corporate sites around the globe, nested within hierarchies of parent companies, subsidiaries, and manufacturing sites. Furthermore, the petrochemical industry is interconnected with upstream and downstream industries through myriad technical, economic, and logistical processes. Even at the level of specific sites, the concentrated geographies of petrochemical industrial complexes operate as highly complex systems, with integrated industrial infrastructure, waste processing systems, dedicated private emergency services, and zones for different uses: bitumen, liquefied petroleum gas, butyl polymers. Not surprisingly, given the scale of its operations, the petrochemical industry relies on the tools of complexity science (for example, modeling financial risk) as one of its many fields of expertise.[97]

Yet complexity, in itself, was hardly an insight. In fact, complexity often prevents insight. How was it possible to understand such a complex industrial system? I sought to penetrate the complexity as I continued with my research, participating in many petrochemical conferences and training sessions, speaking with a wide range of industry stakeholders, visiting several petrochemical complexes and fenceline communities, and triangulating qualitative and quantitative sources of data about pollution, environmental health, and corporate responsibility.

Theories of complexity and complex systems have roots spanning several intellectual traditions, including biology, ecology, mathematics, and cybernetics. These roots later extended to socio-ecological systems theory, neoliberal complexity economics, and sociological systems theory. Complex adaptive systems are highly resilient and self-regulating through circular feedback, and they have the remarkable ability to absorb external shocks.[98] Many complex systems seem to share these autopoietic properties, from the biological cell to the global capitalist economy.[99]

Arturo Escobar's vision of "designs for the pluriverse" draws connections between complexity theory and self-organizing autonomous Indigenous movements in Latin America.[100] These movements in defense of territory and place are based on relational ways of understanding the world, seeing all life as interconnected and part of complex systems, and as non-dualistic, with an ethics of communalism and care. The dominant capitalist and colonial worldview, by contrast, is based on simplifications and dualisms, and the failure to grasp complexity. The economist Kate Raworth makes a related point, noting that systems thinking is the most ecologically attuned way of understanding the economy as a dynamic, complex adaptive system, as opposed to traditional economic models of the "economy-as-machine."[101] Decades of interdisciplinary research on socio-ecological systems have also focused on the interdependence of social and ecological systems, including complex adaptive systems.[102] However, complex-systems thinking is also a key area of focus within neoliberal economics and science.

In the 1940s, the neoliberal philosopher Friedrich Hayek promoted complexity economics, based on the idea that complex systems such as the market are unknowable, with uncertain futures, and thus should not be subject to intervention.[103] Jeremy Walker and Melinda Cooper argue that in the twenty-first century, many corporations and governments have adopted similar models of "neoliberal systems thinking" in their strategies to manage uncertainty and complexity, by designing resilience into systems.[104] Examples include financial risk management; geo-engineering and climate science; Big Data and the new complexity science; and security responses to climate change, natural disasters, pandemics, and terrorism. For Walker and Cooper, neoliberal systems thinking is effectively "a call to permanent adaptability in and through crisis."[105] The authors worry about the capacity for neoliberal complex systems to absorb critique, but they underestimate the volatility and vulnerability of these systems.

William Connolly proposes an alternative view of complexity theory that recognizes its contentious origins but emphasizes its political possibility for "experimental intervention in a world that exceeds human powers of attunement, explanation, prediction, mastery, or control."[106] Connolly argues that economic markets are imperfect and volatile precisely because they interact in the real world with many other complex systems.[107] Writing nearly a century before, Gramsci made similar insights on the complexity of modern political systems. Stuart Hall observed that one of the most significant contributions of Gramsci was to point to the "increasing complexity of the interrelationships in modern societies between state and civil society. Taken together, they form a complex 'system' which has to be the object of a many-sided type of political strategy, conducted on several different fronts at once."[108] According to Hall, this has implications for how "to unravel the changing complexities in state/civil society relationships in the modern world and the decisive shift in the predominant character of strategic political struggles."[109] If disruption and unraveling are possible, then this points to limits in the capacity for complex systems to absorb external shocks. What is the critical point whereby a system (such as petrochemical entanglement and proliferation) could become destabilized?

Despite seemingly universal properties of complex systems, in reality of course, they are not all the same. They have different characteristics and breaking points. The petrochemical industry is a complex adaptive system, with the powerful capacity for self-reproduction even in the face of profound shocks. The industry is primed for responding to threats, from challenging negative perceptions of plastic waste and toxic disasters, to doing business amid economic sanctions and civil war. The industry navigates complexity at different levels, on the one hand through engineering it, and on the other hand through taming it. Thus, for the petrochemical industry, complexity represents both an opportunity and a threat. The challenge for everyone who is concerned about sustainability, justice, and public health is to find a way of disarming the harmful features of the system without destroying everything else in the process.

Loops are a recurring and recursive theme in complex systems. We need to break out of the loops that perpetuate excessive petrochemical consumption, pollution, and waste. Systematic multiscale approaches are required to address the complex systems underpinning environmental inequalities. To do so, we must first recognize the limitations. It is difficult to extend systematic analyses and critical engagements across different scales in terms of geography, in terms of values, and even in terms of ontology. It involves continually shifting attention between micro and macro levels, and grappling with conflicting forms of science, knowledge, and politics.

Structure of the Book

The global petrochemical industry is under considerable pressure to transform, but competing visions, interests, and values are at stake. The opening two chapters of this book juxtapose two opposing worldviews of the vast territorial expansion of the global petrochemical industry: the military-strategic vantage point of industry, and the grassroots resistance of polluted fenceline communities. Chapter 1 reveals that despite internal differences, the petrochemical industry has a collective operational logic based on geopolitical strategies to address a range of complex, uncertain, and risk-laden scenarios. This deep-rooted logic drives relentless expansion at the expense of disadvantaged populations, and it underpins the industry's responses to crisis. In stark contrast with corporate worldviews, chapter 2 shows how fenceline petrochemical communities around the world have witnessed firsthand the unjust burdens of toxic exposure and employment blackmail. Grassroots activists have fought protracted battles to hold corporations accountable for the costs of clean up or relocation, with some victories but many failures.

For decades, fenceline environmental justice struggles have highlighted the toxic impacts of industry, but with few impacts beyond the level of individual corporations. However, as chapter 3 discusses, some people living in fenceline communities have widened their base of support through multiscalar activism, connecting to broader concerns over plastic waste, climate change, toxic pollution, and land rights. Other fenceline community activists have adopted more subtle, microscale forms of resistance within contexts of political repression, gathering strength as they wait for opportunities for future escalation. Multiscalar activism can be risky, but it can also raise the political visibility of fenceline issues, while exerting pressure on corporations from a powerful angle: the future survival of the industry. Chapter 4 confronts this existential angle head-on, examining the competing stakes of the planetary petrochemical crisis for the future of the petrochemical industry and for multispecies life on Earth.

The petrochemical industry is on a path of profound transformation, but its trajectory remains uncertain. Chapters 5 and 6 examine the dilemmas of just and sustainable petrochemical transformation, challenging the unsustainable capitalist growth imperative while recognizing the embedded problem of petrochemical dependency across multiscalar material and cultural systems. There are significant barriers to radical industrial transformation, not least the powerful interests of petrochemical corporations. Multiscalar activism is an important tool of resistance, but enforceable regulations and fundamental changes to growth and consumption-driven models of capitalism are also required. To conclude, this book sketches out a vision for an alternative petrochemical planetary politics.

1

The Petrochemical Game of War

The water is served in glass, rarely in plastic. The networking tables are high and circular. Most participants are men over the age of fifty. Maps detail petrochemical investments around the world, with arrows showing the flows between countries. They resemble the maps of flight paths that you see in airline magazines, or preserved plans from old military campaigns.

I have been an interloper at dozens of these global petrochemical industry events, paying the hefty registration fees and declaring my professional identity.[1] My first was a petrochemical conference in Amsterdam in 2016, where I immediately stood out on the list of eighty-odd participants. "So, you're a sociologist," a leading industry representative said, singling me out during a coffee break. "Why are you interested in petrochemicals?"[2] I was directed to Sarah, a corporate sustainability consultant, who told me about her work with multinational companies. A geologist by training, she seemed to have faith in the idea of a virtuous circle of economic and environmental sustainability. But later that afternoon, when the corporate executives unveiled their grand new investment plans, Sarah turned to me in a hushed voice: "These plans completely contradict their commitments to the Paris Agreement!" she exclaimed. "Especially the coal investments in China. Why doesn't anyone say anything about this?"

I observed similar outbursts of moral objection at many of the petrochemical events, alongside the usual talk about the threat of regulations and the price of crude. Some outbursts, like Sarah's, appeared spontaneous. Others were more rehearsed, part of a soul-searching repertoire that was standard in these spaces. "What do I say to my granddaughter when she asks me about climate change?" asked a petrochemical executive during a panel discussion about the future of polymer markets in 2019.[3] There were other eruptions, too, betraying different commitments. "Who here likes the color green?" a petrochemical speaker scoffed about the public backlash over fracking.[4] Over time, I learned that internal conflicts could in fact be productive rather than disruptive for companies in contested industries, showcasing their apparent capacity for self-reflection and dialogue.[5]

Participants at these events came from a range of industry and professional backgrounds, including not only petrochemical, plastics, and oil company representatives, but also corporate lawyers, chemical engineers, management consultants, market analysts, refinery operators, catalyst merchants, food packaging company representatives, shippers, and precious-metals specialists, to name just a few. Each participant brought a different professional and personal perspective to the events. Ultimately, even the most self-critical corporate narratives looped back to the script: the industry was under assault, but its capacity for innovation and problem-solving would save it. As an industry analyst commented in the lead-up to the UN Climate Change Conference (COP26) in Glasgow in 2021:

> The chemical industry is really good at problem-solving. The challenges of decarbonization and net zero: if we state the goals, that allows the industry to change. The science is there. There's things that can support the industry in creating these solutions. The policies have to be aligned in order to not constrain the industry by saying, "We need you to get to net zero, but you can't do this, and you can't do that."[6]

Industry events are curated performances, offering few clues about the inner workings of individual corporations. However, they do offer clues about the strategic world of the industry. Most of the elements of the corporate petrochemical world are taken for granted by participants—the fierce geopolitical positioning, the calculated risk-taking, the faith in technological solutions, the boom-and-bust cycles, and the adversarial relationship with regulators. These are all part of the thrill of the game. Rooms buzz with excitement during times of high profitability, and they slump when profits are dipping.

The discussion topics are grouped like pieces in a game of Risk, the classic board game of strategic conquest, carving up the globe into contested geopolitical blocks: "Iran and Russia: Latest Developments and Impacts of Sanctions on Petrochemicals Product Flows"; "China's Expansive One Belt, One Road Initiative Impact on the Petrochemical Industry."[7] Each player competes for the domination of feedstocks. "Global Crude Oil Outlook"; "Consequences of the US Shale Gas Boom on the Downstream Petrochemical Industry." The players march from regional feedstock locations to global markets in olefins, aromatics, and derivatives, across different technologies and regions. "The Dark Days of Benzene"; "Crude Oil to Chemicals." Alliances are forged to tackle the obstacles: "Climate Change's Influence on Future Business Ventures"; "Plastics Sustainability"; "COVID-19 and the Crude Oil Crash: Supply Chain Resilience in the Petrochemical Industry." The winners take home the biggest share of the global profit, and there is a scramble over the remaining pieces.

There is talk of "bear fights" in petrochemical markets; "boxing matches" between regional competitors; and environmentalists having "a knife edge to our throat." There are references to "nails in the coffin" for losing players; and the ultimate risk of being "killed, stone dead." Yet there are also "saviors in the export markets," and various strategies for "winning the war."

This chapter aims to "see like the petrochemical industry" on a strategic level, to gain insights for critical intervention.[8] My analytical approach examines the operational logic of the industry in terms of a game, including its playing field, rules for success, and strategies. These terms are all commonly used within the industry, as indeed they are in many other industries, along with direct references to "the game." By seeing the world in terms of a game, where material control, technological prowess, and market domination are the ultimate goals, petrochemical players become detached from the real-world implications of their actions.

On one level, the petrochemical industry operates like most other contested industries within global capitalism: it pursues profit relentlessly, while engaging in wars of position to combat threats and maintain hegemony.[9] Yet on another level, the petrochemical industry has its own ways of operating, which stem from its path-dependent history of collusive practices, including illegal cartels and tacit cooperation to gain market control.[10] The industry is embedded in geopolitical conflicts over access to raw materials and markets, based on technologies developed in actual wars, and deploys military models for navigating complexity and risk.

The geopolitical origins of the petrochemical game of war can be traced to colonial histories of the Great Game between Russia and Britain over control of Central Asia, the Scramble for Africa, and oil exploration in the Middle East.[11] In *Savage Ecology*, Jairus Grove contends that war is a "form of life" that has made the world through centuries of geopolitical violence.[12] Grove defends this expansive definition of war, which goes beyond the "real war" of military conflict, arguing that "politics, colonialism, settlement, capitalism, ecological destruction, racism, and misogynies are not wars by other means—they are war."[13] While this argument is compelling, my analysis of the petrochemical game of war is somewhat closer to the classical version.

War is not just a metaphor. The petrochemical industry produced deadly toxic gases that were used in both world wars: phosgene was used as a chemical weapon during the First World War, which is sometimes referred to as the "Chemists' War," and hydrogen cyanide was used by the Nazis in the gas chambers during the Second World War.[14] That war brought unprecedented demands for synthetic rubber, high-octane aviation fuel, nylon, and other petrochemical products, produced for a range of military uses.[15] In the aftermath of the Second World War, the German chemical company BASF emerged out of the remnants of IG Farben, which operated a concentration camp at one of its petrochemical complexes during the Nazi period, and the first directors of BASF were tried as Nazi war criminals.[16] Other petrochemical companies—most notoriously Shell—have been implicated in human rights violations, including the murders of environmental activists.[17] Doing business in conflict zones was a standing agenda item in many petrochemical conferences that I attended. In 2022, the devastating Russian invasion of Ukraine underscored the extent of global and military dependence on fossil fuels. Major oil, gas, and petrochemical companies posted record profits in 2022, and were widely criticized for immoral profiteering from the energy crisis.[18]

The analogy between warfare and corporate strategy may seem exaggerated, but I did not set out to find it. When I started my investigations, I knew about the petrochemical industry's long history of "deceit and denial," as the historians Gerald Markowitz and David Rosner call it, hiding knowledge about the toxic health hazards of their products.[19] However, I was surprised at the extent to which industry leaders habitually and explicitly deploy military language and tactics. In regular business meetings, corporate representatives talk openly about their opponents in terms of war, particularly environmentalists, regulators, and the public. Throughout its history, the industry has often tended toward collusion, including formal, tacit, and illegal forms of market control, particularly when faced with threats.[20]

Today the industry positions itself within a world of "volatility, uncertainty, complexity, and ambiguity" (VUCA), a concept that was first advanced by the US military to describe post–Cold War contexts, which has since become a twenty-first-century management buzzword.[21] The industry also uses several other concepts which have military origins, including the very ideas of "strategy" and "logistics." The art of navigating the petrochemical industry through intensifying existential threats involves multiscalar tactics of "toxic expertise"—expertise about toxic hazards, and the toxic nature of expertise itself.[22]

James Scott argued that authoritarian modern states attempted to order nature and society through "state simplifications." Countering these "pernicious" modern state logics, which led to human tragedies and disasters, Scott emphasized "the indispensable role of practical knowledge, informal processes, and improvisation in the face of unpredictability."[23] Macarena Gómez-Barris observed further that "extractive capitalism literally 'sees like the state,'" which means "violently asserting its rule over human and nonhuman populations."[24] Gómez-Barris cautioned, however, that "if we only track the purview of power's destruction and death force, we are forever analytically imprisoned to reproducing a totalizing viewpoint that ignores life that is unbridled and finds forms of resisting and living alternatively."[25]

Throughout this book, I argue that both perspectives are needed to counter the destructive forces of global capitalism. On the one hand, we need to find alternative ways of living and thinking and to highlight forms of resistance. On the other hand, we need to critically examine the driving logics of powerful industries, which are neither simple nor entirely predictable.[26] In fact, many industries within global capitalism, including the petrochemical industry, have incorporated complexity thinking into their schematic ways of operating.[27] The petrochemical industry has refined its strategies for securing, maintaining, and expanding its power. While there is danger in overestimating its totalizing worldviews, there is also danger in underestimating them.

A Brief History of the Playing Field

The extraordinary rise of petrochemicals in modern society occurred in the aftermath of the Second World War. It was accelerated by the large-scale, technology-driven demands of the war effort, and then shifted in the postwar period toward new mass consumer markets for plastics. Oil companies in the United States (such as Standard Oil, Shell, Mobil, Amoco) built the first petrochemical plants near their refineries in the 1920s and 1930s to find uses for the by-products of oil refineries.[28] During the same period, scientists in Western European and American chemical companies (such as DuPont, Dow Chemical, Union Carbide, IG Farben, Solvay, Imperial Chemical Industries) synthesized a number of chemicals derived from coal, wool, and alcohol to find cheap replacements for a wide range of natural products such as wood, glass, rubber, and textiles.[29] The potential of oil as a major petrochemical feedstock (raw material input) became evident in the lead-up to the Second World War, as refining and chemical processes were developed for military purposes.

According to the business historian Alfred Chandler, the postwar growth of the petrochemical industry can be traced to two scientific and technological "revolutions": first, the polymer revolution in the 1920s and 1930s, led by Western European and American chemical companies, when scientists discovered most of the major synthetic polymers (plastics and other resins) in use today; and second, the petrochemical revolution in the 1930s and 1940s, when oil companies began to produce experimental high-octane gasoline for the US army.[30] Chandler argues that the "first movers" in the polymer and petrochemical revolutions—chemical companies and oil companies—achieved world market dominance in petrochemicals through the strategy of continually commercializing new products based on scientific and technological developments, creating strong barriers to entry through economies of scale and scope. However, there were other strategic barriers to entry too: chemical producers in the interwar period controlled the market explicitly through national and international cartels.[31]

Peter Spitz, a chemical engineer who worked in the American petrochemical industry from 1956 until the early 2000s, has written extensively about the history of the industry, drawing on his experiences at Esso Engineering, a division of the Standard Oil Company (which became Exxon Corporation in 1972), and as an industry consultant.[32] In *Primed for Success*, Spitz accounted for the tremendous power of the IG Farben cartel, which was created in 1925 to rebuild Germany's chemical industry, avoid duplication among German producers, set pricing, and keep out competitors. According to Spitz, "It is hard to appreciate today the extent to which German firms controlled the world's organic chemistry before World War II." The IG Farben cartel, which included BASF, Bayer, and Hoechst in Germany, gradually expanded to have a "sometimes controlling interest in 379 German and 400 foreign firms."[33]

Spitz was particularly interested in the influential role of scientific exchanges between Standard Oil and IG Farben between 1925 and 1939 in the development of the petrochemical industry. In the book's introduction, he casually noted his inspiration for researching this wartime history:

> With the help of Dieter Ambros, then a high level executive of Henkel, and a good business friend, I spent an afternoon in Mannheim, Germany, with his father Dr. Otto Ambros, earlier an executive of I.G. Farbenindustrie, who headed up a complex that made Buna rubber during World War II at a plant near Auschwitz and was convicted as a war criminal because he had employed "slave labor." Rehabilitated, he told me about his postwar experiences working for W. R. Grace's chemical business, but he also recounted stories of his career at I.G. Farben.[34]

The matter-of-fact way in which Spitz describes this friendly meeting with a convicted Nazi war criminal is unnerving. He puts quotation marks around slave labor, as if to question its validity, while "rehabilitated" is assumed with a single word. Between 1947 and 1949, twenty-three directors of IG Farben were tried by the US Military Tribunal sitting in Nuremberg for war crimes and crimes against humanity, including using slave labor from the concentration camps; supplying the toxic gas Zyklon B to the concentration camps; conducting medical experiments on prisoners; producing synthetic rubber and fuels required by the Nazi war of aggression; and plundering foreign property in the German-occupied territories.[35] Of the accused, thirteen directors were convicted.[36] The IG Farben trial was a hallmark case, the first attempt in legal history to hold business leaders responsible for corporate crimes.[37]

By his own admission, Spitz's career was closely tied to the legacy of IG Farben. He had his "baptism of fire" in the late 1950s and early 1960s at

Standard Oil ("in a real sense," he quips, due to "fires and explosions"), designing a petrochemical plant based on reports that American chemical executives had brought back from Germany after World War II.[38] Indeed, historians have detailed how US oil company managers and scientists came to Germany immediately after the war to visit petrochemical industrial facilities and gather millions of pages of technical documents, resulting in "technology transfer" through "war booty."[39] Ultimately, Spitz justifies Standard Oil's controversial collaboration during the Nazi period by saying that it was an unequal exchange: Standard Oil gained more information from IG Farben than vice versa, which, he claims, ultimately helped the Allied forces to win the war.[40] While Spitz's ethical and logical reasoning is clearly flawed, his detailed insider's account demonstrates the significance of deadly war technologies for the rise of the petrochemical industry.[41]

The Second World War broke up the cartels. In 1941, the United States conducted an antitrust investigation into Standard Oil and its six subsidiaries for conspiring with IG Farben to restrict trade in synthetic oil and rubber around the world, indicting three corporate leaders, who resigned in 1942 due to pressure from stakeholders.[42] However, as Diarmuid Jeffreys explains, "Standard Oil itself survived. In time of war no government is going to force the collapse of its biggest national oil business—no matter how disgracefully its top management has behaved."[43] In 1951, IG Farben was disassembled into different companies, including BASF, Bayer, and Hoechst, which each had their own legal identities, and thus did not carry liability for the crimes of the conglomerate.[44] Anti-cartel legislation in the United States and Europe emerged after the war, although tacit cooperation continued.[45] As historian Adam Hanieh points out, five of the "Seven Sisters," the transnational companies that dominated the global oil industry between the mid-1940s and the 1970s, were US-owned, and after the war, nearly all of the world's production capacity for ethylene ("the world's most important chemical") was located in the United States: "There was thus a mutually reinforcing relationship between the rise of American hegemony, the shift to an oil-centred global energy regime and the revolution in commodity production inaugurated by petrochemicals."[46]

The petrochemical industry expanded rapidly in the postwar years, following "an extensive public relations campaign (by industry) to promote petrochemical products, particularly plastics, as materials that would transform the lives of Americans."[47] The industry promoted plastics as essential to modern consumer life, including cars, appliances, carpets, toys, foam insulation, piping, packaging, crockery, nylon stockings, and many other everyday products. The leading countries in petrochemical production were the United States, followed by Japan, Germany, France, and the United Kingdom, countries with high GDPs and disposable income to spend on the new consumer goods.[48] To increase petrochemical capacity, oil and chemical companies built a vast number of petrochemical facilities, mainly located adjacent to refineries or within refinery complexes in coastal areas, for access to oil feedstocks and supply-chain networks. The largest clusters were located along the Gulf Coast of the United States near existing oil and refining infrastructure, and near major ports in Europe, fueled by imperial oil supplies from the Middle East.[49] Petrochemical production also globalized in the postwar period, and several petrochemical projects were built in the Middle East, South America, Africa, and Asia.

"From its basic origin as a satellite of the petroleum, coal and chemical industry, petrochemicals has emerged as an industry of its own," Monsanto executive Eric Yates declared in his keynote speech to the inaugural meeting of the European Petrochemical Association (EPCA) in 1967 in Deauville, France.[50] The EPCA was established with the aim of finding a new meeting place for the growing "global petrochemical family" in Europe, beyond their roots in the US National Petroleum Refiners Association (NPRA) as the junior partner to oil and gas. Yates declared that the petrochemical industry had achieved "phenomenal growth" in the 1960s and that this was forecast to continue, but he cautioned that problems arising from such growth were becoming apparent.[51]

Tellingly, Monsanto was already working to find solutions to two of these problems. The first problem that the industry faced was the publication of Rachel Carson's *Silent Spring* in 1962, which raised public alarm about the toxic consequences of DDT (dichlorodiphenyltrichloroethane) and other pesticides on health and the ecosystem. As the biologist and environmentalist Barry Commoner recalled, "Monsanto, which long knew about PCB [polychlorinated biphenyls] toxicity and must have known as well about its close similarity to DDT, nevertheless viciously attacked Rachel Carson for her views on the hazards of DDT and other pesticides."[52] The second problem was the industry's discovery in 1964 that many workers in vinyl chloride plants suffered from acro-osteolysis, a degenerative bone condition. Quietly, Monsanto gathered information in vinyl chloride plants about the extent of the occupational disease—which was widespread—and then conspired with other petrochemical companies to hide the information from the public and the workforce.[53]

Shortly after the EPCA was founded, the boom years came to an end. The 1973 oil crisis led to downsizing and restructuring in the industry.[54] New competitors entered the market, including state-owned enterprises in Brazil, Saudi Arabia, Taiwan, India, South Korea, and China. In the aftermath of the oil crisis, several chemical companies formed illegal cartels, which were later rooted out by the European Commission in the 1980s.[55] This led to a period of intensified global competition and overcapacity in several petrochemical commodities.[56]

During the 1970s and 1980s, a series of major chemical disasters and accidents resulted in new environmental regulations on both sides of the Atlantic, including in the United States the Toxics Release Inventory Program in 1986 to regulate chemicals and the Superfund Act in 1980 to clean releases of hazardous substances, and in Europe the Seveso Directive in 1982, aimed at preventing major accidents with hazardous substances. The worst disaster was the Bhopal gas leak in 1984, which caused the immediate deaths of between 3,800 and 15,000 people.[57] The response from industry insiders was to seize the opportunity presented by the disaster for corporate takeover: "For [Union] Carbide the disaster was not just the gas leak, tragic as that was. It was the response to that tragedy, in the emerging market for corporate control in the United States. Within days of the news of Bhopal, the vultures began to circle, being that Union Carbide's breakup value far exceeded its current market value."[58] Faced with a wave of environmental regulations and public protests over the health effects of toxic petrochemicals, petrochemical corporations began to adopt the strategy of anticipating legislation through self-regulation, a strategy which they have refined ever since. For example, chemical industry associations around the world adopted the Responsible Care program, which was initiated by the Canadian chemical industry in 1985, and it began to lobby governments to block and delay further regulations.[59]

In the 1990s, the industry witnessed further global restructuring, with several mergers between leading American and European companies, foreign direct investment in emerging economies, and numerous joint ventures. Rather than interpreting this period as a shift away from traditional collusive practices within the petrochemical industry, Hubert Buch-Hansen and Lasse Henriksen argue that mergers and acquisitions can be seen as "the pinnacle of market control; constituting the moment when two competitors stop competing and join forces."[60] In fact, despite periods of restructuring, the petrochemical industry had a remarkably stable corporate leadership concentrated in the United States, Western Europe, and Japan up until the end of the twentieth century.[61] Many of the top petrochemical corporations at the turn of the twenty-first century were the original leaders from the interwar era, and several remain dominant to this day, such as BASF, Dow, and ExxonMobil.

In the first two decades of the twenty-first century, corporate power across the petrochemical playing field gradually shifted, with China overtaking the United States and Europe as the world's largest petrochemical producer and other emerging economies becoming global players.[62] In a corporate network analysis of the global petrochemical industry conducted in 2017 and 2018, Thomas Verbeek and I found that the industry remained dominated by an established North Atlantic corporate elite (that is, in Europe, North America, and Japan), but that this hegemonic power has been challenged by isolated corporate networks in emerging economies, as illustrated in figure 1.1.[63] This echoed findings from research on global corporate elite networks, which demonstrates the relative lack of integration of corporate elites in China and Asia with dominant North Atlantic corporate elite networks.[64]

But our multiscalar analysis also revealed more nuanced patterns, including both isolation and integration in the global petrochemical industry: "While corporate elite networks in emerging economies remained isolated from the established elite core, corporations in emerging economies have integrated with Western companies through joint ventures [figure 1.2] and spatial interlocks in petrochemical hub cities [map 1.1]."[65] On a spatial level, the petrochemical industry is integrated through strategic regional concentrations of petrochemical facilities, particularly in the Eastern United States, in Western Europe, and along the Asia-Pacific coast, where leading companies from different parts of the world are collocated. In the shift to a multipolar world, the global petrochemical industry remains dominated by a handful of key corporations, which are highly competitive but also increasingly interdependent.

The petrochemical playing field has distinctive features, but it is by no means homogeneous: each company has its own history, culture, identify, and strategic interests.[66] Each company has also had its share of scandals and disasters, from war crimes and human rights abuses to deadly explosions and the toxic poisoning of fenceline communities.[67] The key players include vertically integrated international oil and gas companies (such as the supermajors ExxonMobil, Shell, and British Petroleum); diversified chemical companies (for example, BASF, Dow, Formosa Plastics, and Mitsubishi

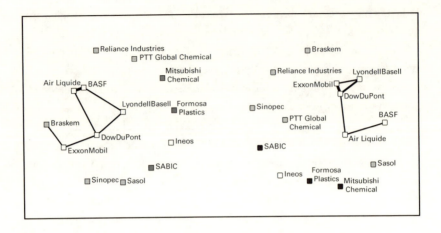

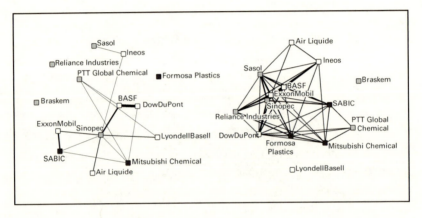

Figure 1.1. Corporate board interlock network analysis of the global top ten petrochemical companies and four additional corporations from three emerging companies in 2017–18. The analysis is based on indirect interlocks through other companies (left) and through policy-planning institutes, other organizations, and states (right). Note: White squares are companies based in Europe and the United States; dark-gray squares are post–World War II Asian entrants; light-gray squares are companies from emerging economies. Source: Verbeek and Mah, "Isolation and Integration."

Figure 1.2. Joint venture interlock network based on direct joint venture integration (left) and through joint ventures with the same external companies (right). Source: Verbeek and Mah, "Isolation and Integration."

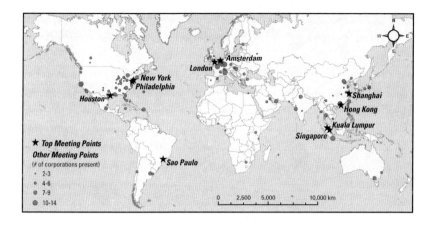

Map 1.1. Meeting points where the subsidiary networks of American and European corporations integrate with those of corporations from other parts of the world. Source: Verbeek and Mah, "Isolation and Integration."

Chemical); national state-owned oil and gas companies (such as Chinese Sinopec, Saudi Arabian SABIC, and Brazilian Braskem); specialized downstream petrochemical companies (for example, LyondellBasell); and other companies that do not quite fit (such as INEOS, which started out as a "pure-play" petrochemical company and later expanded into oil and gas).[68]

Most of the leading petrochemical players have moved up and down the value chain at some point in their histories, from raw material extraction through to refining, petrochemicals, and plastics, although not always successfully. Vertical integration stretched some companies too thin—for example, oil companies that extended all the way down the value chain to plastics, later retreating to their "core capabilities."[69] Despite interconnections across the value chain, there are subtle distinctions between the upstream and downstream industries. During research interviews, several petrochemical and NGO representatives told me that, by and large, the further you went upstream, toward oil and gas, the less cooperative people were with each other, and the further you went downstream, toward the consumer-facing plastics industry, the more friendly and collaborative people were. A corporate representative from ExxonMobil Chemical remarked that even within the same vertically integrated company, the petrochemical and oil divisions rarely spoke to one another.[70]

I got the clearest sense that there were differences between upstream and downstream players when I attended an oil industry event, International Petroleum Week (IP Week) in London in February 2020, just before lockdown due to COVID-19. Echoing the staged confessional moments that I had witnessed at petrochemical events, the corporate representatives at IP Week made a great deal of show about engaging in "uncomfortable conversations" about climate change and asking the question, "Will this be the last cycle?"[71] External speakers were invited to make provocations, and several speakers chastised the industry directly, saying that they had to stop funding climate change denial and lobbying. Watching the room, these interventions had an almost comic effect, as if they were scolding naughty children. There was practically no response. The industry presenters spoke only to what their specific companies were doing, all positive things about new technologies and strategies. One oil company executive shrugged and said that his company would continue with oil for as long as it could, noting the problem that "the bit that is actually challenged in our company is frontier oil exploration."[72] Over coffee, a media participant revealed that the real action at IP Week would take place later, by invitation only, at the extravagant parties hosted by the richest oil companies. It was here, in a highly securitized five-star hotel, surrounded by oil elites, that I felt most acutely that the petroleum world was not only incommensurable with my own but also detestable.

By contrast, the industry representatives in petrochemical-specific events were more energetic, often buzzing with excitement over the latest projects and technologies, and more expressive about the game of adversity and competition. One of the oil industry analysts at IP Week mentioned that they needed to learn from the petrochemical industry about methods for collaborating across the value chain to respond to sustainability threats, citing the example of circular economy recycling initiatives.[73] I realized the difference: although petrochemicals are entwined with oil, in terms of its material politics, the petrochemical industry operates a tighter game, more exposed to market fluctuations, with its reliance on vast quantities of cheap feedstocks.[74]

"The dirty little secret of the industry," confided a petrochemical workshop instructor to a room of budding petrochemical managers, "is that the only plant that the petrochemical industry builds specifically is for ethylene. All the rest are by-products of other industries, which can be good or bad."[75] Although the global petrochemical industry has grown and profited exponentially, it still operates in the shadow of the upstream players. In comparison with the upstream sector, the petrochemical sector is less profitable (for now), but it also offers a hedge against downturns in oil and gas prices and against threatened oil markets during energy transitions. Crude oil prices and petrochemical profits tend to be inversely related, and thus vertical integration between oil and petrochemicals is a key corporate strategy for managing volatility in commodity prices.[76] For example, the oil-and-petrochemical major ExxonMobil profited during the first two years of the pandemic due to the strong pandemic-driven demand for single-use plastics; and then in 2022, the company reported unprecedented profits due to the rise in oil prices following the Russian invasion of Ukraine.[77]

During each year of my research, industry experts expounded on the implications of major disruptive or unpredicted events for the petrochemical playing field: the COP21 Paris Agreement (2015), Brexit and the election of Trump (2016), the withdrawal of the United States from the Paris Agreement (2017), the public backlash over marine plastic waste (2018), rising global attention to the climate emergency (2019), the COVID-19 pandemic and the crude oil crash (2020), the "Great Texas Freeze" (2021), and the Russian invasion of Ukraine (2022). They also made new predictions about the future growth of different petrochemical markets. Their predictions rarely proved accurate, and the only constant throughout the period was volatility and uncertainty.

Box 1.1. Regional Profiles in the Global Petrochemical Industry

In 2011, China emerged as the top petrochemical producer in the world, overtaking the United States and Europe.[a] China's state-owned petrochemical industry has been driven by the national quest for self-sufficiency. Uniquely within the global petrochemical industry, China uses coal as one of its main petrochemical feedstocks, despite the high economic and environmental costs, but it also relies heavily on crude oil imports. By 2018, China had consolidated its leading global position not only economically but also in terms of technology and innovation.[b] It developed the first crude oil to chemicals (COTC) mega-project in 2019, and despite construction delays during the COVID-19, further COTC projects are being built. In January 2021, China became the world's largest importer of liquified natural gas (LNG), with increased economic growth in the pandemic recovery.[c] In the long term, volatile oil prices and climate change targets could undermine the viability of coal-based and methanol-based feedstocks in the Chinese petrochemical industry.

In 2000, the US petrochemical industry was starting to stagnate.[d] However, the US shale gas revolution turned the fortunes of the industry around in the years following the economic recession of 2008. Shale gas (natural gas derived from hydraulic fracturing) offered a cheap, abundant, and accessible feedstock to the US petrochemical industry. This was a complete game changer, giving the United States a strong feedstock advantage, particularly when oil prices were high. Despite several years of growth in US petrochemicals, industry analysts issued warnings about a downturn from overcapacity at the end of 2019.[e] The crude oil crash in 2020 temporarily overturned the shale gas feedstock advantage, but the COVID-19 pandemic also delayed the overcapacity crisis, due to delays in capacity building and the rise in demand for single-use plastics during the pandemic.[f]

In the 2000s and early 2010s, European petrochemical companies struggled to compete, given their high feedstock costs (reliant on naphtha from crude oil, primarily from Russia, Norway, Iraq, Saudi Arabia, and the United Kingdom).[g] Throughout Europe, there were site closures and minimal investments. However, European markets slowly recovered after oil prices dropped and petrochemical markets expanded. In 2017, new large-scale investments in Europe were announced for the first time in decades, many relying on transatlantic shipments of LNG from fracked shale gas in the United States.[h] Many European refineries and petrochemical companies struggled to survive in 2020 due to the impacts of COVID-19, despite increasing demand for single-use plastics products, which favored some producers. In February 2022, the Russian invasion of Ukraine dramatically increased oil and gas prices in Europe, making European petrochemical companies reliant on Russian oil and gas feedstocks less competitive.

In the Middle East, state-owned companies have pursued large-scale petrochemical investments in order to diversify from oil. Similar to the United States, the Middle East has benefited from "advantaged" gas feedstock, while Latin America, Japan, South Korea, and Taiwan have struggled to compete, particularly until the fall in oil prices; but like Europe, they have slowly rebounded.[i] Following the example of the Middle East, Russia also turned to petrochemicals as a way of overcoming its reliance on oil.[j] It is unclear how different regions and countries will be affected by the long-term impacts of the pandemic, climate change and plastics sustainability policies, the energy crisis, and economic sanctions on Russian oil and gas supplies as a result of its invasion of Ukraine.

a. Hong et al., "China's Chemical Industry."
b. CEFIC, "Facts and Figures 2020."
c. Chen Aizhu and Marwa Rashad, "US Supplies Give China Muscle to Become Major Force in Global LNG Trade," Reuters, February 13, 2022.
d. Geiser, *Materials Matter*, 54.
e. Çetinkaya et al., "Petrochemicals 2030."
f. Malik et al., "Impact of COVID-19"; Peng et al., "Petrochemicals 2020."
g. Eurostat, "Oil and Petroleum Products."
h. The investments were by the British firm INEOS, which rose to be among the top ten global chemical companies in 2005, with its £5 billion takeover of Innovene, BP's petrochemical business. European investments were based on shipping shale gas in super-containers across the Atlantic. See Andrew Ward, "Ineos to Spend €2bn on Expanding Petrochemicals Capacity," *Financial Times*, June 12, 2017.
i. Çetinkaya et al., "Petrochemicals 2030."
j. Vladimir Soldatkin, "Russia Eyes Petrochemicals as Answer to Crude Oil Reliance," Reuters, May 18, 2018.

The Rules for Success

The petrochemical playing field has changed considerably over the past century, but throughout its history the industry has been shaped by two rules for market success: first, geopolitical advantage in access to cheap raw material feedstocks (primarily oil and gas); and second, scientific and technological advantage, creating strong market barriers to entry. Both rules are enduring features of the petrochemical "game," as the brief history above illustrates. However, in the twenty-first century, players have also used different corporate strategies for gaining market domination in an increasingly complex global playing field. In this context, some industry analysts have proposed further rules for success, including core capacity building, digital analytics, risk management, flexibility, diversification, and vertical integration.[78] These rules are more contentious, particularly "unrelated diversification," which some analysts consider to be a strategic error.[79]

Location has long been a major factor for success in the petrochemical industry because of the need for large volumes of cheap feedstocks and access to supply chain logistics. Petrochemicals are highly exposed to international competition.[80] As my instructor explained at the beginning of a three-day training course on the petrochemical industry: "In order to get an understanding of the global petrochemical industry, you need to look at the different regions. Only then will it make sense."[81] He then summed up his thirty-eight years of experience working for a major American petrochemical company in one line: "Gases are expensive to ship across an ocean; liquids are cheaper."[82] The take-home message was that "there are pockets of regional advantage with gas as a feedstock because of shipping costs." The twenty-first century has been characterized by regional asymmetries, with "advantaged" gas feedstock in the United States and Middle East, and rising petrochemical consumption in China, India, and other emerging economies.[83]

Scientific and technological advantages have also been essential for achieving political and economic power within the petrochemical industry. As noted above, being a first mover in scientific and technological innovation has been historically a key to corporate success.[84] This explains how a handful of Western chemical and oil companies were able to gain market control in the early development of the industry. However, being a first mover does not ensure success; companies need to continually upgrade their technologies and fight off competitors. For example, Imperial Chemical Industries (ICI) was once the largest petrochemical company in the United Kingdom, and one of the original members of the interwar cartel led by IG Farben.[85] After years of decline in the UK petrochemical sector, the Dutch company AkzoNobel took over ICI in 2007. A chemical industry consultant who worked for ICI in the United Kingdom for thirty years reflected on the significance of war for the industry's technological developments:

> So, at the end of World War I, the UK sat down and had a think and there were... I think it was four or five major chemical companies said, "Hey look, we've got absolutely stuffed by the Germans, who were vastly more inventive and creative than we are. We don't have a good chemical industry. What we should do is pull everybody together, people making stuff from the fledgling organic chemistry companies, the inorganic chemistry, the whole thing, and we're going to pull the whole lot together." The whole shooting match came up here—and in World War II, as an example, ICI, I think, had forty-four major chemical plant projects as part of the war effort and delivered every single one on time, on budget, with full effect in this. It was a brilliant, brilliant, brilliant effort.[86]

Similarly, a polymer scientist who had also worked for ICI commented, with a touch of nostalgia, that most of the innovations in the petrochemical industry had happened during the Second World War. He stated bluntly that real change in the petrochemical industry would happen only through war or legislation.[87]

In fact, despite the importance of scientific and technological innovation for the petrochemical industry between the 1920s and 1950s, Chandler argues that the industry can no longer be considered high-tech because "chemical science no longer generates basic new learning to stimulate commercialization of fundamental products."[88] This is ironic given the strong discourse of technological innovation that the industry uses today. It also explains the palpable mood of excitement that I observed among catalyst engineers and polymer scientists at the Future of Polyolefins Summit in Antwerp in January 2019.[89] In the wake of the global public backlash over marine plastics waste, they relished the opportunity to work on technological "solutions" to design recyclability into products, in order to make it possible to comply with the target of making all plastic recyclable in Europe by 2030.[90] They were also piloting new research in chemical recycling, involving breaking plastics back down to their molecular level, but with challenges due to its high toxicity and carbon footprint.[91] In other words, legislation, rather than war, had given the industrial scientists the opportunity to innovate.

In the twenty-first century, some corporate players have succeeded in overcoming long-standing barriers to entry through deploying new strategies of market domination. For example, the private company INEOS rocketed into the top ten global petrochemical companies in the 2000s, borrowing tools from venture capitalism by buying "unloved" petrochemical assets from blue chip major companies and effectively flipping them.[92] Chinese state-owned Sinopec, the second largest chemical company in the world in 2021 (in terms of sales), has also defied the rules for success, driven by regional ambitions of market self-sufficiency to become a leading global player due to the high level of demand for petrochemicals in China.[93] By contrast, BASF has retained its number one position as top global chemical producer for several years, dethroned only briefly in 2018 following the merger of Dow and DuPont, and ExxonMobil (what remains of Standard Oil) has remained firmly in the top ten.[94]

A leading industry analyst observed that the year 2018 was "the sixth year of an extended upcycle in global chemical markets—characterized by robust demand, tight supply, and strong profitability. This extended period of profitability has caused a surge in reinvestment planning activity in North America, the Middle East, China and other Asia locations."[95] At the same time, a report by McKinsey and Company warned that "the rules for success" in the petrochemical industry, long based on "stark regional asymmetries," were about to change.[96] The report predicted that there would be "slower demand growth in emerging economies and less abundant advantaged feedstocks" over the next decade. However, the rules for successes are constantly changing. In 2019, the petrochemical industry was heading into a downcycle, but COVID-19 and the crude oil crash of 2020 turned its fortunes around. There was a surge in demand for single-use plastics, and the petrochemical industry fared remarkably well during a global recession. In the longer term, its future remains highly uncertain, with intensifying sustainability pressures, ongoing geopolitical tensions, and regular supply chain disruptions.

Strategies

To see like the petrochemical industry, on a strategic level, it is important to examine what drives the industry, in terms of its visions, plans, and goals. The industry shares many of its approaches to strategy with other modern organizations, and indeed, the very idea of strategy itself has military origins. However, the industry's strategies are also distinctive: it defaults to its foundational practices of collusion whenever possible in response to major opportunities or threats. In this section, I begin by situating corporate strategy within the context of strategy on a more general level. Then, I discuss strategic visions within the petrochemical industry, focusing on the illustrative example of the global chemical company INEOS. Next, I shift to a sociological analysis of corporate strategies in terms of wars of position, detailing the petrochemical industry's collusive strategies in relation to two specific threats: the toxic effects of industry, and the overlapping threats of global environmental and health crises. My argument is twofold. First, the industry's approach to threats is mechanistic; it treats them all simply as obstacles to achieving the goals of the game. Second, its strategies are reinforced ideologically through an instrumental capitalist process that Escobar calls "self-alchemization," whereby "humans, finally, learn how to operate like individuals by construing themselves as raw materials for endless improvement."[97]

Strategy is a well-established field of research within business and management studies, one that Gerry Johnson and colleagues define as "the long-term direction of an organization," including a mission, vision, purpose, and objectives.[98] Martin Shaw, a sociologist of war, argued that the modern concept of strategy originated in war but gradually diffused into wider societal usage in the 1960s, losing its military association.[99] He was worried about this trend. "From the standpoint of the sociology of war and militarism," Shaw reflected, "the strategization of society could be seen as part of the militarization of social life."[100] Anticipating Scott's analysis in *Seeing Like a State*, he was critical of strategy because it failed to consider complex social relations and the consequences of war.[101] Shaw traced the historical connections between war and bureaucratic planning and strategy, suggesting that "the success of war-mobilization led state controllers to think in terms of long-term 'planning' of the social and economic order, and to the broad development of 'social policy.'"[102]

Writing about the development of logistics, Deborah Cowen unveiled similar connections between the military and corporate spheres of war and trade, arguing that logistics began as a military art, was adopted in the postwar period by civilian corporations, and that the two spheres, military state and capitalist economy, are deeply entangled. The key to this system of entanglement, as mentioned in the introduction, is the global supply chain, which arose out of military arts and logics.[103]

The petrochemical industry relies on its global supply chain for the violent extraction of raw material feedstocks, including oil, gas, coal, and biomass. Oil is one of the resources most associated with armed conflicts, and it is the core traditional feedstock of the petrochemical industry.[104] The fracking of shale gas, the main petrochemical feedstock in the United States, has been highly controversial due to its association with groundwater contamination, toxic health effects, and earth tremors.[105] Coal is one of the dirtiest petrochemical feedstocks, developed as an alternative to crude oil during the oil embargo under apartheid in South Africa, and used today in China, at tremendous financial and environmental cost, to feed the national drive for "self-sufficiency."[106] Despite the problems with "virgin" (new fossil fuel-based) feedstocks for petrochemical production, virgin feedstocks are difficult to replace and come with their own set of problems: bio-based (from sugar or biomass) and recycled "feedstock" pose social and environmental challenges to scale, and they fail to address issues of toxicity, carbon intensity, and extractive land use, including competition with the food system.[107]

Beyond supply chain injustices, perhaps most obvious evidence of the military origins of corporate strategy today is war gaming, developed by the military as a strategic application of game theory involving playing out a series of moves and countermoves to understand the "enemy."[108] War games have been used in a range of organizational contexts—for example, healthcare restructuring and climate change disaster scenarios.[109] Petrochemical war games include conventional disaster scenarios, but they also extend to the everyday discourses and practices of the industry. When industry leaders engage in role-play within the petrochemical game, they often do so with mythical rather than military figures. These mythological figures relate to scripted roles within corporate "visions." In organizational strategy, vision "typically expresses an aspiration that will enthuse, gain commitment and stretch performance."[110] In other words, an effective strategic vision should attract its followers through motivation and enticement. In the petrochemical industry, this works through using myths, which gloss over toxicity and violence, and replace them with heroic leaders and "essential" products. The corporate vision of the petrochemical giant INEOS exemplifies this phenomenon.

ALCHEMICAL VISION   In 2018, the self-made billionaire Jim Ratcliffe and communications specialist Ursula Heath published *The Alchemists*, a book about the first twenty years of INEOS.[111] The choice of the title is revealing. The medieval precursor to modern chemistry, alchemy was concerned with transforming basic substances into gold and finding the "elixir of life." On the one hand, alchemy seems like an unflattering analogy for a major corporation—a discredited and foolhardy practice in modern scientific terms. On the other hand, alchemy sounds magical and heroic, fitting with the rags-to-riches narrative of Ratcliffe, who highlights his northern English working-class background throughout the book. Alchemy also sounds better, somehow, than petrochemistry: it is better to be associated with dreamers and mystics than with toxic pollution.

The early pages of *The Alchemists* outline the achievements of Ratcliffe and INEOS over the past twenty years.

> [This period] has seen INEOS grow from a small obscure chemical company in Antwerp to, quite frankly, a colossal enterprise today. Now we have chemical plants the size of the City of London. We have over 100 chemical sites worldwide. We have annual sales of $60 billion, comparable to the GDP of a medium-sized country. We produce 50 million tonnes of chemicals and 50 million tonnes of oil and oil products. We own 1 billion barrels of oil still in the ground. We have eight tanks shuttling shale gas from America to Europe. We have a car company, a clothes company and a football club, not to mention my hotel business. It's difficult to keep up sometimes.[112]

When I first read this passage, I was taken aback. This was like a laundry list of corporate excess, the kind that an environmental justice campaigner could have drawn up. As I kept reading the brazen prose, about how Ratcliffe stood up to unions and took a bold yet calculated approach to risk,

I wondered how this could really be the public relations-friendly face of INEOS. Yet this account was carefully crafted and largely consistent with other petrochemical worldviews. At the fiftieth anniversary meeting of the European Petrochemical Association in 2016, EPCA published a history of its achievements that portrayed the industry's key leaders as bold, risk-taking innovators.[113] This was unsurprising: Tom Crotty, president of EPCA and director at INEOS, wrote the foreword, and an interview with Peter Spitz was featured in the report.

The fantasies of alchemical transformation and mystical role-play serve as powerful ways of hooking participants into the game. In petrochemical training workshops, my instructors spent a great deal of time marveling at the history of scientific innovation for each of the polymers discovered in the early twentieth century, including anecdotes about eccentric inventors, patent wars, and chemistry in-jokes.[114] At a training workshop on petrochemical markets, my instructor described how the industry's chemists and engineers "fix" problems of balancing chemical supply and demand through "our bag of tricks to fool Mother Nature" (through using different chemical reactions in order to make higher-value molecules).[115] On several occasions, industry representatives delighted in showing their knowledge of plastics through guessing games—for example, in the following exchange with a petrochemical executive:

> EXECUTIVE At the beginning, even entering in a factory where you see something from nothing, and you then end up with a final product; I think it is really interesting. And many times when I speak with people, I can explain what is the material that you are using—for example, for that glass which you maybe don't have an idea—it's maybe nice to know... So, if I asked you what kind of material is that, maybe it would be...?
>
> RESEARCHER I'm going to get it wrong. I'm going to guess polyethylene.
>
> EXECUTIVE Hmm [*negative*]
>
> RESEARCHER Oh, I'm still learning... [*laughter*]
>
> EXECUTIVE No way a glass is made of polyethylene... So you need a material which can resist at least eight, eighty-five degrees before becoming soft. So polystyrene is the right one. And don't put hot tea or hot coffee in polypropylene glass. It will not resist. So, when you see this transparent glass near the big bottle of water, they are made of polypropylene and they are designed only for water, not for hot drinks. Okay?[116]

The corporate executive's fascination with polymer science exemplifies Escobar's observation—inspired by the work of ecofeminist scholar Claudia von Werlhof—that within the dominant patriarchal capitalist worldview, "the technological imagination is powerful, even more so perhaps when depicting the final alchemic fantasy of a world that no longer depends on nature."[117]

The anthropologist Laura Bear makes a related argument that capitalist decisions are based not only relaying information but also on "technologies of imagination" that invoke an invisible realm, generating symbolic meaning and creating "truth events" that "reveal a hidden order to the world."[118] Empirically, Bear focuses on the case of "populist speculators" who were port authority bureaucrats in India, men who gave business advice alongside religious advice and drew on a range of sources, both material and spiritual. In this sense, the relationship to divination in capitalism was literal. By contrast, in the case of the petrochemical industry, there is no literal invocation of religion or spirituality; instead, everything is discussed in rationalistic scientific and economic ways. However, there is a kind of magic overlaid onto the functioning of the material economy itself: the invisible realm is the transformative power of petrochemistry to make plastics "from nothing."

Corporate petrochemical visions illustrate the compulsive drivers within capitalism to pursue endless growth, regardless of the destructive effects, and to venerate technology as if it was a god. On the world petrochemical stage, industry leaders like Jim Ratcliffe cast themselves not only as innovators but also as saviors, mavericks, and pioneers. These mythical, hegemonically masculine figures serve to justify corporate plunder by creating the illusion that gold really can be made from nothing. Like gold, the modern miracle of plastics is illusory: there are hidden toxic costs in its production and consumption. The illusory nature of plastics also relates to corporate deception, since the public's desire for plastics was manufactured by the industry, and its toxicity was deliberately concealed for many years. I now turn to a more Gramscian understanding of strategy, as constituting a war of position involving arsenals of expertise to deny, deflect, and anticipate threats, while co-opting the potential solutions.

LEGACIES OF COLLUSION   Born out of powerful industrial cartels, the modern petrochemical industry has a long history of collusive corporate strategies. In the immediate postwar period, plastics were new substances with unknown health effects, and industry operated on the basis that plastics were considered "safe until proven dangerous."[119] At first, the industry controlled scientific research about petrochemical toxicity, privately researching the health effects of its products and then preventing the public from finding out. Then, once the toxic health effects of petrochemicals were made public, the industry worked to deflect responsibility and to anticipate regulations through self-regulation and lobbying. Today, the industry still deploys core tactics of deflection, but it also draws on models of complexity science to navigate risks and uncertainty, hiding violence and injustice behind a veil of toxic expertise. When faced with existential threats, the industry draws on its foundations in collusion, collaborating across the industry to control technical expertise and to neutralize public controversies.

In the mid-1960s, the petrochemical industry discovered that vinyl chloride, the basis for hundreds of consumer plastics products, was linked to acro-osteolysis as well as to several rare cancers. As historians Markowitz and Rosner have detailed, American and European industry leaders conspired for years to conceal scientific evidence about the health effects of vinyl chloride, benzene, and other toxic petrochemicals, which were evident even at low levels of exposure, leaching into fenceline communities.[120] When the link between petrochemicals and cancer was finally made clear to regulators and the public in 1974, the industry acted swiftly to control the scandal and delay regulations. Workplace limit thresholds for toxic substances were put in place, and hundreds of vinyl chloride aerosol products were taken off the market.[121] However, the industry denied the health risks associated with toxic pollutants in petrochemical fenceline communities and funded their own studies by professional epidemiologists.[122]

For decades, the petrochemical industry has continued to use tactics of outright denial as well as "strategic ignorance" to manufacture doubt and uncertainty about toxic risks.[123] Their corporate strategies for protecting markets have also evolved and adapted over time, typically in relation to crises. In a longitudinal study of environmental "triggering events" in the controversial US chemical industry between 1962 and 1993, Andrew Hoffman examined how corporate strategies gradually shifted from defensive to proactive stances.[124] Hoffman described the chemical industry as an "extreme case" of a controversial industry where environmental concerns emerged earlier and with greater intensity than in other industries. The triggering events included the 1962 publication of Rachel Carson's *Silent Spring*, the celebration of the first Earth Day in 1970, the chemical disasters at Love Canal in 1978 and Bhopal in 1984, and the rise of environmental regulations including the enactment of the Toxics Release Inventory in the United States in 1986 and the Montreal Protocol on Substances that Deplete the Ozone Layer in 1987. Between the 1960s and the 1990s, the industry shifted from defensive strategies of challenging regulations toward proactive strategies of addressing environmental issues, notably through the Responsible Care program, a voluntary industry initiative.[125]

By the early twenty-first century, corporate sustainability had emerged as a mainstream business strategy. As Peter Dauvergne argues, there is now a strong business case for corporations to engage proactively with sustainability "to help mitigate reputational risk, add to the bottom line, create new product lines, enhance brand loyalty, and increase their power."[126] After years of honing its strategies, the petrochemical industry has developed a multipronged approach to navigating sustainability pressures, consistently lobbying to block, delay, and water down regulations, while defending its products and positioning itself as integral to solutions.[127] In the first months of the COVID-19 pandemic, for example, the industry acted swiftly to lobby governments to reverse single-use plastics bans and to stall circular economy projects, highlighting the essential role of plastics in fighting the virus.[128] As far as possible, the industry seeks to shape regulations to align with its interests: opposing product bans, monopolizing technological control over complex infrastructures and systems, and narrowing the scope of attention to issues of waste rather than production.

The industry is also renowned for its lack of transparency, which is linked to anticompetitive practices. Lara, a reporter who had previously covered the oil and gas industry, told me that she was surprised by the lack of transparency in the petrochemical industry. For example, it was unwilling to disclose when its sites stopped operating, whereas that would be reported within minutes by the oil and gas industry. Lara said that the oil and gas industry is more regulated, due to concerns over insider trading without open information, but observed that the petrochemical industry (in her experience and that of her colleagues) was much less transparent, and it invoked antitrust legislation as a reason for not speaking about issues.[129] A chemical regulations campaigner at an environmental law NGO echoed this view, noting that transparency of the data on chemicals was "a huge problem, but when you work on chemicals there are a lot of secrets."[130] The campaigner went on to describe the incredible resistance within the petrochemical industry to the 2007 European REACH regulations, particularly when companies were asked to register not only the chemicals that they used but their company names.[131]

In my research, I was impressed by the extent of corporate knowledge about regulations. Industry insiders knew the complex details of multiple regulations, across local, regional, national, and international levels, and their implications for various markets. These included regulations for chemical production, use, and sales; persistent organic pollutants; single-use plastics; pollution monitoring; emissions reductions; climate risk disclosure; international shipping pollution; the trade and disposal of hazardous waste, and myriad others. Up-to-date knowledge about constantly changing regulations is vital for industry market forecasts so as to identify potential threats as well as opportunities. When China's National Sword policy came into effect in March 2018, banning imports of plastic waste, industry analysts were enthused about the opportunity to sell more virgin resins to make plastic products in China. As one petrochemical representative put it, "China could be the savior in the export market."[132]

The concept of "volatility, uncertainty, complexity, and ambiguity" (VUCA), developed by the US military following the Cold War, underpins the industry's adaptive approach, using complexity science as a tool for forecasting and navigating risks and threats.[133] I first heard about VUCA at a petrochemical conference in Rotterdam in 2018, when industry experts discussed the future impacts of "disruptive technologies in the plastics value chain" and coordinated an industry-wide response to the public backlash over the marine plastics crisis.[134] Oliver Mack and his colleagues apply VUCA to the strategic world of business, identifying complexity as the key concept, "a situation, where interconnectedness of parts and variables is so high, that the same external conditions and inputs can lead to very different outputs or reactions of the system."[135] The petrochemical industry views the world in VUCA terms, where crude oil prices, regional market outlooks, toxic disasters, consumer-product bans, labor and environmental regulations, war and conflict zones, sanction regimes, and energy geopolitics all impact the smooth running of business.

There are many approaches for navigating corporate risk and uncertainty, of which VUCA is just one. Within business and organizational studies, the strategic position of an organization is typically evaluated according to macro-environmental factors, including political, economic, social, technological, ecological, and legal factors (known as PESTEL). A PESTEL analysis of British Petroleum (BP) in 2016, for example, showed "a preponderance of threats over opportunities," related to tensions in oil-producing regions, economic decline, and decreased car usage in Western countries as well as legal, political, and infrastructural threats due to climate change and rising legal costs for pollution.[136] In later chapters, we will return to the theme of escalating threats to the petrochemical industry and their implications for critical intervention.

Critical Intervention

The petrochemical game of war originated in literal war and conquest, with a disturbing global history of collusive practices, including illegal cartels and the deliberate misuse of science and technology. The petrochemical industry has become more sophisticated at dealing with complexity, risks, and uncertainty, while its compulsion to expand toxic petrochemical production has been unwavering. Given the scale and aims of this chapter, my analysis has necessarily involved its own omissions and simplifications. However, after researching the petrochemical industry for the past several years across multiple sites and from various angles, I have realized that one can only ever scratch the surface of the overt and latent violence in this industry. Collusive practices run deep.

What are the implications of this analysis for critical intervention? After all, environmental justice activists have long recognized the need to engage in battle against polluting corporations, either directly, through blockades and protests, or indirectly, on the terrain of science. I suggest that there are three main implications. First, corporate petrochemical warfare has become increasingly complex, adaptive, and sophisticated, requiring new methods of resistance. Second, as the polymer scientist who had worked for ICI told me, real change in the industry will happen only through war or legislation. Following this observation—which is also a simplification, but a telling one—throughout this book I argue that deep industrial transformation will require protracted battles across multiple fronts and scales. Third, the petrochemical industry has exposed its vulnerability to systemic threats through activating its highly responsive defense systems. This relates to the "wild cards" of the game, including the marine plastics crisis, the school climate strikes, COVID-19, and supply chain disruptions from extreme weather and geopolitical conflicts. Seeing like the petrochemical industry, on a strategic level, helps to identify weaknesses in its corporate logics and defenses.

2

Enduring Toxic Injustice

and Fenceline Mobilizations

— Oh, it is awful, you'll be sleeping, and you smell this—I knew I don't have gas, I have electric. And they got to be so potent in your house, and I think, "Oh my God, I forgot to turn the stove off." And you jump. Oh gosh! But it's so strong you can hardly breathe. (Poppy, St. James Parish, "Cancer Alley," Louisiana, May 2016)[1]

— It smells at times. I mean you would think somebody had sparked off a match in your house. And then you shut all of your windows because it's absolutely stinking of sulfur, which can't be healthy. (Keith, Grangemouth, Scotland, October 2019)

—— Because I live on the fifth floor, we always smell something pungent at night, around ten o'clock. We even have to close the windows. We often call the government hotline to complain. (Zhao, Nanjing, China, March 2016)

—— I've had dust in my back garden, and to be honest, sometimes I can't sleep because the noise is so bad. I tell you it's that bad. And if the flares are going up, we turn our lights off in the house and we can all see what's going on. It lights the garden. And this year has been a pretty terrible year because you just can't separate it. There's no peace. (Arthur, Grangemouth, October 2019)

—— And you step out and you smell something funny, and you get a headache immediately, so we're at the point now that we don't spend a whole lot of time outside. My grandson, I won't take him to the park here. (Edith, St. James Parish, May 2016)

—— There is even worse pollution here [in the petrochemical complex] than in the community because there are power plants, polystyrene, oil refineries around. Especially there is always a layer of dust on the cars. Sulfur dioxide and sulfide from the power plants create an obvious white layer on my car. (Yang, Nanjing, March 2016)

—— So many people have so many cancers and diabetes. And so many have heart failure, respiratory—you know—it is, it's just very disheartening. Very disheartening. (Rose, St. James Parish, May 2016)

—— Over these years, I feel there are more people getting cancer. I'm not sure if it's associated with the working environment. Somehow, I feel there must be some connection. (Li, Nanjing, March 2016)

—— You know, people have got depression. That's one that's associated to it because you open your back window and there's the biggest industry in the world and you can't get near it. (Daniel, Grangemouth, October 2019)

—— There was an accident concerning alkene last year. The year before, a large oil refinery suffered from a heavy explosion, which killed all the fish in the Macha River. Chemical wastes were leaked. It was declared, however, that there was no harm done to the environment. (Wang, Nanjing, March 2016)

—— I've been here when the explosions have happened and when the cat cracker went up. I mean, they had to leave guys on that pipe for a few days. They had to leave the dead people there until they could recover the bodies because the place was so hot, and they couldn't get it to cool down. (Davina, Grangemouth, October 2019)

—— When we heard it, my neighbor called me. "Aunty," she said, "Did you hear that too? Has someone moved a house, or what?" So many times, that plant does explode or have an explosion up there, and it shakes the whole house. (Daisy, St. James Parish, May 2016)

—— And the locals have been protesting. INEOS went to the high court to get an injunction to stop the people from protesting more or less outside the fracking there, eh? (Malcolm, Grangemouth, October 2019)

—— People come to the company to protest ("make noise"), rather than to the local government. They come to ask that their houses are demolished, and they are relocated, or else to protest when the fish in their privately owned fishponds die. (Sun, Nanjing, March 2016)

—— The company has not approached the community. Not the citizens. They do whatever it is they do with the government part at the state level.... Oh, we protested, gave our petitions, citizens signed, but it happened anyway. (Elias, St. James Parish, May 2016)

—— They like to treat us as if we don't exist, and if we dare step out of line and challenge them, they throw everything at it that they can even to the point of telling lies. (Davina, Grangemouth, October 2019)

━━━━━━━━━━ Around the world, petrochemical plants are located on the edges of industrial cities, ports, and rivers, near to low-income, working-class, and minority ethnic communities. These communities have unique histories, but as the residents quoted above attest, they also share common experiences. Exposed to foul smells, toxic water, air, and soil, incessant noise and dust, high rates of cancer and other diseases, periodic explosions, and state and corporate neglect, countless people living and working in petrochemical communities have mobilized over toxic pollution. Environmental justice activists refer to communities living on the frontlines of toxic exposure as "fenceline communities," "frontline communities," or "sacrifice zones."[2] Over the past half century, there have been many fenceline struggles over petrochemical pollution, from the "working-class environmentalism" regarding toxic exposures in factories and communities in 1970s Italy, to grassroots environmental justice activism in "Cancer Alley" in Louisiana since the 1980s, to anti-PX (paraxylene) protests in cities across China in the first two decades of the twenty-first century, to recent struggles against petrochemical expansion in Scotland.[3] Yet after decades of activism, why has toxic petrochemical injustice continued and in some cases even intensified?

This chapter examines environmental justice and labor mobilizations in different petrochemical fenceline communities around the world, focusing on the problem of enduring toxic injustice. Methodologically, it is based on a thematic review of data from the Global Petrochemical Map, an online participatory mapping resource produced by the Toxic Expertise project, which features seventy-five case studies of petrochemical areas in regions around the world.[4] The analysis also integrates findings from qualitative case study research in the United States, Scotland, and China.

Looking across the planet at different petrochemical community mobilizations, what lessons can be learned, and what are the limitations and possibilities for change? To address these questions, I will trace two divergent yet interconnected types of community mobilization over the impacts of the petrochemical industry: First, *environmental justice activism*, following the movement that emerged in the United States in the 1980s and then expanded to become a mobilizing discourse in fenceline petrochemical communities around the world. Second, *labor protests*, once at the forefront of environmental justice activism over toxic industrial pollution, but increasingly disconnected from environmental justice movements.

This is a timely comparison. Over the past few years, the importance of alliances between labor and environmental justice concerns has regained political and academic attention in debates about the need for just transitions to protect displaced workers and communities from risk, harm, and disadvantage during low-carbon transitions.[5] Since the 1990s, the solidarities between labor and environmental justice movements have gradually eroded amid decades of industrial restructuring and "job blackmail," whereby industry forces workers to choose between their health and their livelihoods.[6] At the same time, the toxic injustices of petrochemical exposures have magnified for both workers and communities, leading to increasing local frustrations and protests, with relatively few labor-environmental (or "blue-green") coalitions.[7] The "jobs versus environment" dilemma is a powerful narrative in many petrochemical communities and can be difficult to overturn.[8] Indeed, there are considerable barriers to forging a collective oppositional politics to petrochemical harm, which might be capable of transcending polarized perspectives, national boundaries, and systemic social inequalities.

My analysis aims to account for the limitations of petrochemical fenceline community struggles in creating systemic change thus far, while recognizing the hard-won achievements and identifying possibilities for escalating resistance. One of the main challenges in grassroots environmental justice struggles is that responsibility for proving harm lies with communities, not with corporations.[9] The acute and chronic health effects of working and living with petrochemical pollution have been widely documented, including cancer, respiratory illnesses, autoimmune diseases, and neurological disorders.[10] However, the "safe" threshold levels of environmental exposures to toxic petrochemicals remain disputed and notoriously difficult to isolate from other environmental factors.[11] Faced with workplace and fenceline struggles over toxic pollution, the petrochemical industry has repeatedly denied the health risks associated with its products, concealing epidemiological evidence and emphasizing the uncertainty of science as a delay tactic.[12] Thus communities have focused their efforts on proving the damages, leaving them with a reduced capacity to address the structural issue of "expendability" within wider systems of environmental racism, settler colonialism, and toxic injustice.[13]

Some communities have won uphill battles against powerful corporations for compensation and relocation, but such victories are rare, and often hazards are displaced onto other vulnerable communities.[14] The perpetual displacement of harm underscores the limitation of the widely used environmental justice concept of the "sacrifice zone" to describe contaminated fenceline communities.[15] As David Pellow argues, "entire *populations* are viewed as expendable (within society), not just particular, localized communities and spaces. The implication of a 'sacrifice zone' is that one could presumably move away to safety, but the implication of expendability is that there is no escape."[16] Pellow's critical take on environmental justice resonates with Eve Tuck's call for communities, researchers, and educators to reconsider the long-term impact of "damage-centered research" in Indigenous and other disenfranchised communities, where pain and loss are documented in order to hold those in power responsible for damages, including in cases of environmental racism.[17] Tuck writes: "It is a powerful idea to think of all of us as litigators, putting the world on trial, but *does it actually work*? Do the material and political wins come through? And, most importantly, are the wins worth the long-term costs of *thinking of ourselves as damaged*?"[18]

Yet it *is* possible to confront issues of environmental injustice, including toxic petrochemical harm, while also avoiding damage-centered research. Tuck's proposed alternative to damage-centered research is to adopt a desire-based framework that does not fetishize damage but instead focuses on "survivance" and building alternative possibilities.[19] Rather than interpreting Tuck's criticism of damage-centered research as a call to avoid research on environmental injustice, we can interpret Tuck's intervention as critical to the wider goals of community activism, resistance, and resurgence in struggles for environmental justice.[20] This highlights the need for environmental justice scholars and activists to address systemic issues of decolonization, racial capitalism, and settler colonialism, both materially and culturally, across interconnected histories and futures.[21] At the crux of these issues is the problem of enduring toxic injustice.

The following analysis will trace toxic injustice through the entangled histories of environmental justice and labor struggles in petrochemical communities.

Environmental Justice Activism

Since the beginning of the petrochemical age, residents and workers in polluted petrochemical communities have endured toxic exposures and contaminated water and land. One of the first petrochemical disasters was recorded at Minamata, Japan, in 1956, when the Chisso Chemical Corporation, a fertilizer and petrochemical company, dumped methylmercury into Minamata Bay, causing the death, severe poisoning, and injury of thousands of people.[22] Around the world, there have been countless cases of deadly petrochemical explosions, toxic waste dumping, industrial accidents, chemical leaks, and contaminated water, land, and air, both historically and in the present day. This happens wherever the industry operates, to a greater or lesser extent of severity, because the industrial process of petrochemical production necessarily entails the management of "unruly" toxic and explosive substances, which are difficult to contain.[23]

Throughout the 1970s and 1980s, a series of chemical disasters revealed the deadly human costs of toxic industrial hazards: the explosion of a chemical reactor in Seveso, Italy, in 1976, which covered thousands of people in dioxin; the discovery of a leaching chemical dump with alarming health effects in a predominantly white, working-class residential community in Love Canal, New York, in 1978; and the Bhopal gas tragedy in 1984, by far the worst industrial disaster in history.[24] Each of these high-profile cases raised public awareness about the risks of the chemical industry and spurred the growth of the antitoxics movements and new environmental regulations, as discussed earlier. The Seveso disaster led to a 1982 European Union law on major accident hazards, commonly known as the Seveso Directive. It also provided the impetus for new collaborations between petrochemical factory workers, fenceline communities, labor physicians, ecologists, and politicians in the Italian Left, in a movement that scholars call "working-class environmentalism."[25] Love Canal is widely cited as the beginning of the US antitoxics movement, and led to the creation of the Superfund Act of 1980, a tax on the oil and chemical industries to fund the clean-up of hazardous waste sites.[26] In the aftermath of Bhopal, a number of international and national regulations were established, including the US Toxics Release Inventory in 1986 and India's first Environmental Protection Act in 1985. Global antitoxic activists also mobilized in response to Bhopal, using the phrase "no more Bhopals" to advocate for international chemical regulations.[27] While these disasters galvanized antitoxic movements, Robert Bullard argues that many "Black Love Canals" were ignored by public authorities during this same period, such as the case of Triana, Alabama, in 1978, a rural, Black community with significant DDT water contamination, where residents' complaints were recognized only after they raised a class action lawsuit.[28]

The first national protest by Black activists over toxic injustice in the United States occurred in 1982, against the siting of a PCB (polychlorinated biphenyl) landfill in a Black-majority community in Warren County, North Carolina. The protest did not prevent the landfill from going ahead, and 414 protesters were arrested.[29] However, the collective resistance in Warren County sparked a number of protests across the United States over toxic siting decisions, and it is widely cited as the beginning of the environmental justice movement, which brought together civil rights, antitoxic, and public health activists. The protests led to the landmark 1987 United Church of Christ study "Toxic Wastes and Race in the United States," which identified national patterns of unequal toxic waste facility siting in relation to race.[30] In 1990, Bullard addressed the issue of environmental racism in his seminal book *Dumping in Dixie*, arguing that it was important for grassroots groups "to know that there have been citizen victories," but also warning that they "should be prepared to remain in environmental justice struggles for years and possibly generations to come."[31]

One of the key battlegrounds over environmental justice in the 1980s was in the Mississippi Chemical Corridor, also known as "Cancer Alley," an 85-mile stretch of former slave plantation land along the Mississippi River between New Orleans and Baton Rouge with a high concentration of petrochemical facilities and oil refineries. In the early to mid-twentieth century, numerous plantations were sold to petrochemical companies, which were attracted by cheap natural resources and weak labor and environmental regulations. By the early 1980s, Louisiana had surpassed New Jersey to become the most polluted state in the United States, with rising local concerns over industrial hazards.[32] In 1984, the petrochemical company BASF locked out 370 workers from its largest American plant in Geismar, Louisiana, in an effort to purge the workforce of the Oil, Chemical, and Atomic Workers (OCAW) union. During the five-and-a-half year BASF lockout, new alliances were forged between labor and environmental justice activists, who shared concerns over the health impacts of toxic chemicals on workers and communities.[33] The BASF workers put up "Welcome to Cancer Alley" billboards and have been credited with coining this term.[34] In 1988, a coalition of labor unions, environmental groups, and civil rights activists took part in the Great Louisiana Toxic March from Devil's Swamp, north of Baton Rouge, to New Orleans. This coalition formed the basis for other environmental justice struggles in Cancer Alley over the ensuing decades.

Throughout the 1990s and 2000s, marginalized petrochemical fenceline communities around the world organized grassroots struggles over toxic exposures. In their efforts to hold corporations accountable for toxic pollution, fenceline community activists often formed alliances with scientists, lawyers, and other experts, and conducted their own health surveys and pollution monitoring.[35] Environmental justice campaigners also shared organizing tactics and tools with other fenceline communities in different parts of the world. The idea of the "bucket brigade," for example, a low-cost device for citizen air pollution monitoring developed in California in 1995, led to the founding of the Global Community Monitor in 2001, which helped fenceline communities develop their own bucket brigades in South Africa, India, Thailand, Canada, and in other parts of the United States. In Cancer Alley, bucket brigades were valuable tools for the environmental justice struggles of the Concerned Citizens of Norco in the Black community of Diamond, culminating in a community buy-out from Shell in 2002.[36] Community-led bucket brigades in marginalized Black communities in post-apartheid South Africa led to new national air quality legislation in 2004.[37] Grassroots activists of the Indigenous Aamjiwnaang First Nation located in "Chemical Valley" in Sarnia, Ontario, also campaigned against oil and petrochemical projects, including bucket brigades and other forms of pollution monitoring, biomonitoring, health surveys, and legal action.[38] In recent years, there have also been community-led struggles over toxic petrochemical pollution in Europe, including in southern France and northeast Spain.[39]

Another US environmental justice concept that has "traveled" is the idea of the "sacrifice zone." In 2011, the Chilean branch of the NGO Oceana International directed a letter-writing campaign at Chilean president Sebastián Piñera, naming Mejillones, Tocopilla, Huasco, Coronel, and Las

Ventanas as "zones that have been destined for sacrifice, forgotten by successive governments that have continued permitting the installation of new industrial contaminators even when the impact on the health of people and the environment has been immense."[40] Las Ventanas, the biggest industrial complex in Chile in the Puchuncaví-Quintero bay, including thermoelectric plants, copper smelters, cement plants, and nearby oil and petrochemical facilities, was the central focus of these campaigns.[41] In 2018, a cloud of toxic gases enveloped the Quintero and Puchuncaví communities, which led to a protest over the Puchuncaví-Quintero sacrifice zone, involving industrial action by trade unions and the fishing industry, joined by a mobilization of local groups and families.[42] The following year, the Supreme Court of Chile released a ruling acknowledging that the Chilean state had continually violated the constitutional right for people in the Puchuncaví-Quintero bay to live in a non-polluted environment. However, according to Efren Legaspi, a resident of Puchuncaví-Quintero bay, the state failed to apply any of the health or environmental measures that it was ordered to put in place.[43]

Indeed, hard-won environmental justice gains are frequently rolled back, given the relentless proliferation of petrochemical projects. Even in the case of Cancer Alley, where notable environmental justice victories have been won in Convent (1996) and Diamond (2002), toxic petrochemical production has only expanded. In 2014, the US Environmental Protection Agency's National Air Toxic Assessment found that the risk of getting cancer from air pollution was 95 percent higher for people living in Cancer Alley than elsewhere in the country. At the time of writing, this industrial chemical corridor includes seven out of ten census tracts with America's highest cancer rates.[44] In March 2019, a coalition of community, environmental justice, civil rights, and religious leaders in Cancer Alley organized the March against Death Alley, renaming Cancer Alley as "Death Alley," to highlight the continuing environmental injustices in the area.[45] A leading environmental justice activist in St. James Parish expressed his frustration about all the deaths and illnesses from pollution over the years: "We don't want to see it go on any longer. We want to make sure that instead of everything exacerbating into something that's way beyond what we can even imagine happening today, and today is enough. So, imagine if we don't stop it. It can grow even more out of hand to the point where St. James will become uninhabitable."[46] We will return to the continuing toxic battles in Cancer Alley in chapter 3, in a slightly more hopeful spirit, by examining multiscalar mobilizations of resistance against oil and petrochemical proliferation.

Although many petrochemical fenceline communities have shared ideas of environmental justice, most struggles have developed independently in response to local conflicts, often using different kinds of mobilizing discourses. For example, anti-PX protesters in China avoid the language of justice altogether, using instead the state's own laws of environmental protection to frame their euphemistic "strolls" as forms of "rightful resistance."[47] As geographer Anna Lora-Wainwright observes, residents of polluted industrial areas in rural China frequently adopt "resigned activism," where their range of activism is tempered by their acceptance of pollution.[48]

Another term, the "environmentalism of the poor," converges with the global environmental justice movement, but it has a stronger focus on poor and Indigenous peoples involved in resource extraction conflicts, whose livelihoods, values, and cultures depend on the environment.[49] The thesis of the "environmentalism of the poor," according to Joan Martínez-Alier, "is that in the many resource extraction and waste disposal conflicts in history and today, the poor are often on the side of the preservation of nature against business firms and the state."[50] Indeed, environmental injustice in zones of resource extraction relate to global patterns of "ecologically unequal exchange," in which rich countries absorb biophysical resources from poor and vulnerable communities and destroy their natural environments.[51] Threats to health and livelihoods are compounded in many of these conflicts, with threats of violence and detention for taking action.

An example of the "environmentalism of the poor" is the Movement for the Survival of the Ogoni People, founded in 1991 by Ken Saro-Wiwa, which campaigned over the health and livelihood impacts of the oil industry on the Ogoni people, a marginalized minority ethnic group from a region of the Niger Delta.[52] In 1995, the military dictatorship executed Saro-Wiwa and his colleagues for their opposition to Shell and the Nigerian state. After years of delays in US courts, in 2017, four widows of activists brought a case to the Netherlands against Shell for its human rights abuses in the Niger Delta. In June 2020, more than 40,000 Nigerians from the Ogale and Bille communities in the Niger Delta took a case to the UK Supreme Court over the impacts of toxic pollution from Shell, which is headquartered in London.[53] The Supreme Court ruled in February 2021 that the two communities could bring legal cases for compensation and clean-up to Shell in the English courts.[54] The enduring struggles over the Niger Delta highlight global disparities in the intensity of the toxic injustice of the oil and petrochemical industries, a theme that parallels issues of labor injustice.

Labor Protests in the Petrochemical Industry

There is a long history of resonance between environmental justice and labor struggles: fighting for healthy and safe workplaces, communities, and environments; standing up for dignity, recognition, and equity; and protesting the violence of social and ecological expendability. Environmental justice activists and scholars frequently invoke the slogan that "the environment" includes those spaces "where we live, work, and play."[55] One of the original principles of environmental justice set out at the First National People of Color Environmental Leadership Summit in 1991 "affirms the right of all workers to a safe and healthy work environment without being forced to choose between an unsafe livelihood and unemployment. It also affirms the right of those who work at home to be free from environmental hazards."[56] Moreover, workers in toxic industries played a key role in the early history of the environmental justice movement, as they were often the first people to encounter toxic environmental hazards.[57] Many chemicals and hazardous substances are known to cause cancer and other illnesses because of workplace exposures, for example in the cases of asbestos, benzene, and vinyl chloride.[58]

Between the 1960s and the 1980s, labor movements in the United States and Italy forged alliances with environmental and health movements in collective struggles for safe and healthy environments.[59] In the United States, trade unions and health professionals worked together to investigate the health risks of hazardous chemicals and substances. Their campaigns led to the passage of significant legislation, including the Occupational Safety and Health Act of 1970, the Environmental Protection Act of 1970, the Clean Air Act of 1970, and the Clean Water Act of 1972.[60] The concept of the "just transition," now a mainstream climate policy term, originated in the US labor movement in the 1970s and 1980s, which sought to bridge labor and environmental concerns by advocating for assistance to workers who lost their jobs in polluting and hazardous industries.[61] In Italy, workers and scientists also collaborated to push for stronger environmental and health regulations.[62] Their efforts led to major environmental and health reforms, including the Labor Statute in 1970 and the Public Health System in 1978. The alliances between workers and communities in Italy shared many similarities with those in the United States, but the political philosophy of "working-class environmentalism" in Italy was also distinctive in articulating a view of ecology that put "workers' bodies formerly at the center of a true environmentalism . . . both inside the factory and outside in the local space."[63]

Since the 1990s, however, there have been increasing rifts within many fenceline petrochemical communities over the "jobs versus environment" dilemma.[64] Amid globalization, technological advances, and labor outsourcing, there has been a gradual decline since the 1990s in the postwar "social contract" between the petrochemical industry and local communities, particularly in the United States and Europe. In recent decades, most labor protests in petrochemical plants worldwide have related to wages and conditions rather than to health or environmental issues.[65]

Meanwhile, the concept of the "just transition" has gained international policy recognition and expanded to include a wide range of social groups and concerns, but it remains contentious. In practice, as we will discuss in chapter 5, just transition debates tend to focus on industries where job losses have already occurred, primarily in coal, rather than anticipating future transitions in difficult-to-decarbonize industries such as petrochemicals.[66] According to estimates from the International Labour Organization (ILO), approximately 20 million workers are employed by the global chemical industry worldwide, including workers in the global chemical, pharmaceutical, and rubber and tire industries, but excluding oil, gas, coal, and refinery workers.[67] Thus far, just transition debates have gained limited attention, in either policy or practice, in the petrochemical industry, with the exception of cases of plant closures.[68] However, the petrochemical industry is facing increasing social and political pressure to decarbonize and to limit its production of toxic and wasteful products. This will have implications, ultimately, for both direct and indirect jobs in the industry. Within this context, issues of labor injustice should be considered along with those of environmental injustice, particularly for the global petrochemical workers who work in the most precarious and dangerous jobs.

Over the past decade, there have been several labor protests by outsourced migrant petrochemical workers in Saudi Arabia, the United Arab Emirates (UAE), and other Gulf countries over unpaid wages and wage arrears. According to the ILO's 2015 figures, more than 80 percent of the private sector workforce in Saudi Arabia and the UAE are migrant workers, employed under the coercive *kafala* (visa-sponsorship) system, which "gives employers excessive control over them, including the power to prevent them from changing jobs, escaping abusive labor situations, and, for some workers, leaving the country."[69] Migrants occupy jobs at different hierarchical levels, for example as shop-floor workers, staff managers, and senior managers, and thus they are positioned differently in relation to the *kafala* system.[70] On average, migrant workers are paid just over one-third of the salaries of Saudi workers in equivalent jobs, with salaries determined based on country of origin.[71] Despite reforms to the controversial *kafala* system in 2021, trade unions are not recognized within Saudi or Emirates law, and migrant workers do not have the right to strike or the right to collective bargaining.[72] The fear of deportation means that migrants tend to avoid direct confrontation through strikes or protests, using instead other forms of resistance such as sabotage and, in extreme cases, suicide.[73]

Given the lack of civil rights and freedom of information in these countries, it is difficult to obtain reliable information about public protests. While there have been several studies showing severe contamination and deadly explosions in petrochemical facilities in Saudi Arabia and the UAE, environmental protests have been rare.[74] However, there have been a number of media reports of labor protests, several involving police violence. In July 2007, 1,300 migrant workers from the Habshan Gas Complex Expansion project in Ruwais, near Abu Dhabi in the UAE, went on strike, demanding that their employer (the Greece-based Consolidated Contractors International Company) increase wages and grant a yearly trip home.[75] After four days the UAE armed forces broke up the strike, with conflicting reports over the number of deaths and injuries, resulting in the resignation of 300 workers.[76] In October 2018, the Saudi police fired on hundreds of migrant construction workers in the city of Dhahran, who were protesting over unpaid wages from Saudi Aramco's contractor Azmeel, killing an unspecified number of protestors.[77] According to a Pakistani news outlet, in January 2019, a number of Pakistani workers were shot dead by the police in Jubail, a major petrochemical complex in Saudi Arabia, for protesting over unpaid wages.[78]

Beyond scattered media reports, it is difficult to find information about public protests in these countries, and more difficult still to learn everyday working conditions. In one report, journalist William T. Vollmann offers rare insights from informal interviews with Pakistani and Indian migrant workers from the Ruwais refinery, conducted in autumn 2016 with the help of a translator from Rajasthan.[79] Workers were afraid of being taken away by the police for the smallest misstep, and they were not permitted to have cameras on their cell phones, ostensibly due to corporate concerns over industrial espionage. One worker described his living space as follows: "One hall and ten people. Blanket one by one. Three bed on wall, like this: top, middle, bottom. Each man has one cupboard with lock, but all money you have you must keep with you. Many bathroom is there; no kitchen. Free, paid for by company . . . I am here only for working, only for eating."[80] Vollmann reflected: "Would you call these laborers exploited? Mr. Rana Saqib's missing finger (from a workplace accident), and that common complaint about not getting enough 'oxygen,' not to mention the fear they so often showed (from the police), made me feel relieved not to be in their shoes."[81]

The interviews with refinery workers in Ruwais share many themes with interviews that Xinhong Wang and I conducted with migrant petrochemical workers in peri-urban Nanjing in China in 2016 (see figure 2.1).[82] Given the lack of employment opportunities in their hometowns, migrant petrochemical workers in Nanjing worked in the most hazardous jobs, lived in the closest proximity to the plants, and tolerated the heavily polluted working and living conditions.[83] Under the *hukou* system of household registration in China, rural migrants lack rights to welfare, local schools, health services, and employment protections. Many migrant workers in China have been unable to claim compensation from their employers for occupational diseases, such as pneumoconiosis, as without labor contracts they have been unable to obtain official diagnoses from government-designated hospitals.[84] A common refrain among migrant workers who we interviewed in Nanjing was, "But what can we do?"[85] This sentiment was related to frustration over political powerlessness rather than indifference. As one migrant worker scoffed, "They are all the Communist Party's factories, so why do we complain to the Communist Party?"[86]

Although there were no labor (or environmental) protests reported in Nanjing during the time of our research, there have been a number of labor protests by migrant workers in cities and industries throughout China over the past decade about unpaid wages and discriminatory treatment.[87] Strikes in China are illegal, and thus labor protests have occurred spontaneously, without the support of trade unions.[88] Migrant workers have typically sought to resolve labor issues through legal disputes first, and only then escalated their protests. However, as in Saudi Arabia and the UAE, illegal labor protests in China are risky, often resulting in violent clashes with the police with many injuries, deaths, and arrests.[89] Precarious migrant workers in toxic industries have been rendered "expendable" within global capitalism, which, as Cedric J. Robinson observed, has been "influenced in a most fundamental way by the forces of racism and nationalism."[90]

While the labor injustices of precarious migrant workers in the petrochemical industry are extreme in China and the Gulf countries, reliance on outsourced labor is endemic to the industry as a whole. Since the 1960s, the global petrochemical industry has increasingly relied on technological

Figure 2.1. Petrochemical transport company and coal power plant, Nanjing, March 2016. Photograph by Xinhong Wang.

innovation and automation to replace labor, resulting in the shrinkage of the core workforce, alongside an increase in technical knowledge and skill levels.[91] Relatedly, there has been a decline in the number of secure jobs and an increasing reliance on outsourced workers who work a wider range of tasks, including core logistics and maintenance operations as well as peripheral tasks such as cleaning, gardening, and security.[92] This resembles what Barry Bluestone and Bennett Harrison call "the hourglass economy" in their classic study of deindustrialization in America, where jobs cluster at high and low skill and income levels.[93] In fact, the petrochemical industry in Europe has experienced significant "labor deindustrialization," the contraction of manufacturing as a share of total employment. In a study of community and industry relations in Grangemouth, Scotland, Lorenzo Feltrin, David Brown, and I introduce the concept of "noxious deindustrialization" to convey the simultaneous occurrence of job losses and socioeconomic decline on the one hand, and continuing industrial activity and toxic pollution on the other—resulting in the fragmentation of industrial social contracts.[94]

The petrochemical town of Grangemouth is an exemplar of noxious deindustrialization but also of the limits of organized labor to challenge new

ENDURING TOXIC INJUSTICE

modes of petrochemical expansion in the twenty-first century. Grangemouth has a strong working-class identity. It was a petrochemical "boom town" in the 1960s but has endured a slow and painful history of socioeconomic decline since the 1970s. Although there have been a handful of vocal environmental activists in the area over the years, organized labor protests have been a more defining feature in the town. In 2005, the private petrochemical company INEOS, owned by self-made billionaire Jim Ratcliffe, bought the Grangemouth refinery and petrochemical complex from BP and weathered the financial crisis in 2008 with an aggressive restructuring program.[95] In 2008, members of the union Unite went on strike for two days to protect their pensions, and INEOS backed down. During an industrial dispute in 2013, INEOS effectively blackmailed the union, threatening to close down the plant if the workers did not accept the withdrawal of their final-salary pension scheme, a three-year freeze on wages and industrial action, and other compromises regarding their conditions.[96] The union capitulated, and workers had to reapply for their old jobs, losing two leading shop stewards and 30 to 40 percent of their directly employed workforce. However, instead of opening up job opportunities in the deprived local community, due to the skills gap, INEOS hired new workers from farther afield in the United Kingdom, and existing employees worked overtime. As a local representative put it, "What we have now is what we refer to as DIDOs, or drive in and drive out. People drive into work and they drive out at night. They take their well-earned cash with them and they spend it elsewhere."[97]

The increasing physical separation of many workers from fenceline petrochemical communities is one of the main barriers to bringing together labor and environmental justice concerns. When many petrochemical plants were built in the middle decades of the twentieth century, residences for workers were built close by. Over the years, with rising awareness of pollution and the increased outsourcing of employment, workers who can afford to do so have moved away from fenceline communities. Our research in Nanjing also revealed this dynamic: directly employed petrochemical workers lived away from the petrochemical fenceline, while migrant workers lived in close proximity to refineries and petrochemical plants.[98]

There have been some examples of "blue-green" labor and environmental justice coalitions in petrochemical fenceline communities—for example, port and refinery workers in the United States fighting for emissions regulations.[99] However, much of the literature on labor and environmental justice glosses over the acute differences in local conditions for struggle and possibilities for action, particularly when organized protests are repressed either violently or through other forms of coercion. There are structural gaps between labor and environmental justice protests at a global level, where the toxic injustices are uneven and dispersed and multiple social inequalities overlap and agglomerate in existential struggles over livelihoods. In later chapters, I will discuss this dynamic further and demonstrate how multiscalar activism has the potential to stitch some of these movements together.

The Challenge of Enduring Toxic Injustice

Both the fenceline community and the workplace are central sites of political struggle against the social and environmental harms of the petrochemical industry, with interconnected histories and futures. As this chapter has detailed, there are many challenges to forging stronger environmental and labor connections in contexts of declining industrial employment, fragmented trade unions, deep social inequalities, and polarized attitudes about working for oil and gas. On a planetary scale, the obstacles to forming transnational labor and environmental solidarities are even greater, with the rise of authoritarian and populist governments and the brutal repression of activists.

While the global environmental justice movement has grown over the past half century, toxic injustice has endured, underpinned by the problem of expendability, which manifests differently in time and place. Fenceline community mobilizations are episodic, typically escalating in relation to specific disputes and then returning to less fractious community-industry relations.[100] In many social and environmental justice conflicts over oil extraction and petrochemical pollution, people face violent repression and the loss of livelihoods and ancestral lands in addition to toxic exposures. Even in cases where there have been environmental justice victories, toxic exposures continue to aggregate and accumulate. Outsourced migrant workers in the global petrochemical industry work in the most dangerous jobs and lack basic employment protections, yet for the most part they remain disconnected from environmental struggles.

At this critical conjuncture, it is important to recognize the many achievements of environmental justice struggles around the world, even if the material and political wins do not always come through.[101] "Those on the environmental justice front lines have been living, dying, and fighting for a long time," Julie Sze observes, suggesting that there is much to be learned from environmental justice movements, which offer "important guidelines to troubled times" in terms of resistance, concepts, and living practices.[102] Remembering and rekindling the connections between diverse labor and environmental justice struggles could have important implications for multiscalar resistance against the destructive power of the petrochemical industry.

3

Multiscalar Activism and Petrochemical Proliferation

Over the past few years, there has been a groundswell of environmental justice activism around the world. In 2016, the #NoDAPL resistance movement against the construction of the Dakota Access Pipeline at Standing Rock attracted international media attention and solidarity from many Indigenous tribes and climate activists. The demonstrators at Standing Rock opposed the pipeline because it threatened Indigenous land, water, and sacred burial sites, and they faced widely documented police repression.[1] Despite the hostility of the Trump administration, important alliances were forged at Standing Rock, inspiring and intensifying further mobilizations.[2] That same year, on the other side of the world, the global Break Free from Plastic movement was launched, which grew out of decades of grassroots resistance to toxic plastic-waste incineration in Southeast Asia and called for "a future free from plastic pollution."[3] In 2017 and 2018, the marine plastics crisis hit international media headlines, featured in the final episode of David Attenborough's BBC series *Blue Planet II* and in *National Geographic*'s Plastic or Planet campaign, which galvanized the growing anti-plastics movement. In 2018, the Fridays for Future school climate strikes began, inspired by Swedish climate activist Greta Thunberg, and the Intergovernmental Panel on Climate Change (IPCC) published a stark report, warning that the world needs to reach net-zero emissions by 2050 or face untold climate catastrophe.[4] Since then, international climate activism has escalated dramatically, coalescing with a wide range of interconnected environmental justice campaigns.

Within this context, the global petrochemical industry has faced tremendous public pressure to transform, from both the downstream side of plastics and the upstream side of fossil fuels. Within just a few years, sustainability, the circular economy, net zero, and other environmental, social, and governance concerns have risen to the top of petrochemical industry agendas, presented as both threats and opportunities in relation to corporate success.

Building on the question of enduring toxic injustices in fenceline petrochemical communities, this chapter argues there are emerging yet fragile possibilities for fenceline communities to put additional pressure on the industry through what I call "multiscalar activism." In this form of activism, social and environmental justice issues beyond the local toxic effects of industry, such as climate justice, plastic waste, urban smog, systemic racism, and land rights, have broadened the base for community resistance. The concept of multiscalar activism links to the strong tradition of alliances within the environmental justice movement, but it also describes a planetary phenomenon, which extends solidarity beyond the spatial and discursive boundaries of the fenceline community. Multiscalar activism involves processes of "articulation," defined by Stuart Hall as "moments of arbitrary closure" within long-term political and cultural struggle, in which different elements temporarily unite.[5] It combines multifrontal nodes of activism across the petrochemical planet, which can work separately as well as in conjunction, at various points of articulation in wider struggles.

Since I began my research on the petrochemical industry, I have observed emerging forms of multiscalar activism in different petrochemical fenceline communities accompanying the rise in global public concern over the climate and plastics crises. In some cases, multiscalar activism was articulated through overt forms of coordinated action between different social groups and movements. In other cases, state violence and repression led to different manifestations of multiscalar activism, operating across low-profile contexts, which percolated at various critical moments. Multiscalar activism is contextual and relational, following Liboiron and Lepawsky's theory of scale as "a way to think about systems and relationships."[6] It can involve scaling up, but also scaling down, wide, across, and in multiple directions.[7] These diverge struggles form part of a wider environmental justice battle on multiple fronts and scales against the harmful expansion of the oil, petrochemical, and plastics complex.

Twin Dynamics of Resistance and Proliferation

In Naomi Klein's study of capitalism and the politics of climate change, Klein concludes with a sense of optimism about the promise of "Blockadia," which "is not a specific location on a map but rather a roving transnational conflict zone that is cropping up with increasing frequency and intensity wherever extractive projects are attempting to dig and drill, whether for open-pit mines, or gas fracking, or tar sands oil pipelines."[8] Since then, the movement against fossil fuel extractivism has gathered pace on an unprecedented global level, aligning with fenceline petrochemical community struggles. Solidarity has been forged across multiple social groups in resistance movements, from farmers to fisherfolk to school children. However, most of the pipelines, fracking wells, and petrochemical plants in question have nonetheless been built.[9]

Alongside mounting public resistance over the past decade, the global petrochemical industry has also witnessed a phenomenal period of sustained growth. These twin dynamics of popular resistance and petrochemical proliferation are intimately related, with new waves of resistance coalescing as extractive petrochemical investments encroach ever farther into new territories. In the United States alone, petrochemical corporations invested more than $200 billion in 333 petrochemical projects between 2008 and 2018, benefiting from cheap shale gas feedstocks.[10] With the forecasted decline in transportation fuel through the energy transition, state-owned national oil companies in Saudi Arabia and China have diversified into new petrochemical manufacturing processes that convert crude oil directly into petrochemicals. These new multi-billion-dollar crude-oil-to-chemicals (COTC) projects are predicted to have ten times the capacity of existing world-scale petrochemical plants, and they have started to come online.[11] While some petrochemical investments have been pushed back, the vast majority have continued to expand irrespective of increasing popular resistance. In fact, they show no signs of abating. What explains this disjunction between resistance mobilizations and petrochemical expansion, and what does it mean for the possibilities of activism?

One explanation for this trend is the self-perpetuating role of market forecasts in facilitating capital investments. While petrochemical industry leaders have a penchant for airing existential crisis, they consistently deny that ecological crisis is that much of a threat. Invariably, they return to a script in which industry comes out ahead, pointing to market forecasts for increased demand in plastics and green technologies. At the height of the public backlash over the marine plastics crisis in 2018, the executive director of Petrochemicals Europe stated confidently, "All major studies show substantial market growth for petrochemicals worldwide, which is certainly linked to the fact that 95% of all manufactured goods are made from petrochemicals."[12] The director was referring to a 2018 report by the International Energy Agency (IEA), which found that petrochemicals were "rapidly becoming the largest driver of global oil consumption" and predicted that petrochemicals would account for nearly half of global oil demand by 2050.[13]

Following the historical crude oil price crash of 2020 and the increased demand for single-use plastics throughout the pandemic, the IEA ramped up its forecasts for future growth in petrochemicals. A 2021 report outlined oil market uncertainties but remarked optimistically that "the petrochemical industry remains a pillar of growth over the forecast period. Ethane, LPG [liquid petroleum gas] and naphtha [petrochemical feedstocks] together account for 70% of the projected increase in oil product demand to 2026."[14] Echoing this view, energy historian Daniel Yergin predicted that there would be resilient oil futures for decades to come, regardless of climate protests, bolstered by US fracking, expanding plastics markets, Russian geopolitics, and exceptional growth in China.[15] Environmentalist Bill McKibben countered in a skeptical book review, "Yergin understands oil markets . . . but he's behind the curve on the volatile mix of activism, engineering and climate science that seems to be reshaping the energy world in real time."[16] I would like to agree with McKibben, but it is difficult to make declarative statements about the future of oil and petrochemical markets in the midst of uncertainty and conflict.

My point is not about the reliability of forecasts to predict the actual future; it's that the very act of making market predictions reinforces dominant narratives and existing systems. Political economist Peter Newell argues that the IEA has been known to overestimate growth in fossil fuel markets, creating a self-fulfilling investment cycle. "Within energy forecasts," Newell writes, "demand is always projected to increase, so the essential work of the models is to work out which energy sources and technologies are able to close the energy gap: often foreclosing questions of reducing demand or the adoption of energy efficiency and conservation measures."[17] Sociologists Olivier Courtyard and Elizabeth Shove make the related observation that strategies of "predict and provide—in which planners anticipate future 'need' and build capacity capable of meeting it—have acted as self-fulling prophecies: generating the very forms of demand to which investments and infrastructures are allegedly a response."[18] Thus, it is not surprising that the IEA predicts future oil growth through the energy transition, driven by petrochemicals and plastics.

By and large, given the dominant priorities of economic growth, the relentless quest for petrochemical expansion around the planet has gone unchallenged by governments. Yet the pressure for profound petrochemical transformation is mounting. Key figures in the climate divestment movement have started to question the oil industry's growth projections for plastics, which would become "stranded assets" in the transition away from fossil fuels.[19] On February 28, 2022, the IPCC issued another major report about the climate emergency, warning that the "point of no return is now in sight," which commentators called its "bleakest assessment yet."[20] The same week, the United Nations Environment Assembly in Nairobi agreed on a landmark mandate to negotiate a global treaty on plastic pollution, across every stage of the lifecycle of plastics, from fossil fuel extraction through to refining, petrochemical production, plastics consumption, and waste disposal.[21] The significance of this news was overshadowed by the Russian invasion of Ukraine, which brought a different kind of attention to the problem of fossil fuel dependence, resulting in the unprecedented severing of multiple state and corporate ties to Russian oil and gas, alongside renewed impetus for oil drilling and fossil fuel expansion elsewhere. According to Somini Sengupta, ten days after the invasion, US oil companies were "suddenly upbeat again."[22] Months later, the oil industry posted record profits.[23]

Many environmental justice struggles are protracted, involving uphill battles against powerful corporations and states. The most "successful" environmental justice campaigns, in terms of achieving remediation, compensation, or relocation, have involved coordinated action beyond the local level, gaining media attention, public support, and solidarity across different regional and national contexts.[24] This chapter argues that the significance of environmental justice struggles goes beyond material achievements by challenging dominant narratives and ideologies, building on long histories of resistance, and fostering new forms of solidarity. In what follows, I will explore the theme of multiscalar activism through a series of interconnected cases that cut across fenceline petrochemical communities, beginning with Indigenous resistance to pipeline expansion and climate change in North America, then following the petrochemical flows to China, before delving into diverse forms of multiscalar activism that unite both contexts, and finally considering the plastics lifecycle approach of the global anti-plastics movement.

Converging Resistance in Cancer Alley:
Pipelines and Petrochemicals

Indigenous resistance to fossil fuel infrastructure, including direct actions and legal battles over land rights, has become one of the most powerful forms of environmental justice activism. There is a long history of Indigenous resistance to oil and gas pipelines. Two of the most widely reported pipeline battles are the #NoDAPL resistance movement at Standing Rock in 2016, which attracted more than 10,000 protestors, and the mobilization against the proposed Keystone Pipeline XL between 2008 and 2015, which also attracted considerable media and political attention. Both proposed oil pipelines would traverse sovereign Indigenous lands, waters, and sacred sites, and were opposed by Indigenous tribes, environmental activists, landowners, and many members of the public. If built, the pipelines would contravene the right to "free, prior and informed consent" for land use and development on sovereign Indigenous territories, which are protected in the United Nations Declaration on the Rights of Indigenous Peoples.[25] These controversial pipeline projects reached the highest level of political intervention, with US presidents using their powers to decide whether to block or permit them. The Obama administration vetoed the construction of the Keystone Pipeline XL in 2015 and temporarily blocked the Dakota Access Pipeline in 2016. In early 2017, within days of taking office, President Trump signed an executive order to approve both pipelines. Then, in 2021, President Biden shut down the Keystone Pipeline XL once again, but delayed action to shut down the Dakota Access Pipeline while waiting for an environmental assessment following the 2020 Supreme Court ruling that the pipeline was illegal because the operator's federal permit violated the National Environmental Policy Act.

Across North America, there have been a number of other Indigenous mobilizations against pipelines that have aligned with environmental activists, farmers, and frontline communities, extending a "network of resistance" based on interconnected struggles.[26] An inspiring example is the Unist'ot'en Camp, which has reoccupied Wet'suwet'en land in northern British Columbia since 2009 and resisted the Enbridge Northern Gateway Pipeline, the Chevron Pacific Trail Pipeline, and the TransCanada Coastal GasLink Pipeline. The Unist'ot'en Camp's resistance campaign is part of a long history of Wet'suwet'en resistance to settler colonialism, which led to the landmark Delgamuukw decision in 1997 by the Supreme Court of Canada that the Wet'suwet'en and Gixtsan had never ceded their land and thus retained their aboriginal title.[27] The Unist'ot'en Camp extends their politics of resistance to pipelines beyond their region, considering the multiscalar impacts of development on neighboring regions and wider ecologies, including interconnected ecosystems and climate change.[28]

One of the key points of convergence in multiscalar activism has been in environmental justice battles over pipelines in fenceline petrochemical communities. For example, in 2013, the Aamjiwnaang community in Sarnia-Lambton town in Ontario, also known as "Chemical Valley," connected their long-standing struggles against toxic petrochemical exposures to broader regional campaigns against the proposed Enbridge Line 9 tar sands pipeline, which would terminate in Sarnia on unceded Aamijiwnaang land.[29] In the United States, tribal leaders also demonstrated against fracking developments in Pennsylvania, from the fracking wells to the pipelines and petrochemical infrastructure.[30]

In Cancer Alley in Louisiana, the Bayou Bridge Pipeline project was a catalyst for new forms of multiscalar activism in the region. The Bayou Bridge Pipeline is the final link of the Dakota Access Pipeline, dubbed the "tail end of the Black Snake" by environmental justice activists, terminating in St. James Parish in Cancer Alley.[31] As such, it brought two major environmental justice movements together: first, the growing Indigenous resistance movement against oil and gas pipelines, just months after the #NoDAPL protests at Standing Rock; and second, the environmental justice struggles of Black fenceline communities fighting against toxic petrochemical pollution and environmental racism in Cancer Alley. The two movements found common cause in their strong opposition to the transcontinental pipeline, and in their shared concerns about the threat that it posed to fragile wetland ecosystems and to community health.

Just over 162 miles in length, the Bayou Bridge Pipeline is a crude oil pipeline across eight waterways of Louisiana's Atchafalaya Basin, the largest floodplain swamp in the United States. A joint venture between Energy Transfer Partners (the same company that built the Dakota Access Pipeline), Phillips 66, and Sunoco Logistics Partners, the permit application for construction was announced in October 2016 in a joint public notice by the US Army Corps of Engineers and the Louisiana Department of Natural Resources. In June 2017, Reverend Harry Joseph, the pastor of St. James Parish, filed a lawsuit against the pipeline in a case put forward by the Tulane Environmental Law Clinic. The residents of St. James Parish were already embroiled in battles against two new multi-billion-dollar methanol plants in the region, and this was yet another major hazard that they did not want in their community. In interviews with journalists, Reverend Joseph described local frustrations with the ongoing health hazards in Cancer Alley in eloquent phrasing: "We are sick and tired of being sick and tired."[32] The same month, Indigenous water protectors set up a prayer and resistance camp blocking the pipeline construction called *L'eau est la vie* ("Water is life"), founded by Cherri Foytlin, of Diné and Cherokee heritage, carrying on the legacy of the water protectors from Standing Rock.[33] Many of the activists at the camp had been at Standing Rock. For the water protectors, the affirmation "water is life" (or Mni Wiconi) relates to the idea of "being a good relative," which extends to the water, land, animals, and human world.[34]

The Bayou Bridge Pipeline struggles were reported in the media, drawing comparisons with Standing Rock. Several of the members of the Indigenous resistance camp faced felony charges under anti-protest laws that framed pipelines as "critical infrastructure."[35] However, the Bayou Bridge Pipeline resistance did not reach the same iconic levels of international solidarity and public attention as Standing Rock, attracting dozens as compared with thousands of activists. Law scholar Adam Crepelle, who describes the Bayou Bridge Pipeline conflict as part of a broader "Standing Rock in the Swamp," examines the contrast between the unprecedented public interest in the Sioux's resistance at Standing Rock and the lack of recognition of the Houma's rights to protect their land, water, and air in Louisiana. According to Crepelle, the Houma are neither well known nor federally recognized, as compared with the Sioux, but the Houma's battles with the oil industry have a longer history. Furthermore, the implication of a lack of federal recognition is that "the Houma have suffered discrimination because of their Indian blood while simultaneously having their Indian ancestry questioned."[36] Indeed, according to activists, the Indigenous resistance camp at Bayou Bridge Pipeline was criticized for drawing supporters from outside Louisiana. In the 2019 documentary film *L'eau est la vie (Water Is Life): From Standing Rock to the Swamp*, Cherri Foytlin responded to this allegation, saying: "So what? It's not my fault Energy Transfer Partners made enemies all up and down the country. . . . They made the enemies themselves. So yeah, a lot of people want to come down to fight."[37] Foytlin also pointed out that the resistance camp was led entirely by a network of Indigenous women who were local to Louisiana.

Indigenous water protectors joined their struggles with those of grassroots environmental justice activists who were fighting against the proliferation of the petrochemical industry in St. James (see figure 3.1). Climate and environmental groups from nearby metropolitan areas also came to join the resistance movement. The Toxic Expertise project organized three research trips to St. James between 2016 and 2018.[38] During the first trip in spring 2016, the main environmental justice activism against petrochemical expansions was led by the Baptist Church, with the support of local environmental organizations such as the Sierra Club and the Louisiana Bucket Brigade. By autumn 2017, with the increased public attention to the area due to the Bayou Bridge Pipeline, several other environmental organizations had become active in the area. At organized pipeline resistance events, speakers and participants observed multi-faith Christian and Indigenous ceremonial practices. Differences in religious belief were set aside out of respect for the leadership across different faith-based organizations, notably the Baptist Church in St. James and the Indigenous Environmental Network, a coalition of environmental justice groups.[39] The coalition was interesting in light of recent Indigenous criticisms of the US environmental justice movement for failing to take seriously the question of decolonization.[40] In the pipeline resistance events, some of the activists discussed solidarity in terms of their different yet interconnected histories of slavery and colonization.[41] When we asked a leading environmental activist how she stayed positive in light of the weight of petrochemical advances in her state, she responded that it was the people, the friendships, and the solidarity.[42]

The Bayou Bridge Pipeline was eventually completed as planned in 2019. On many levels, it could be interpreted as a defeat, not only in material terms but also symbolically, especially in comparison with the critical mass behind the #NoDAPL resistance at Standing Rock. On another level, the legacy of multiscalar activism over Bayou Bridge could be interpreted in a more positive

Figure 3.1. Residents signing a wooden cross in protest against the Bayou Bridge Pipeline in St. James Parish, Louisiana, September 2017. Photograph by Thom Davies.

light. While the pipeline resistance dispersed, fenceline community struggles over petrochemical pollution in St. James were emboldened. The increased media, environmental, and political attention to the pipeline resistance in Cancer Alley brought the wider problem of environmental injustice and racism in the region to wider attention. Grassroots environmental justice organizations continued to engage in forms of multiscalar activism, building new coalitions and networks.

A grassroots environmental justice organization, RISE St. James, led by Sharon Lavigne, received national recognition for leading a fight against the proposed $9.4 million fourteen-plant petrochemical complex in St. James Parish by the Taiwanese petrochemical company Formosa Plastics.[43] The Formosa complex would more than double the area's toxic air pollution, release up to 13 million metric tons of greenhouse gases a year, and more than triple exposure to cancer-causing chemicals, which are staggering estimates in an area that is already infamous for toxic pollution.[44] In January 2020, a coalition of local environmental groups, including RISE St. James, the Center for Biological Diversity, the Louisiana Bucket Brigade, and Healthy Gulf, filed a lawsuit against the US Army Corps of Engineers for issuing an unlawful

CHAPTER 3

wetlands permit to Formosa Plastics, which failed to evaluate the water, air, and health impacts of the proposed facility and failed to adequately protect burial sites of enslaved Black people who were discovered on the property.[45]

In June 2020, Lavigne and other local community leaders took Formosa Plastics to court so that they could visit the gravesites legally to honor their ancestors on Juneteenth, which commemorates the emancipation of African American slaves. "I feel like our ancestors are shouting and rejoicing in heaven about what we did for them today," Lavigne commented in an interview after the Juneteenth ceremony.[46] Lavigne was motivated by the widespread protests over racial justice that followed the police murder of George Floyd the month before. "We are seeing change that should have been here a long time ago," she said. "Building the [Formosa] plant in a Black community shows that they just want us to die off."[47] Some environmental justice activists drew direct comparisons between the phrase "I can't breathe" and environmental racism, referring to the disproportionate burden of toxic pollution in communities of color.[48] Robert Bullard, widely recognized as the "father of the environmental justice movement," put it this way: "We are talking about *what* we breathe."[49] The Black Lives Matter movement put the spotlight on systemic racism and the violent disregard for Black lives, including environmental racism, which has long been endured in Cancer Alley.

In January 2021, President Biden mentioned "Cancer Alley" and "environmental justice" by name in his announcement of a new executive order to tackle climate change and pollution: "With this executive order, environmental justice will be at the center of all we do addressing the disproportionate health and environmental and economic impacts on communities of color—so-called fenceline communities—especially . . . the hard-hit areas like Cancer Alley in Louisiana or the Route 9 corridor in the state of Delaware."[50] This announcement was met with optimism by local environmental groups, who noted that the term "Cancer Alley" was rarely mentioned even in state-level politics, and that it was significant for it to be mentioned by a US president.[51] In March 2021, United Nations human rights experts wrote a report that condemned the concentration of toxic petrochemical plants in Cancer Alley as a form environmental racism that "poses serious and disproportionate threats to the enjoyment of several human rights of its largely African-American residents, including the right to equality and nondiscrimination, the right to life, the right to health, right to an adequate standard of living and cultural rights."[52] The UN report drew international attention to half a century of toxic injustice and environmental justice activism in the region. The environmental lawsuit against the Formosa Plastics permit was dismissed, but in summer 2021, the US Army Corps of Engineers announced that they would commission a full environmental impact review of the planned expansion, which would likely delay the project by more than two years.[53]

Only time will tell how much difference these environmental justice "victories" will make to the health, environment, and wellbeing of people in St. James Parish, in the Atchafalaya Basin, or indeed elsewhere among the dense web of fossil fuel infrastructure connecting pipelines to petrochemical projects to petrochemical markets around the world. The multiscalar activism surrounding pipelines and petrochemical plants is part of a powerful network of resistance involving different communities and social groups across North America, but this activism tends to stop at the border, as crude oil, ethane, and liquified natural gas tankers set off to petrochemical markets in Europe and Asia.

Petrochemical Shipping Flows

In December 2021, China entered into the "longest and largest" liquified natural gas (LNG) trade deal with the United States, from two sites in Plaquemines Parish, Louisiana, involving the US company Venture Global and the state-owned China National Offshore Oil Corporation (CNOOC). According to Shi Chenggang, chairman of CNOOC's gas and power division, the trade deal marked a step toward meeting China's climate commitments: "As China's largest LNG importer, CNOOC is committed deeply not only to the mission of securing China's gas supply, but also to the climate goals of building a carbon-neutral China by 2060."[54] By early 2022, China was poised to become a "major trading force in the global LNG trade," overtaking Japan in 2021 as the world's largest importer of LNG, with imports increasing by 18 percent to 79 million tons.[55]

China's increased use of LNG has particular significance in terms of climate policy, given China's continued reliance on coal, the dirtiest of all fossil fuels. In energy transition debates, natural gas is typically positioned as a "transition fuel" because it releases fewer carbon emissions than oil or coal.[56] Many climate policymakers would therefore see this as a positive step. However, LNG exports from the US are far from climate friendly: the gas is extracted by fracking, which releases considerable methane emissions (a worse greenhouse gas than carbon), uses toxic chemicals that contaminate water and land, requires large amounts of water, and damages health.[57] Furthermore, fracking wells decline very quickly, losing the majority of their productive capacity within just a few years. The ecological implications of the fracking boom are evident in a toxic trail of spent fracking wells and a continually shifting frontier of fracking exploration, with over 1.7 million fracking wells in the United States as of 2021.[58]

The United States first started exporting its fracked ethane (a petrochemical feedstock) in 2016, when the UK petrochemical giant INEOS pioneered the development of the world's largest shipping multi-gas carrier, which could transport fracked ethane, LNG, and other liquified gases from the United States to Europe. In January 2021, the world's largest single shipment of ethane was transported to China from Energy Transfer's terminal in Nederland, Texas. As if these ships weren't large enough, in February 2022, INEOS launched an even larger ethane carrier to transport US ethane and other petrochemical gas products to Europe and China.[59]

The surge in China's LNG imports has been driven not only by its climate and energy security ambitions but also by its plans to ramp up economic growth. The LNG imports followed record high exports of US crude oil to China from Louisiana's offshore supertanker port in January 2021, as Asian buyers stockpiled oil in anticipation of a post-pandemic recovery.[60] The petrochemical sector witnessed considerable growth in demand for single-use plastic packaging and personal protective equipment (PPE) during the pandemic, with the largest growth occurring across petrochemical markets in China. This growth was expected to continue. In a talk for IHS Markit on plastic resin (petrochemical) markets in the United States and China in spring 2022, Joel Morales, executive director of Polyolefins Americas, commented: "What we've seen in the last couple of years has been nothing short of amazing for polymer consumption."[61]

Intensifying petrochemical and fossil fuel expansion in the United States, concentrated in the Gulf Coast, is directly tied to growing markets in China as well as to other markets around the world. In St. James Parish in Louisiana, a key source of local controversy has been over the $1.85 billion YCI Methanol One (petrochemical) greenfield investment project, a partnership between the Chinese company Yuhuang Chemical Industries and Koch Methanol. This mega methanol project was announced by Yuhuang in 2014 and began construction in 2017, but it stalled because of strong opposition from environmental justice groups, permit disputes, cost overruns, and construction delays. At the time of writing, the project continues to develop with the financial backing of Koch Methanol, and it has a planned production capacity of 1.7 million metric tons of methanol per year, primarily for plastics markets in the United States and in China.[62]

MULTISCALAR ACTIVISM

Petrochemical Growth and Anti-PX Protests in China

China became the world's largest petrochemical producer by revenue in 2011, overtaking the long-dominant United States and Europe.[63] Since then, the industry has continued to grow at a remarkable pace, led by three state-owned enterprises: Sinopec Group, China National Petroleum Corporation (CNPC), and China National Offshore Oil Corporation. According to industry forecasts, China is expected to account for 29 percent of all new global petrochemical capacity additions between 2021 and 2030.[64]

The rapid growth of the petrochemical industry in China in the twenty-first century has contributed to increasingly acute problems of pollution, with a number of heavily contaminated rivers and days of high smog. During this period, environmental protection emerged as a top government priority in China. In 2007, "ecological civilization" became the goal of the Chinese Community Party, and the phrase was later elevated to the party's Constitution in 2012 and the Constitution of the People's Republic of China in 2018.[65] However, as Yifei Li and Judith Shapiro argue, state-led environmentalism in China is accomplished through coercive mechanisms of political and social control over research funding, industrial subsidies, and media programming. Within this context, "environmental NGOs and scientists are forced to cooperate with the state if they wish to survive, playing a delicate game of testing boundaries and carefully monitoring the prevailing political winds."[66] Most environmental activists in China have thus adopted strategies of "embedded activism," "rightful resistance," and "soft confrontation" by pushing for changes within the legal and political constraints of the state.[67] In everyday life, residents in heavily polluted areas of rural China often engage in subtle forms of "resigned activism," oriented toward protecting families from the immediate harms of pollution.[68]

Despite abundant government propaganda on the safety of paraxylene (PX) and the government's restrictions against mass demonstrations, many planned petrochemical projects in China have met with public resistance due to concerns about environmental and health risks.[69] Inspired by the first anti-PX protest in 2007 in Xiamen, which resulted in the relocation of a PX project, there have been a number of anti-PX protests in China, which were loosely structured, voluntary, mass activities initiated by individuals rather than organized movements.

Environmental conflicts in semi-authoritarian countries are often articulated within wider demands for social and political reforms.[70] In a study on protests against the construction of a bridge in Istanbul in Turkey, a "country coping with, instead of being defined by, democracy," Aimilia Voulvouli argues that the protests were "transenvironmental," extending beyond immediate environmental concerns to issues of democratic rights.[71] In the more restrictive context of China, where social gatherings can be punished as crimes against social order, anti-PX protests can be understood as "transenvironmental," in which "rightful resistance" over environmental protection offers a relatively safe channel for the public to express their frustrations over deep-rooted social and political problems. However, the wave of anti-PX protests in China abated with the tightening of civil society restrictions under Xi Jinping.

The first anti-PX protest in China happened in Xiamen, Fujian Province, in June 2007, when several thousand urban residents demonstrated against the planned siting of a petrochemical plant in their city. The protests were framed as a "collective stroll" (*jiti sanbu*) by people to "legitimize their action as peaceful and apolitical."[72] The mass protests were animated by extensive media coverage of opposition to the PX plant from 105 national committee members, including Zhao Yufen, a professor at Xiamen University. Christoph Steinhardt and Fengshi Wu argue that the anti-PX campaign in Xiamen in 2007 was a "transformative event," one based on alliances between elites and ordinary citizens that were the outcome of intersecting processes of street mobilization and policy advocacy.[73] Ultimately, the Xiamen anti-PX protests were successful in stopping the project. However, following patterns of the displacement of toxic harms to more vulnerable communities, the planned petrochemical project was moved from Xiamen to the Gulei Peninsula in Zhangzhou, also in Fujian Province, where there have since been major explosions in 2013, 2015, and 2017.[74]

Xiamen inspired several large-scale anti-PX protests in cities and regions across China, despite government propaganda insisting on the safety of PX and media suppression about the protest events.[75] In 2011 in Dalian, a typhoon caused toxic leaks from chemical tanks at a PX plant, leading to anti-PX protests that resulted in the relocation of the plant. In Ningbo in Jiangsu Province in 2012, large-scale demonstrations in urban Ningbo followed smaller protests by villagers living in the Zhenhai district over a planned petrochemical expansion project, which the local government agreed to stop.[76] In 2012, there was an environmental campaign in Kunming in Yunnan Province to prevent a new refinery project, but the project went ahead with construction.[77] As Sibo Chen argues, the media reporting of anti-PX protests was highly skewed, both within the Chinese media, which characterized protesters as irrational, and within Western media, which framed the protests as urban middle-class forms of liberal resistance.[78] In fact, urban and class dimensions were more complex, including rural peasants, in the case of Ningbo, and marginalized cities and urban districts, in the cases of Dalian and Kunming.

The 2014 anti-PX protests in Maoming, "the oil town of the South," resulted in bloody confrontations between the protesters and the police.[79] In contrast with other cities in China where anti-PX protests occurred, Maoming was economically dependent on the petrochemical industry. Residents were fed up not only with toxic pollution but also with the corruption of local officials; in 2014, two former party secretaries in Maoming were sentenced to "death with reprieve" (a two-year suspended sentence before execution in China's criminal law) for corruption.[80] Furthermore, Maoming lacked an organizational basis of support from environmental organizations, and the protests were organized spontaneously through social media. The local protests were fueled by anger and a complete lack of trust in the government, escalating to direct action and rioting, which were violently repressed by the police.[81] The protests failed to gain media attention or public sympathy, and they also served as a cautionary tale about the limits of environmental protests in China. Since Xi Jinping came to power in 2013, the Chinese government has dramatically increased the repression of civil society groups, jailing dozens of human rights lawyers and NGO activists.[82] In 2016 in Chengdu, riot police arrested a number of residents who were suspected of putting facemasks on statues to protest over smog in the city.[83] In the aftermath of a deadly explosion at a petrochemical plant in Jiangsu Province in 2019, which killed seventy-eight people and injured 617, the police swiftly suppressed media reporting and detained several journalists.[84]

During the time of our research on the petrochemical industry in China, anti-PX protests were subsiding in frequency. People who had been involved in the Xiamen anti-PX protests in 2007, or who had witnessed the Tianjin explosions in 2015, were reluctant to share their stories. By 2018, with a new law coming into force in China that required all foreign environmental NGOs to register with the authorities, there was heightened political sensitivity to doing research on environmental issues in China, particularly in relation to state-owned enterprises. Rather than focusing on sites of reported protest or controversy, we decided to examine residential areas located close to petrochemical sites, starting with Nanjing, a leading traditional base of the petrochemical industry in China.[85]

The Turnip and the Mole

Located along the lower reach of the Yangtze River, Nanjing is a heavily polluted megacity with a dense concentration of chemical industry areas and a high number of smog days. The city is surrounded by hills in three directions and water in another, which traps polluted air and prevents an easy escape route in the event of a disaster. The protests over pollution in Nanjing have been small in scale and highly localized. At the time of writing, the largest environmental protest to have been reported in Nanjing was a campaign in 2011 to save urban trees.[86] However, discreet forms of multiscalar activism have been taking place through the work of local environmental organizations on the monitoring and reporting of pollution.

According to Li, a project leader for a local environmental organization, most of the environmental organizations in Nanjing and indeed throughout China focus on "individuals."[87] Her own organization takes a different approach, focusing on issues rather than on individuals. Li described an important strategic insight that her student-led environmental organization had learned in Nanjing after nearly two decades of work on raising environmental awareness. Up until 2016, their primary focus had always been on "cultivating individuals." In particular, they aimed to "initiate" individuals, which "means to push for changes on an individual, from their mindset to their action." However, in 2016 they decided to shift to an issue-based approach, motivated by their collaboration with the Institute of Public and Environmental Affairs environmental research organization in China, which focused on pollution issues, environmental information disclosure, and data transparency. Li recalled that it was a valuable learning process: "We were like a blank canvas and tagged along with their investigation and research to learn by doing."[88] They learned that by focusing on local issues, rather than on cultivating individuals, they could help to solve practical matters, such as the problem of excessive discharge from the sewage treatment plants in a chemical industrial park.

At first, they had tried the "individual" approach with their environmental projects in Nanjing. Li reflected: "But then we realized it's much more difficult to do it here. Why? In Jiangsu, let's look at Nanjing first: the culture here has its characteristic. The people here are dubbed 'large turnips.' Why? It's from the saying, 'every turnip to its hole.'" In other words, each person has their own position. In comparison with the cities where she had worked and lived in China, Li and her colleagues felt that the "culture" in Nanjing was more reserved and less open to collaboration: "If one is forced into hugging, it'll be awkward. And even if they are made to hug and hold each other, they just do it for formality. It wouldn't work. But that's fine, we just need to find other ways."

In 2016, Li's organization decided to shift their strategy from an individual to an issues-based approach, based on their "learning." They started a project focusing on environmental issues in the Yangtze River's Nanjing section, including environmental monitoring of the chemical industry. Paralleling the work of other environmental NGOs in China, they worked with the companies and with the local government to report their findings and make recommendations. Many of their activities could be described as forms of "embedded activism," which change over time, working within the constraints of existing social and political structures, guided by pragmatism and careful attention to the possibilities of change. One aspect of their work that was perhaps distinctive was their philosophy of learning and adapting their strategies to local contexts in their efforts to find practical "solutions." For example, Li noted that there were some rare instances of people who were willing to speak out to try to make a change, but she also emphasized that in heavily polluted places, "The government is looking very closely at the people and that stops people from talking about things. It's a place-specific risk. If the pollution is rather bad in that place, people there don't dare speak out." When asked about the concept of "environmental justice," Li said that this was only a "loanword," and that at most, people would ask, "Why did it happen to our village? Why me?" Recognizing that each person has their own position, or "every turnip to its hole," is an important insight for reflective and pragmatic environmental change.

On one level, the possibilities and limitations of environmental activism over petrochemical pollution in the Yangtze River in China are radically different from those in the Atchafalaya Basin wetlands in Louisiana. However, there are also important similarities with the locked-in petrochemical infrastructure concentrated in both regions, the continuing expansion of controversial projects, the repression of dissent, and the everyday activism that continues.

Multiscalar activism is not only about "scaling up" activism; it is also about burrowing below, to concealed levels, both in terms of space and in terms of time. In the aftermath of the armed repression of the resistance camp at Standing Rock, Nick Estes invoked the important yet under-recognized figure of the mole in revolutionary struggles for social and environmental justice:

Karl Marx explained the nature of revolutions through the figure of the mole, which burrows through history, making elaborate tunnels and preparing to surface again. The most dramatic moments come when the mole breaks the surface: revolution. But revolution is a mere moment within the longer movement of history. The mole is easily defeated on the surface by counterrevolutionary forces if she hasn't adequately prepared her subterranean spaces, which provide shelter and safety; even when pushed back underground the mole doesn't stop her work. In song and ceremony, Lakota revere the mole for her hard work collecting medicines from the roots underfoot. During his campaign against US military invasion, to protect himself Crazy Horse collected fresh dirt from mole mounds. Hidden from view to outsiders, this constant tunneling, plotting, planning, harvesting, remembering, and conspiring for freedom—the collective faith that another world is possible—is the most important aspect of revolutionary work. It is from every life that the collective confidence to change reality grows, giving rise to extraordinary events.[89]

Connecting Struggles along the Plastics Value Chain

Time and again, I am amazed by the spirit and perseverance of activists who refuse to give way to pessimism and instead continue to fight, spurred on by solidarity with other activists and by anger at the many injustices that they see. One of the most important multiscalar environmental campaigns to align with fenceline petrochemical struggles on a planetary level, led by grassroots movements in Southeast Asia, is over the issue of plastic pollution. Between 2017 and 2018, public alarm over the marine plastics crisis rose to unprecedented levels around the world, as people responded to harrowing media images of turtles and seabirds entangled in plastics. This new attention added strength and numbers to the growing global anti-plastic movement, which had been fighting against plastic pollution for decades. A key point of intersection between fenceline petrochemical struggles and anti-plastic campaigns is over the issue of environmental injustice across the whole plastics lifecycle, from fossil fuel extraction to petrochemical production to plastic consumption, waste, and disposal.[90]

Contrary to popular perceptions that grassroots environmental activism over the problem of plastic packaging waste began in Europe and North America, it began, in fact, in the early 1990s in South Asia, with citizen movements to ban plastic bags, which were accumulating in sewers and drains, causing flooding, and killing animals. Bangladesh was the first country to legislate against plastic bags in 2002 due to clogged drains during a major flood; it was followed by a number of countries in Southeast Asia and Africa, and then by countries in Europe and North America in the 2000s.[91] Plastic bag bans have been fought by the plastics and petrochemical industries, particularly in the United States, through lawsuits, lobbying, and advertising campaigns.[92] The problems of plastic waste are evident around the world, but they are particularly concentrated in Asia and Africa, with cities and shorelines now heaving with plastic that is destroying livelihoods, wildlife, and ecosystems. This distressing accumulation is connected to decades of environmentally unjust practices by corporations and governments, including the aggressive marketing of nonrecyclable single-use "sachets" (single portions of food and hygiene products) to low-income groups in Asia and Africa by plastics companies to open up new growth markets; the unjust transnational disposal of contaminated plastic waste from high-income to middle- and low-income countries, either through trade or dumping, which many activists and scholars term "waste colonialism" or "toxic colonialism"; and the related transnational transfer of dirty technological "solutions," such as waste incineration.[93]

The unjust international trade in toxic plastic waste came to international attention in 2017, when China announced its National Sword policy, banning the import of contaminated postconsumer plastics and scrap metal. Since 1992, China had taken in more than half of the world's scrap plastic for recycling, but due to concerns over pollution from plastic waste incineration, the government decided to refuse the contaminated imports.[94] This single policy move marked a major disruption in global recycling systems, exposing the inadequacy of North American and European recycling schemes to handle their own waste, and prompting a flood of shipments of scrap plastic to countries in Southeast Asia and subsequent bans and restrictions to stem the flow.[95] In May 2019, the Basel Convention on the Control of Transboundary Movements of Hazardous Wastes and Their Disposal adopted an amendment to their original convention, which for the first time classified most plastic waste as "hazardous." The amendment was fiercely opposed by the petrochemical and plastics industries, and it was met with cautious optimism by environmental activists.[96] By including plastic waste in the definition of hazardous waste, developing countries now had the right to refuse shipments from other countries, as the law required prior informed consent. However, in practice, the unequal trade has continued, linked to long histories of colonialism and debt, whereby poor countries rely on financial compensation for receiving toxic shipments.

The Break Free from Plastic movement was launched in 2016, a coalition of environmental NGOs and individuals around the world, with more than 11,000 members (organizations and individuals) to date.[97] Von Hernandez, the global coordinator for the movement, won the Goldman Environment Prize in 2003 for his work campaigning against toxic waste incinerators in the Philippines, which had led to the world's first national waste incineration ban in 1999. While working as the first Asia toxics campaigner for Greenpeace, Hernandez realized that rich countries were not only exporting toxic waste to developing countries; they were also exporting dirty technologies, such as waste incineration. As Hernandez explained in an interview: "The plastics industry loves incineration because it makes the problem 'disappear.' What it actually means is that you transform the problem from a waste problem to a toxic air pollution problem. So, there's definitely a public health argument against incineration, because the local communities become victims. There has been study after study linking greater incidence of cancer in communities living around incinerator plants."[98] This insightful analysis has implications for considering the industry's promotion and development of "chemical recycling" technologies in response to the plastic waste crisis, a pilot technology still in development that breaks plastics back down to their molecular structure in highly carbon-intensive and toxic processing plants.[99] Effectively, environmental campaigners argue, chemical recycling is another word for incineration.[100]

The Break Free from Plastic movement has played a crucial role in countering damaging industry narratives about solutions. In July 2022, the Ocean Conservancy retracted its 2015 report *Stemming the Tide* and issued a public apology to hundreds of environmental organizations for the harm caused by, first, promoting waste incineration and waste-to-energy as acceptable solutions, without acknowledging the role of these technologies in supporting continuing plastic production and pollution; and second, blaming countries in East and Southeast Asia for plastic pollution, while ignoring the "outsized role" of rich countries, particularly the United States, in generating and exporting plastic waste to this region.[101]

Since Break Free from Plastic was launched, the movement has grown, bringing together a range of different tactics across its membership, including NGO reporting and campaigning, legal advocacy, and supporting diverse communities, organizations, and individuals to work toward common aims. It has brought a critical, systemic analysis to the plastics issue, drawing attention to ways that plastics fuel the climate crisis and relate to issues of systemic environmental racism and injustice. The movement's coordination team also recognizes different capacities for action, offering toolkits for different kinds of campaigns, whether it is advocating changes in consumption patterns, pushing for a "plastic-free" university campus, organizing a local community-based campaign, or pushing for new legislation. For example, the movement supports the US Break Free from Plastic Pollution Act, first introduced in Congress in 2020 and then reintroduced with stronger environmental justice language in 2021.[102] In this respect, the movement employs both an individual-based and an issues-based approach, to borrow Li's classification from Nanjing, and it also brings NGO activism into greater dialogue with grassroots community-based approaches. Other influential organizations in the anti-plastics movement include the Centre for International Environmental Law, which has produced reports on the relationship between plastics and health and climate, and the Global Alliance for Incinerator Alternatives, which campaigns against plastic waste, sachets, and incineration, and is rooted in grassroots zero-waste movements in local communities. The flagship Break Free from Plastic campaign is its annual "brand audit," conducted since 2017, when 15,000 volunteers pick up thousands of pieces of plastic waste on beaches and name the top brands in the items of waste that they collect. Coca-Cola, PepsiCo, and Nestlé have consistently come out on top.[103] Increasingly, the Break Free from Plastic movement has moved beyond a focus on the problems of waste and big brands and started to zoom in on the problem of plastics production and the global petrochemical industry.

In 2022, Break Free from Plastic launched a new initiative, called Toxic Tours, which it describes as a "community-led storytelling and mapping experience on the impacts of plastic production on frontline communities," featuring twenty-two communities in ten different countries in Asia, Europe, Africa, North America, and Latin America, with support from local environmental organizations.[104] On an activist level, it builds on the environmental justice idea of the "toxic tour" to invite people to witness and share experiences of toxic pollution, guided by insights from local people, including short video interview clips from residents and activists, accompanied by summaries of the issues in each case. I embarked on the virtual Toxic Tours, which bore some resemblance to the Global Petrochemical Map discussed in previous chapters. What stood out for me was the gravity of the health and livelihood issues: areas classified as "critically polluted" by government authorities; fishermen in India, Bangladesh, and Taiwan unable to sustain their livelihoods due to the poisoning of waterways; animals dying from drinking contaminated water near to petrochemical plants; and people unable to voice their concerns because the "personal risk for individuals is very high" (for example, in Jamnagar, India, the biggest oil refining hub of the world) or because their claims about health risks are routinely dismissed by government and corporate authorities (for example, in Taixi Village, a "cancer village" in Taiwan). The toxic exposures and corporate and state negligence in these frontline petrochemical communities relate closely to toxic exposures due to waste incineration and dumping in vulnerable communities. They highlight the uneven and unequal dynamics of global capitalism, toxic colonialism, and enduring environmental injustice.

Maintaining Hope

Multiscalar activism offers an important source of hope and strength for people living and working in polluted fenceline communities who face multiple forms of social and environmental injustice. By aligning their local struggles with wider movements, they can extend their networks of solidarity beyond the limits of the fenceline and gain political visibility. Within the context of escalating petrochemical proliferation, however, the promise of multiscalar activism is also tinged with disappointment, available only to some communities, and beset with obstacles, including state repression and corporate pushback.

Much as I would like to, I do not share Naomi Klein's early optimism about "Blockadia." After all, Klein spelled out its contours, which were "more reminiscent of civil war than political protest."[105] Echoing this theme, Nick Estes writes evocatively about the #NoDAPL resistance at Standing Rock in 2016 as part of a longer history of war against Indigenous peoples.[106] The word *war* here is not metaphorical. In a polarized world that has been shaped by centuries of colonialism, racial capitalism, and violence, and where vulnerable populations continue to be treated as expendable, it is difficult to imagine how any movement toward a just and sustainable transformation will be achieved peacefully. This has led to an overwhelming sense of disillusionment with political leaders and business elites.

Yet people keep on resisting toxic petrochemical injustices, from multiple perspectives, angles, and positions, according to their different capacities, and often against incredible odds. This chapter has traced only a fraction of the multiple threads of solidarity that interconnect and coalesce across different places, communities, issues, and lands. Diverse people and communities find increasing resonance in their struggles for environmental justice, often extending their solidarity and support beyond their own communities, issues, and borders. Indigenous pipeline resistance mobilizations are both inspiring and humbling in the compassionate ways that they "articulate the politics of territorial defense within a multiscalar conception of responsibility that stretches to follow development impacts."[107] Similarly, the growing anti-plastics movement has drawn attention to the commonalities between vulnerable frontline communities facing toxic exposures to plastics production as well as to waste incineration, highlighting points of convergence in a deeply uneven and unequal world. The recognition within environmental justice movements that it is OK to "fail" is also a profound insight—that caring can be an important form of activism, a form of burrowing, hiding, and gathering strength. Still, material gains matter. Multiscalar activism can foster new solidarities, confrontations, and victories, but it can also dissipate quickly, while oil and petrochemical production continues to expand. In the context of a planetary petrochemical crisis, will escalating resistance ever be sufficient to halt the course of petrochemical proliferation?

4

The Competing Stakes of the Planetary Petrochemical Crisis

What happens when opposing existential planetary crises collide? On one side, there is the intensifying threat of the petrochemical industry to planetary life, and on the other side, there is the threat of planetary ecological crisis for the future of petro-capitalism. Caught up in the crosshairs is the multitude of ways of living entangled in petrochemical systems. The planetary petrochemical crisis is one of the most crucial yet neglected existential threats of our times. At this critical juncture, the pathways forward are fraught with conflicts and dilemmas. This chapter investigates the competing stakes of the planetary petrochemical crisis, tracing their roots, contradictions, and contingencies.

Within just a few years, these overlapping and intensifying ecological crises have spiraled to dizzying heights. In 2019, the threat of the climate emergency rapidly overtook the plastics and pollution crises in terms of public alarm, following the IPCC report on global warming of 1.5°C and the Fridays for Future school climate strikes. Reports about the existential planetary threat of the climate crisis surged, many drawing connections between social and ecological crises of overconsumption, biodiversity loss, and social and economic inequalities.[1] Then, after one of the worst wildfires in modern history in Australia, came the coronavirus pandemic, with ecological roots in "zoonotic spillover" (disease transmitted from nonhuman animals to humans) from the destruction of wildlife habitats due to deforestation. Following a year of delay due to the pandemic, the COP26 climate conference in Glasgow finally went ahead in 2021, but it was deemed a "failure" by most activists and observers.[2] Meanwhile, extreme weather events fueled by climate change continued to set records around the world. In 2022, an international team of environmental scientists published a groundbreaking new study that found that humanity has exceeded the safe planetary boundaries for plastic and chemical pollutants.[3]

Many people recognize that these crises are interconnected, with common roots in the global capitalist system, which is founded on deeply unjust and unsustainable growth dependent on fossil fuels and embedded in colonial histories and logics. It has become common knowledge that the fossil fuel industry has a long history of climate denial, delaying climate action, and political lobbying.[4] Furthermore, there is increasingly widespread intergovernmental consensus that the world needs to transition away from fossil fuels, even if there are conflicts about the timelines, pathways, debts, and obligations of different countries, industries, and communities.

Although there are rising public concerns about the ecological crisis, for the most part the role of the petrochemical industry in fueling the crisis has evaded scrutiny. The global industry has kept out of the spotlight due to its low public visibility, in the middle of the fossil fuel-to-plastics value chain, dispersed across thousands of production sites and millions of supply chain nodes worldwide. Most of the attention from environmental activists has focused on the big players at opposite ends of the value chain: the oil majors and the brands that make so much plastic stuff. The worst players have been singled out, for example Exxon, which has faced climate litigation for deceiving the public about climate change, and Coca-Cola, which was named the world's worst plastic polluter for the fourth year in a row in 2021 in Break Free from Plastic's global "brand audit."[5] Of course, many of the biggest petrochemical companies are also oil companies, including ExxonMobil. Furthermore, many environmental activists and scholars have started to turn their attention to the role of petrochemical companies, also known as "plastics producers," as the source of the problem of toxic and unsustainable production.[6] On the whole, however, the petrochemical industry is not the primary focus of public attention or policymaking. It tends to be treated as just one toxic polluting industry among others, and a relatively small player in relation to the bigger, more profitable upstream oil and gas industry. However, as I will argue, the petrochemical industry is more insidious than it appears.

The petrochemical industry positions itself as an "exception" to the current ecological crisis. By this account, petrochemicals benefit society by adding value to oil through creating products from it instead of burning it; saving energy through lightweight materials; creating "essential" products used in medicine, transportation, housing, and countless other everyday products; and always striving for efficiency to reduce environmental impacts and make plastics "circular." Moreover, petrochemicals are presented as the key solution to the ecological crisis, underpinning most green technologies and innovations. When it comes to ecological crisis, though, the petrochemical industry is by no means an insignificant player. Quite the contrary.

Fathoming the Ecological Crisis

For all the collective planetary anxiety about the ecological crisis, it is difficult to fathom. Part of the problem relates to the overwhelming reliance on scientific expertise to understand the "facts" of the crisis, from climate models to reports on biodiversity loss and ocean acidification. Many people can understand the basic facts, observe the increasingly frequent extreme weather events, and see that these are interconnected. They can point to the intense social inequalities and injustices of ecological crisis, the people living on the frontlines of climate catastrophe and toxic pollution, and the culpability of rich countries and fossil fuel industries. However, to appreciate what the ecological crisis demands of people—both individually and collectively, according to their different responsibilities, capacities, and ethical commitments—is more challenging. Collective planetary action is both necessary and urgent, but this is the problem. Writing about the inadequacy of global climate policy for Indigenous climate justice, Kyle Powys Whyte observes: "Consent, trust, accountability, and reciprocity are qualities of relationships that are critical for justice-oriented coordination across societal institutions on any urgent matter. Yet they are precisely the kinds of qualities of relationships that take time to nurture and develop. That is, they are necessary for taking urgent action that is just, but they cannot be established urgently."[7]

Other scholars have made similar observations about the clash between urgency and justice in the context of ecological crisis. At the start of the global financial crisis in 2008, Isabelle Stengers observed that we live in "catastrophic times," where a state of ecological crisis has already shifted to a point of suspension between two histories, one that is familiar, of competition and economic growth, and another that is in the process of happening, of ecological catastrophe.[8] The first historical epoch was founded on modern capitalist beliefs in science, technological innovation, and economic growth as the foundations for progress. However, Stengers observes that this "confidence has also been profoundly shaken. It is not the least bit ensured that the sciences, such as we know them at least, are equipped to respond to the threats of the future."[9] Faced with the second epoch of ecological catastrophe, Stengers warns, "we are as badly prepared as possible to produce the type of response that, we feel, the situation requires of us." She asks, "To what does it [this change of epoch] oblige us?"[10] Stengers posits that the term "Anthropocene" is successful because it reinforces dominant ways of thinking, as "the grand new narrative in which Man becomes conscious of the fact that his activities transform the earth at the global scale of geology, and that he must therefore take responsibility for the future of the planet."[11]

Indeed, many scholars have criticized the concept of the "Anthropocene" as a universalizing and anthropocentric narrative. For example, Whyte observes: "'Anthropogenic climate change,' or 'the Anthropocene' . . . are not precise enough terms for many Indigenous peoples, because they sound like all humans are implicated in and affected by colonialism, capitalism and industrialization in the same ways."[12] Drawing on ecofeminist Val Plumwood's idea of the "master story" of domination,[13] which reinforces hierarchical dualisms in society (masculine over feminine, culture over nature), Stefania Barca argues that the Anthropocene represents a new "master's narrative." This narrative appears to offer a way for "humanity" to save the planet from climate change through technology, but it is actually based on the "denial and backgrounding" of colonial, gender, class, and species relations.[14] Other scholars have offered alternative terms to name the Anthropocene epoch instead, such as the "Capitalocene," the "Plantationocene," the "Wasteocene," and the "Chthulucene" (named after a spider, by Donna Haraway, attending to "multispecies stories"), each connoting different origins and characteristics of our times.[15] While there are disagreements among these scholars, each points in different ways to perspectives that connect human and nonhuman (or "more-than-human") worlds.

The idea of colliding epochs, informed by different worldviews and ethical commitments, has been echoed in other scholarship. Dipesh Chakrabarty's distinction between the planetary and the global (discussed in the introduction) is not only descriptive but also advocates a different way of thinking, seeking to resolve the contradictions of the "conjoined histories" of species and capital. Chakrabarty asks: "How do we relate to a universal history of life—to universal thought, that is [i.e., climate change]—while retaining what is of obvious value in our postcolonial suspicions of the universal?"[16] While Chakrabarty shares postcolonial criticisms of the universalizing "we" of the discourse of the Anthropocene, he insists that deep-time species-thinking cannot be folded into a critique of capitalism: "The crisis of climate change calls for simultaneous thinking on both registers, to mix together the immiscible chronologies of capital and species history."[17] Chakrabarty acknowledges his intellectual debt to Bruno Latour, who also seeks to go beyond "local" versus "global" framings. Latour suggests that the climate crisis can be understood as nature reclaiming its role as an active agent, rather than an inert background, which is shaping the fate of the planet.[18]

In the context of intensifying ecological crisis, several other scholars have engaged with planetary thinking, including "new materialist" reflections on the ontologies of entangled human and natural worlds.[19] These are insightful, but they are not new. Indigenous scholars point out that the "ontological turn" toward recognizing more-than-human worlds fails to acknowledge the fact that they themselves have long made similar arguments. For example, Robin Wall Kimmerer, of the Citizen Potawatomi Nation, writes that in many Indigenous cultures, "the living world is understood, not as a collection of exploitable resources, but as a set of relationships and responsibilities. We inhabit a landscape of gifts peopled by nonhuman relatives, the sovereign beings who sustain us, including the plants."[20] However, Indigenous traditional ecological knowledge (TEK) has often been appropriated and misused. As the Métis/Michif scholar Max Liboiron observes, "Imperialism and colonialism both involve the scientific appropriation of local and Indigenous knowledges, eaten up and digested to create dominant scientific knowledge."[21] Connecting this dynamic with the ontological turn, Métis author Zoe Todd writes that "'ontology' is just another word for colonialism."[22] There is a lot of reparative work to be done when challenging dominant ways of thinking, including humility and recognition.

There is also something significant about the multidisciplinary search for ways of naming and understanding the current epoch of planetary ecological crisis. It points to a kind of convergence that cuts across differences, including between the social and ecological sciences. Political ecologist Andreas Malm argues that the world is in a state of chronic emergency, exemplified by the climate crisis and the COVID-19 pandemic. In this chronic emergency, the drivers of ecological crisis have changed, fusing social and natural hazards and requiring new forms of action: "When the nature of the battlefield shifts this epochally, there will only be time to wash the wounds before new ones are slashed open. Any chance of getting out of the chronic emergency presupposes a different concentration of forces. To be 'radical,' after all, means aiming at the roots of troubles; to be radical in the chronic emergency is to aim at the ecological roots of perpetual disasters."[23] The conclusion, for Malm, is nothing short of "war" against "fossil capital." Having lost faith in the capacity for neoliberal governments to address the climate emergency, he declares that "the time for gradualism is over."[24] Since the disappointment at COP26, many climate activists have echoed Malm's view with rallying calls that "it cannot be activism as usual."[25] In the context of ecological crisis, it is worth heeding the warning by eco-Marxist James O'Connor that "the combined power of capitalist production relations and productive forces tend to self-destruct by impairing or reducing rather than reproducing their own conditions."[26]

Yet despite increasing recognition of the entanglement between human and more-than-human worlds, many environmental scholars, policymakers, and activists still share the same anthropocentric view: that the universal "we" (humans) "must therefore take responsibility for the future of the planet."[27] Even if "our" responsibility is differentiated according to our different capacities, politics, and ethics, there is still the idea that as humans, "we" do have control over nature. There is the glimmer of hope that the violence of centuries of colonialism and environmental destruction can be still undone. There is the assumption that we know what we must do. Phase out the production and consumption of fossil fuels. End deforestation.

Except that these tasks are not simple. Even if agreement is reached on their necessity, they will require deep and painful transformations. There are powerful state and fossil fuel interests involved, but there are also complex interdependencies, including forms of "carbon lock-in" that threaten to intensify rather than halt the ecological crisis.[28] There are climate justice issues with prioritizing dominant climate mitigation and adaptation strategies over issues of loss and damage, a topic of fierce debate at COP climate change conferences, which led to a historic agreement on a loss and damage fund at COP27 in Sharm el-Sheikh.[29] One of the biggest risks with market-led green transitions, however, is that the exploitative systems will end up being reinforced or reinvented rather than reformed or overturned.[30] For example, low-carbon technologies rely on extractive mining, land grabbing, and toxic waste flows that shift environmental justice burdens along supply chains and exacerbate existing social inequalities.[31] Indeed, there are unintended consequences involved for any course of action, with unjust implications for livelihoods, health, cultures, multiple species, and ecosystems. Nobody agrees on what "we" must do or on how to get there. As the rest of this chapter will outline, the competing stakes of the planetary petrochemical crisis shed light on the depths of the collision course.

The Threat of the Petrochemical Industry to Planetary Life

The petrochemical industry poses a fundamental yet overlooked threat to planetary life and ecosystems. It is at the nexus between existential ecological crises of overconsumption, biodiversity loss, climate breakdown, toxic pollution, and overwhelming waste. Many researchers and activists have also highlighted the toxicity of the industry, its climate impacts, and its role in the plastics crisis.[32] At the height of the US fracking boom in 2013, environmental health leader Theo Colborn called for people to make the "fossil-fuel connection" between fossil fuels and petrochemicals, particularly the violence of energy extraction and the dangerous consequences of pollution for public health.[33] In 2019, amid rising public consciousness about the plastics and climate crises, the Centre for International Environmental Law released two reports on the "hidden costs of a plastic planet," focusing on the negative climate and health costs of plastics across their lifecycle, from fossil fuel extraction to petrochemical refining, to consumption and disposal.[34] The report focusing on plastic and climate estimated that the production and incineration of single-use plastics alone would see a rise of carbon dioxide from 815 million metric tons per year in 2019 to 2.8 gigatons by 2050, well beyond the remaining global carbon budget.[35] The report that dealt with plastic and health compiled detailed evidence that "the lifecycle impacts of plastic paint an unequivocally toxic picture: plastic threatens human health on a global scale" and warned that the toxic exposures would increase with rising plastics production.[36]

As the climate crisis outpaced the plastics crisis in terms of public and scientific alarm, biologist Susan Shaw warned that plastics are "the evil twin of climate change," and conservation scientists issued stark warnings that the world faces multiple intersecting ecological crises, which each pose existential threats, including crises of climate disruptions, biodiversity loss, and "ecological overshoot."[37] Petrochemicals are at the heart of the planetary existential threat of ecological overshoot, which "is largely enabled by the increasing use of fossil fuels. These convenient fuels have allowed us to decouple human demand from biological regeneration: 85% of commercial energy, 65% of fibers, and most plastics are now produced from fossil fuels."[38] Moreover, the petrochemical industry is the world's largest industrial consumer of oil and gas and the third largest industrial emitter of greenhouse gases (after iron/steel and cement).[39] Despite these facts, petrochemicals remain largely neglected from public and policy scrutiny, being seen as an "essential" industry that is just one of many sources of environmental pollution, and de-prioritized as relatively minor in relation to the direct burning of fossil fuels in the energy and transport sectors.

In 2001, the biologist and environmentalist Barry Commoner published a paper on the threat of the petrochemical industry to life on Earth, drawing on decades of scientific work and environmental activism.[40] Among the many sources of environmental devastation on the planet, Commoner pinpointed the petrochemical industry as the most significant threat to lives and ecosystems. The petrochemical industry, he argued, created new synthetic materials and products with the aim of making profits, rather than fulfilling specific needs. In this way, the industry "invaded existing markets—soap was displaced by detergents; cotton and wool by synthetic fabrics; glass and steel by plastics; insectivorous birds by insecticides; the plow by the herbicide." Even worse, it "invaded the ecosystem—with the industry unprepared for the biological consequences. And so DDT, aimed at insects, killed birds; polyvinyl chloride film, intended to wrap food, turned trash-burning incinerators into dioxin factories; polyurethane foam, designed to make mattresses, when it smolders kills the sleeper."[41] Commoner argued that the toxic dangers of the petrochemical industry could have been prevented if the industry had proceeded with a precautionary approach. He held up the past mistakes of the industry as a cautionary tale, and he advised that these lessons should inform the industry's new developments in biotechnology. Otherwise, new biotechnological chemicals could also pose great dangers to life and ecosystems on the planet.

Writing more than two decades later, it is important to reflect on these warnings. Commoner criticized the industry for failing to anticipate the toxic risks of synthetic chemicals and for proceeding recklessly in the pursuit of economic growth. "Of course," he wrote facetiously, "we should rejoice in the chemical industry's newly enlightened view that it ought to learn why so many of its synthetic products have been incompatible with the chemistry of living things."[42] Commoner then questioned the industry's delay tactics, noting that public concern over toxic risks was refuted for decades by the industry. This was a powerful and important critical observation, but, if anything, Commoner underestimated the capacity for the industry to continue to ignore the toxic risks of its products. He assumed that scientific knowledge of the risks of synthetic products to life, once made public, should rationally lead to a cautious approach. In other words, he underestimated the extent of the "deceit and denial" and uncertainty campaigns that industry leaders would use to deceive the public about petrochemical toxicity.

Commoner also underestimated the capacity for future exponential growth in the global petrochemical industry. This is understandable, for at the turn of the twenty-first century, the US petrochemical industry was beginning to decline. The sustainable materials scholar Kenneth Geiser described this juncture in the US industry as one of capital limits in an era of globalization:

> The rich natural resources of the nation have been tapped and in some cases heavily drained. The great technical advances in petrochemicals and polymers provided a host of structural and military products and consumer commodities at diminishing costs. However, today many of those materials are made into products throughout the world, often at lower costs. The materials economy is a global economy, and the future of materials development in the United States rests on how well its industries perform in that market and how carefully its resources are used.[43]

In the early 2000s, the US petrochemical industry, like many other heavy manufacturing industries, was witnessing a period of deindustrialization, and its prospects of recovery were uncertain. In this context, Commoner assumed that the future of the chemical industry would be to shift from petrochemicals toward biotechnology, rather than continuing parallel growth in the traditional sector. Neither Commoner nor Geiser anticipated the "petrochemical renaissance" in the United States that followed. The US tapped into new natural resources, namely unconventional oil and gas, exploiting shale gas reserves and exporting tar sands from Canada, despite the known health and environmental consequences of these "extreme" fossil fuels.[44] Nevertheless, the underlying industrial logic that Commoner first identified has remained the same: continuing the reckless path of invading markets, creating demand where there is no need, and ignoring the toxic consequences.[45]

The toxic consequences of petrochemical industry cannot be overstated. Petrochemicals are inherently toxic. There is no way of producing petrochemicals without generating toxic emissions and by-products. Whether the petrochemicals come from fossil fuels (as 99 percent of them do), or whether they come from sugar, biomass, or other "bio-feedstocks," they have the same chemical composition.[46] Moreover, the less-toxic petrochemicals cannot be produced in isolation from the more-toxic ones, due to the "two-for-one principle," that chemical processes involve generating by-products, all of which need to find places to go, whether into new processes and products, or into waste disposal.[47] For example, toxic pollutants that are unique to the petrochemical industry include the BTEX group of volatile organic compounds (benzene, toluene, ethylbenzene, and xylene), which are known carcinogens. Of these, benzene is the most widely monitored in the United States and Europe.[48] BTEX petrochemicals are used to make many different products (many are associated with health effects due to chemical leaching, such as phthalates and bisphenol A), but they are also waste products of polyolefin production (the largest class of petrochemicals, which comprises polyethylene and polypropylene).

Other toxic chemicals include perfluorooctanoic acid (PFOA) and other per- and polyfluoroalkyl substances (PFAS), used in nonstick cookware and firefighting foam, which can cause liver damage, cancer, and reproductive illnesses.[49] Since 1998, DuPont has faced litigation over water contamination from PFOA pollution from its Teflon plants, first in the United States and later in Europe. In January 2021, DuPont, Chemeurs (a spinoff from DuPont), and Corteva (a spinoff from DowDuPont) announced a $4 billion settlement for the historic use of toxic PFAS "forever chemicals."[50] The case closely mirrors the vinyl chloride scandals: researchers revealed that DuPont knew about the toxic health effects of PFAS chemicals since the 1960s, but it covered up the information.[51]

For decades, environmental health researchers and activists have campaigned for stricter chemical regulations, highlighting the problem of "regrettable substitutions," in which hazardous chemicals are replaced by unregulated sister substances (often from the same class of chemicals) which may also be dangerous.[52] The use of regrettable substitutions is a common industry tactic to protect markets and delay regulations—for example, replacing bisphenol A with other bisphenols.[53] Europe is widely considered to have stronger chemical regulations than the United States, particularly since the introduction of the European Registration, Evaluation, Authorisation and Restriction of Chemicals regulations (REACH) in 2007, which was designed to increase data transparency about chemical hazards.[54] However, according to an environmental law campaigner based in Brussels, regulatory agencies in Europe, the United States, and indeed in most countries, take a cost-benefit approach, rather than a precautionary one, to chemicals:

> Everything is turned into euro values or dollar values, or whatever is the currency. Everything is monetized, and then you check if there are benefits, so you say, "Well, we've saved three lives and one life is valued at five million, but since you're going to get cancer in thirty years, we discount . . . so the value of a cancer is like 3,000 Euros," and then on the other side you put the cost for a society for banning the substance, which would be all the loss in income from the company, as if the company would represent somehow the common interest. But we never ask ourselves the question, "Do we really need this?"[55]

The consequence of this cost-benefit logic is that regulators frequently protect company profits over people's health. Several studies have revealed a "revolving door" of key personnel between industry and regulatory agencies.[56] Furthermore, governments and corporations share interests in economic growth. Alongside REACH's aim to protect health and the environment, it also "aims to enhance innovation and competitiveness of the EU chemicals industry."[57]

There are, however, signs of change. In April 2022, following the major scientific report that chemical pollution had crossed a planetary boundary, the European Union unveiled plans for the "largest ever ban" on chemicals, which would focus on whole classes of them, including "all flame retardants, bisphenols, PVC plastics, toxic chemicals in single-use nappies and PFAS."[58] According to the European Chemical Industry Council, this ban would result in the loss of around €500 billion per year, more than a quarter of the industry's annual turnover. This time, though, the threat of economic loss was not enough to convince the European Chemicals Agency. The risks to public health and the environment from these toxic chemicals are too high.[59] A few months later, the Biden administration announced that it would declare two types of PFAS "forever chemicals," hazardous substances under the Superfund Act, which would require companies to report leaks of PFAS and to pay for the cleanup of contaminated sites.[60]

In a recent article on "transitioning the chemical industry," Joel Tickner, Ken Geiser, and Stephanie Baima discuss the dramatic rise of the chemical industry since the Second World War, 90 percent of which is petrochemicals, and its associated environmental and health consequences.[61] Within the context of global climate, toxics, and plastics crises, they argue that petrochemical producers face considerable obstacles to sustainable transformation, notably in terms of costs. However, the authors suggest that there is hope because the industry can learn from its own history of innovation, arguing that since the industry innovated before, during the wars, they can do it again. While the authors recognize the negative environmental and health impacts of the industry, including environmental justice consequences in fenceline communities, they maintain that these harms and injustices can be avoided in the future. Their analysis, while seemingly critical of the industry, neglects the issue of powerful vested interests.

Rather than challenging industry discourses, the authors repeat the industry's own narratives about self-transformation through innovation. They support the industry's claims about a history of pathbreaking innovation, which glosses over mistakes as minor stumbling blocks that it can always fix. The authors write, "Looking to history is instructive because the industry wasn't always as ossified as it is today."[62] In particular, they recall: "Government-directed wartime efforts like investment, guaranteeing demand through military purchasing, encouraging collaboration between firms and end users, and shared patenting and licensing helped the chemical industry to grow rapidly in the United States."[63] Looking to history is indeed instructive, but for different reasons. As we saw in chapter 1, the industry's history of wartime "innovation" and "collaboration" is founded on collusion, deception, and violence. There is no reason to expect that the industry will be capable of just or sustainable self-transformation.

The Threat of Ecological Crisis to the Survival of Industry

"Uncertainty and volatility are key factors for the third year running," declared Rob Westervelt, editor in chief of the industry magazine *Chemical Week*, during the World Petrochemical Conference in March 2022, referring to the start of the pandemic in 2020, the Houston freeze in 2021, and the Russian invasion of Ukraine in 2022.[64] In April 2020, in the midst of the "double barrel blast of COVID-19 and the crude oil crash," a leading industry analyst warned (incorrectly) that "the robust global growth that the industry had become so accustomed to has flattened or is perhaps declining."[65] These statements echoed similar ones that were delivered at industry events in previous years, well before the start of the pandemic.

In a keynote speech to the European Petrochemical Association (EPCA) meeting in 2013, economic historian Niall Ferguson predicted an "end to the petrochemical age," warning delegates about the possibility of a "paradigm shift" involving "fundamental technological disruptions."[66] The fifty-year anniversary meeting of the EPCA in October 2016 addressed the existential theme of environmental threats to the future of the industry directly. They posed the question to their youth debating competition: "How would you imagine your future—with or without the petrochemical industry and plastics?"[67] The debaters who argued "against" the industry did not hold back in their criticisms, highlighting the industry's unsustainable reliance on fossil fuels, its production of toxic pollution and plastic waste, and its continuing contributions to climate change. The debaters who argued "for" the industry emphasized the necessity of petrochemicals for all other industries, including agriculture, manufacturing, food production, medicine, information technology, and alternative energy. They argued further that "the industry is coming to terms with and offering solutions to the most pressing issue of our time: managing climate change and achieving sustainability." The unsurprising outcome of this industry-sponsored debate was that "overall, these young people offered a critical but ultimately positive view of petrochemicals and plastics." According to the conference report, most people were "very optimistic about the industry's capacity to find and fix its own faults."[68]

The petrochemical industry is well versed in the airing of existential crisis. It has been doing this, in some shape or form, since the 1960s. For an outside observer, it is difficult to tell the difference between the performances: some appear heartfelt, others blasé. There are many dynamics that remain hidden offstage.

The industry's response to regulations exemplifies the subtle difference between frontstage versus backstage dynamics. During my research, I interviewed several environmental health campaigners who interacted with big business as part of their advocacy work. They each discussed the problem of industry lobbying to oppose regulations, but they also noted the diversity of the industry. One seasoned campaigner for restrictions on hazardous chemicals told me that it was important to recognize that "there are good industry companies and there are bad companies within industry." When I asked how it was possible to tell the difference, she responded:

If I talk to some of the CEOs at the companies, they're very interested in what's going to come round the corner and clobber them. If they can, they would like to avoid it, so they would like to know what we see on the agenda, what's going to happen in the future: how to put the business in the best shape. At the same time, there are industries that are in the twilight zone of—they're probably sunset industries—if they can get another ten to fifteen to twenty years out of their business, you know, that's what they want. So, naysaying any of the health effects is their best strategy.[69]

This is observation is revealing because, in fact, it doesn't imply that companies are inherently "good" or "bad," but rather that their fundamental interest in profitability and survival determines their willingness to engage with corporate social responsibility. It is also instructive, in a cautionary way, for thinking about the implications of the fossil fuel endgame for shaping future corporate behavior.

At the virtual World Petrochemical Conference in 2021, an industry analyst warned participants that new environmental regulations were on the horizon, observing that "Since the environmental movement emerged in the 1960s, it has been a one-way street towards stricter regulations."[70] Throughout its history, the industry has had an overarching narrative about regulations as threats.[71] In reality, however, the industry views some regulations as more threatening than others, notably any regulations that involve limiting production—for example, bans, taxes, and restrictions on particular products, such as toxic chemical substances and single-use plastics—and any regulations limiting greenhouse gas emissions and toxic releases. It also views some regulations favorably if they are useful for market access. For example, the UK chemical industry was fiercely opposed to Brexit, and one of its main concerns was over the market implications of being excluded from REACH, the main chemical regulations in Europe.[72] In short, industry opposes regulations that pose threats to profits, and it supports regulations that facilitate profits.

The petrochemical industry, while diverse, is well practiced in navigating threats to its business. Each time the industry confronts crisis, it learns lessons, such as how to deflect attention from corporate responsibility, and play one crisis against another.

THE PLASTICS CRISIS "In the 1970s, polymers were the future, and they were going to save the world," a retired chemical consultant told me during a meeting of "chemical stakeholders" in London in 2018. "But now," he said, shaking his head nostalgically, "not so much."[73] The news at the time was filled with images of marine wildlife entangled in plastic debris. "We need to get the image of plastic in oceans out of the public's head," declared a petrochemical executive a few months later. "We need to make plastic fantastic again."[74] In March 2019, the World Petrochemical Conference added a special sustainability seminar to its regular business agenda in response to the public backlash over the marine plastics crisis.

Contrary to appearances, however, the plastics crisis was not as much of a threat as the industry made it out to be. As might be expected, corporate leaders were alarmed over the public backlash against plastics, which threatened their "social license to operate," diminishing markets and opening the door to further bans and regulations. However, market forecasts showed that overall, petrochemical demand would continue to grow, exponentially, irrespective of single-use-plastic legislation and circular economy policies. Increasing consumer demand in China, India, and other "emerging" markets were expected to be key drivers, alongside the role of petrochemicals in green technologies.[75] Besides, the industry had a ready-made response: recycling.

For most of its history, recycling has enjoyed widespread public acceptance as a mainstream solution for environmental waste. In *Recycling Reconsidered*, Samantha MacBride examined the paradox of recycling in perpetuating systems of environmental harm, drawing on insights from her career in municipal waste management.[76] MacBride revealed that the petrochemical and plastics industries promoted the first US recycling programs in the 1980s as a coordinated response to the growing environmental movement. The advantage of recycling, from an industry perspective, was that it facilitated the production of "guilt-free" disposable packaging and placed responsibility for waste disposal on consumers.[77]

Since 2018, the industry's answer to the plastics crisis has been, once again, to promote recycling. This time, the recycling programs would be "circular," to align with the popular circular economy business model of minimizing waste and increasing efficiency, by keeping materials in use for longer.[78] Recycling is the weakest form of the circular economy, as compared with reduction, reuse, and repair. Furthermore, there are significant challenges to achieving "circular" plastic recycling—that is, not relying on "virgin" fossil fuel-based sources. Plastics degrade during conventional recycling processes, and many plastics are too contaminated to be recycled into plastics that have contact with food. To address this problem, industry experts have proposed the circular economy "solution" of chemical recycling, as an alternative to traditional mechanical recycling.[79] Chemical recycling involves breaking plastics back down to their molecular form, returning them to their "virgin" state, free from contamination. However, chemical recycling is still in a pilot phase of development, which means that it will not be scalable for many years. Furthermore, most chemical recycling technologies involve building very large-scale, carbon-intensive, and toxic petrochemical infrastructures.[80] As discussed in chapter 3, many environmental activists maintain that chemical recycling is another word for "incineration."[81]

In the wake of the plastics crisis, the problems with recycling have come into the media spotlight, including the widely cited figure that less than 10 percent of plastics have ever been recycled.[82] In 2020, the US networks National Public Radio and PBS *Frontline* launched an investigation which revealed that the oil and chemical industries spent millions of US dollars to mislead the public about the effectiveness of recycling.[83] Ironically, the petrochemical industry in the United States has started to change its tune about chemical recycling as a circular economy solution. Over the past few years, the American Chemical Council has pushed for chemical recycling to be reclassified as a manufacturing process, rather than waste management, a legislative move to avoid stringent environmental regulations on pollution and hazardous waste.[84] A recent report by the nonprofit Global Alliance for Incinerator Alternatives found that twenty US states have passed legislation to this effect, which could have serious implications for environmental justice.[85]

Beyond chemical recycling, the global petrochemical industry has responded to the plastics crisis—and the related bans and regulations—with a swathe of voluntary corporate sustainability initiatives operating across the petrochemical value chain: the CEO-led Alliance to End Plastic Waste; Operation Clean Sweep (to prevent plastic-pellet loss); and various circular economy pledges to minimize "leakage" (pollution and waste). These voluntary corporate projects aim to contain the threat of the plastics crisis to the industry's markets, passing blame for the "leakage" to consumers and to "poor waste management" in Asia and Africa.[86] Meanwhile, the industry has lobbied aggressively against single-use plastics bans. Faced with industry-level threats to public legitimacy and to future markets due to the growing anti-plastics movement, corporations across the petrochemical value chain have reverted to collusive practices, appearing to be sustainable by co-opting the discourse of the circular economy while protecting toxic and unsustainable markets.

As the media storm over the marine plastics crisis gave way to the even bigger planetary threat of the climate emergency, some scholars started to quarrel about the relative importance of the different crises. In 2019, marine biologist Richard Stafford and geographer Peter J. S. Jones published an article that argued that ocean plastic pollution was a "convenient but distracting truth," drawing attention from the bigger planetary crises of global heating and biodiversity loss.[87] Just before the start of the pandemic, I spoke with a marine scientist working on macroplastics, who noted her increasing discomfort with marine plastics being pitted against "serious climate change topics." This was so prevalent that she found herself apologizing to colleagues about her work, saying "I spotted the plastics by accident, it's not technically my real job," and, "Yeah, I know it's a distraction from the real issues."[88] The industry welcomed this shift in narrative. Climate change is a tricky issue for the industry too, but in different ways.

THE CLIMATE CRISIS Despite its claims to the contrary, the petrochemical industry has long recognized the implications of climate change for its survival. The funding of climate change denial by fossil fuel companies, including by vertically integrated oil and petrochemical companies, has been well documented. The petrochemical industry, however, takes advantage of its position as an "exception in the sustainable development scenario" in the International Energy Agency's oil market forecasts. In this scenario, petrochemical demand for oil will continue to grow even if the Paris climate agreement goals are met, as discussed in chapter 3, due to rising global demand for consumer plastics and green technologies.[89] Indeed, since the 1970s oil crisis, petrochemical industry representatives have argued that lightweight plastics "save" oil by reducing transportation costs. Rather than burning fossil fuels directly, like in fuel markets, they claim that petrochemicals "add value" by processing fossil fuels into plastics to make essential modern products.[90] According to a petrochemical industry trainer, "You are always adding value, that is the name of the game."[91]

During my research on the global petrochemical industry, there were two major climate conferences: COP21 in Paris and COP26 in Glasgow. In the spring of 2016, in the aftermath of the COP21 climate talks, industry leaders at the European Petrochemicals Conference in Amsterdam declared that they welcomed the Paris Agreement.[92] After decades of climate denial perpetuated by the fossil fuel industry, this seemed rather surprising. There was a caveat, however: they welcomed the Paris Agreement, provided that the United States and China stuck to their commitments. The European industry was in a state of depression, floundering after a period of high crude oil prices, which rendered it uncompetitive given its reliance on oil feedstocks, as compared with the cheap shale gas feedstocks from the US fracking boom. Industry leaders said that they hoped the climate agreement would help to balance the "unequal playing field" between different regional players, claiming that the United States and China had an "unfair competitive advantage" due to the stricter environmental regulations in Europe. According to a seasoned oil and gas expert, 2016 was the first year climate change was on the agenda at major industry conferences.[93] Then Donald Trump won the US election, and there were hopeful murmurings within the industry that Trump would spell doom for the Paris Agreement. Despite the rollbacks of the Trump years though, climate change would soon become a standing agenda item.

After Paris, the threat of ecological crisis to business as usual began to percolate through the petrochemical industry, with the dramatic increase in international public attention to the plastics and climate crises. Pressure came not only from regulators and environmental movements but also from investors and litigators. Over the past decade, there has been a dramatic increase in climate litigation, against both states and corporations, with some important victories for the climate movement.[94] The climate divestment movement has also surged, accelerating a shift toward "sustainable" investments, although there are debates about its effectiveness in reducing greenhouse gas emissions.[95] The pandemic provided an unexpected diversion from environmental concerns, and the industry was quick to use the opportunity of the global health crisis to attempt to delay and roll back single-use plastics legislation. However, as one industry analyst cautioned at the beginning of the pandemic: "Sustainability is going to come back with a vengeance."

In fact, the pandemic strengthened the resolve of many governments to accelerate the transition away from fossil fuels through green growth recoveries. In June 2020, the United Nations launched its Race to Zero Campaign, promoting rapid decarbonization across businesses, cities, regions, and investors.[96] The World Business Council for Sustainable Development (WBCSD) set a target of net-zero emissions by 2050 for all its members, including 200 of the world's largest corporations.[97] Oil and gas companies were among the "first movers" to make pledges to become net-zero energy companies by 2050, although many of their efforts backfired, with allegations of greenwashing and loopholes.[98] Indeed, a key activist theme throughout COP26 was "net zero is not zero." In the lead-up to COP26, several petrochemical companies followed suit (many are members of the WBCSD), but they tempered their claims by presenting "roadmaps" to net zero instead of "pledges."[99]

At COP26, the petrochemical industry was conspicuous in both its absence and its presence. I attended COP26 as a UK university delegate, hoping to find some insights into the debates and negotiations, but it was an almost impossible task given the circumstances of logistics and access. It felt like the set of a doomsday film, with the seeming incapacity for anyone to shift the collision course despite their best intentions.[100] On my first day, I attended two side events on the theme of "net zero," held in the same room one after the other: "Net Zero Smoke and Mirrors, a Story of Betrayal: Making the Case against Carbon Offsetting" (with Greenpeace International, Global Witness, Amnesty International, and ActionAid International) and "Transform to Net Zero: Accelerating Non-party Stakeholder Action for 1.5°C" (with the World Economic Forum, Carbon Disclosure Project [CDP], Business for Social Responsibility [BSR], Natura, Dalmia Cement, Microsoft, and Hitachi). Perhaps it goes without saying that each event presented radically different perspectives on the net-zero agenda.

Fossil fuel companies were prohibited from playing an official role at COP26, due to skepticism about their net-zero commitments.[101] Nonetheless, as widely reported in the media, the fossil fuel industry had a strong presence at COP26: more than 503 delegates were associated with fossil fuel interests.[102] In high-level discussions about decarbonization in heavy industry, the steel and cement sectors were present, but the petrochemical sector—one of the other top "hard to abate" industrial sectors—was not. Speaking at a petrochemical conference a few weeks later, an industry leader stated calmly: "The industry is facing the biggest challenge in terms of change ever."[103] However, nobody at the conference seemed particularly worried. As a matter of fact, the conference had a buoyant mood, following the "positive rebound in industry in 2021" due to the surge in single-use plastics demand during the pandemic. Another industry representative remarked glibly that they were "all sailing into uncharted waters" and they just needed to focus on how they could "continue to offer the same materials while reducing emissions and ensuring circularity."[104] In the concluding discussion, the speakers summarized the key takeaway of the conference in one word: "collaboration," a theme that brings us back to the industry's early history of toxic scandals.

THE TOXIC LIABILITY CRISIS Toxicity was the first existential threat that the petrochemical industry faced during the antitoxic campaigns of the 1970s and 1980s. In response, as discussed in previous chapters, the industry developed "deceit and denial" tactics to deflect attention away from the toxic harms of its products and by-products.[105] It continues to use these tactics today, denying the health risks of endocrine-disrupting chemicals and dismissing epidemiological claims about petrochemical "cancer clusters."[106] Environmental health and justice movements have managed to hold some corporations legally accountable for toxic disasters and to push for regulations and bans on specific toxic substances. However, environmental justice struggles over toxic exposures to petrochemical pollution have not yet posed a threat to the industry on an existential level.

Toxicity remains a significant liability threat to the industry, but it is not an issue that the industry tends to air publicly. In the dozens of petrochemical industry conferences that I attended, despite considerable space given to environmental threats to business as usual, the health impacts of petrochemical pollution were rarely, if ever, mentioned. There were discussions about various environmental, health, and safety regulations, but only in terms of understanding the playing field for business operations in different regions. In informal interviews, some corporate participants mentioned cases that were in the public domain, such as that of contaminated water from Teflon containing PFAS "forever chemicals" in the Netherlands in 2016, and the deadly explosions at the BASF petrochemical complex at Ludwigshafen the same year.

When asked about toxic pollution issues during interviews, petrochemical industry representatives tended to dismiss them. A chemical manager in Nanjing, for example, pointed to some chimneys in the petrochemical complex, and said: "You can see all three, you see? The three chimneys that smoke the most? The gas that comes out, in the end, is all water vapor, and it is white. That's why there is no smell. No smell and no pollution. I mean, almost no pollution."[107] A petrochemical executive in Brussels made a similar claim about the relative lack of pollution at his plants:

> There is still space to improve, but I'm sure that the quality of the air that you can breathe in a chemical plant is better than the one that you can breathe in a city—by far, by far, because it's controlled. You don't have the smog coming from the cars, the smog coming from the chimneys and so on because our emissions are all controlled. And because the employees of the employer are working in that factory and they are our asset, the most important resource that we have, we make sure that they can live and work in the right environment as far as emissions are concerned. So, we make, check, control, because this is mandatory by law. But we do it also because we believe this is the right way to do it.[108]

At industry events, the only explicit discussions of petrochemical toxicity happened in training workshops about petrochemical markets. In these workshops, the instructors traced each of the seven basic petrochemicals through their value chains through to their markets, detailing the toxicity and public health concerns of each chemical along the way. For example, they discussed how some chemicals have been banned due to toxicity concerns, such as dioctyl phthalates, outlawed in children's toys in the United States and Europe, and methyl tertiary butyl ether (MTBE), an octane-booster in US gasoline that was banned in 2000 as a carcinogenic pollutant. However, the instructors brushed off most toxicity concerns—for example, remarking that blood bags use phthalates, but "there have been no issues," and introducing the case of MTBE as "the whole stupid story as to why we stopped using this in the US."

This is not surprising. Any admission of responsibility for toxic harm would open the door to corporate blame and liability. Instead, corporations ignore the issue as far as possible, at least in their public appearances, unless they are compelled to do otherwise. This is what sociologist Linsey McGoey calls "strategic ignorance," deliberate practices of obfuscation, which involve "the mobilization of the unknowns in a situation in order to command resources, deny liability in the aftermath of disaster, and to assert expert control in the face of both foreseeable unpredictable outcomes."[109] This does not mean that toxicity does not pose a major threat to the petrochemical industry though. Far from it. Toxicity is ever present, as an inherent and inextricable material part of the industry, continuously erupting into scandals and disputes, across various sites and scales. This explains why, after all these years, the industry still resorts to its campaigns of deceit and denial.

There are some signs that toxicity could resurface as a major liability problem for the industry on a global level. In 2019, the United Nations Environment Program published a report on plastic pollution and its risk to the insurance industry, which examined the risks to global insurance companies as the underwriters, risk assessors, and institutional investors for plastics and petrochemical companies. The report's risk assessment methodology echoed the move toward mandatory climate-related financial disclosures. One of the key risks was related to toxic chemicals in plastic products. In particular, the report highlighted that "phthalates represent the single largest potential products liability risk because of how ubiquitous plastics containing the chemical are and because of the range of harms associated with the chemical."[110] The plans for new legislative bans on whole classes of toxic chemicals in Europe, and for some PFAS "forever chemicals" in the United States, discussed above, are also signs that toxicity could become a bigger problem for the industry.

It is too early to tell whether toxicity will become a full-blown existential crisis for the petrochemical industry. Given the historical record of corporate denial, it seems unlikely that it will happen until it is too late. After all, the planetary boundary for chemical pollution has already been crossed. In the short term, the petrochemical industry seems to be doing just fine. As INEOS director Tom Crotty writes, the industry has "navigated stormy waters and fought its battles," but it continues to grow and profit, "conquering climate change" and other global challenges with "innovative chemical solutions and efficient (as well as effective and innovative) supply chains."[111] After an unexpected year of pandemic-driven plastics demand, an industry analyst exclaimed in April 2021: "We've seen polyethylene producers flourish in ways that no one would have anticipated.... We saw consumer buying habits change, we saw work-from-home culture develop, and e-commerce surged."[112] The following year, amid the "volatility and uncertainty" in oil and gas markets following the Russian invasion of Ukraine, another industry expert reported: "Demand growth has proven to be resilient. Through the recession in 2020, we saw really positive demand growth and it continues to grow now."[113] But in the long term, the endgame for fossil fuels, including petrochemicals, is on the horizon, as the ecological crisis intensifies, and the stakes of inaction rise.

Tipping Points

There are many stakes in the planetary petrochemical crisis. During processes of political, economic, and societal transformation, some people prosper while others experience loss and harm. We have seen this play out historically in the entwined histories of colonialism and capitalism, well before the dawn of the petrochemical age. The fault lines of class, race, gender, and global inequalities have long shaped the divisions of disruption. But never in human history have we faced the existential threat of mass extinction, compounded with accumulating toxic pollution, waste, and systemic injustice. The petrochemical planet is at a critical juncture, on both social and ecological levels. It may even be at a tipping point, or on the verge of one.

The concept of tipping points has been used widely by climate scientists to warn of the escalating dangers of global heating. In a review of the increasing use of "tipping points" within socio-ecological systems research, Manjana Milkoreit and colleagues make the important observation that social and ecological tipping points are often very different, ontologically speaking. They note that scientific definitions tend more toward a "bifurcation" approach, in which a point of no return is passed, whereas social scientific definitions tend to be looser and more metaphorical. Within the social sciences, the idea of tipping points has been used in relation to historical institutionalism, regime shifts, and critical transitions, although typically, societal tipping points are observed only in relation to the past, used to describe ruptures that have already taken place. The authors propose a socio-ecological definition of a tipping point as "a threshold at which small quantitative changes in the system trigger a nonlinear change process that is driven by system-internal feedback mechanisms and inevitably leads to a qualitatively different state of the system, which is often irreversible."[114]

It may already be too late to avoid ecological tipping points beyond the sustainable capacity of the Earth. At the time of writing, five of the nine planetary boundaries have already been crossed, including climate change, biodiversity loss, land-system change, biogeochemical flows, and chemical pollution.[115] The world's political and economic elites are too enamored with market-driven technological "solutions" to crisis, guided by entrenched modern capitalist beliefs in perpetual economic growth and in humanity's ability to control nature. In their 1992 update to the Club of Rome report on the "limits to growth," Donella Meadows and colleagues warned that the planet had already reached a state of ecological overshoot.[116] As Whyte argues, it may also be "too late for Indigenous climate justice" because of the interconnections between "ecological" and "relational tipping points":

> In terms of climate change, the ecological tipping point concerns how the inaction of societies to mitigate their contributions to atmospheric concentrations of greenhouse gases threatens to have irreversible and dangerous effects. The relational tipping point concerns the inaction of societies to establish or maintain relational qualities [of consent, trust, accountability, and reciprocity] connecting societal institutions together for the sake of coordinated action. Such inaction eventually makes it impossible to carry out swift responses to urgent problems without perpetrating injustices. . . . While many people are concerned about crossing the ecological tipping point, the relational tipping point got crossed long ago thanks to systems of colonialism, capitalism, and industrialization.[117]

In recent social scientific debates about "tipping points" within green transformations, there has been an increasing focus on transformations that are still underway, combined with an implicit distinction, on a policy level, between undesirable and desirable transformations.[118] These discussions resonate with calls to "design" just transitions which are based on alternative worldviews.[119] In the next chapter, we will explore the dilemmas of just and sustainable petrochemical transformations.

5

Petrochemical Degrowth,

Decarbonization,

and Just Transformations

We live in an era of intensifying ecological crisis on a scale that represents an existential threat to life on the petrochemical planet—smothered and poisoned by toxic pollution, on the brink of climate catastrophe. Crisis has become the norm, overlapping across social, ecological, and economic spheres. Yet despite increasing public attention to crisis there is also fatigue, fanned by the relentless news cycle, not to mention the COVID-19 pandemic. Scientists warn that alarmist accounts about the climate emergency have not been stark enough, and that there will be dire consequences for life on the planet even with substantial international efforts to reduce emissions.[1] Nothing short of unprecedented collective action on multiple scales is required to respond to the unfolding disaster, which disproportionately impacts marginalized and vulnerable communities. This raises a question: Amid polarized worldviews, crisis fatigue, powerful corporate incumbents, and systemic inequalities and injustices, what kind of planetary collective action is possible?

At this critical juncture, we are poised for a radical industrial transformation that will require collective reckoning with the limits to growth, including the imperative for decarbonization across all industrial sectors. The recalcitrant, dirty yet essential petrochemical industry is a core battleground for such a transformation. The global momentum for decarbonization is an important lever for reducing the damages of the petrochemical industry because it has the potential to demand an end to petrochemical proliferation. Petrochemicals are made from oil and gas, after all, and toxic petrochemical growth is intimately tied to increasing greenhouse gas emissions.[2] Without linking decarbonization to degrowth, however, there is the considerable risk that decarbonization efforts will fail to scale back the toxic and expansive wake of the industry.

Degrowth is a political and ecological movement, with origins in the 1970s "limits to growth" debates, which criticizes the dominant paradigm of economic growth and aims to build a future "in which societies will use fewer natural resources and will organize and live differently than today."[3] The "case for degrowth" has received increasing attention in the context of economic and ecological crises, with its powerful challenge to the logic of extractive fossil fuel-driven growth.[4] Some criticisms of "growthism" have even entered high-level policy. In 2008, the OECD and the European Union launched their "Beyond GDP Growth" campaigns, and several governments and international organizations have developed alternative metrics for social and ecological health.[5] For the most part, though, degrowth remains outside mainstream economic growth-driven policies, and it has little resonance for deindustrialized and disadvantaged communities. By contrast, the concept of "just transitions," which is concerned with protecting livelihoods during green transitions, has achieved widespread international policy recognition, but in practice it fails to address tensions between sustainability and social justice goals.[6] Both concepts are contentious, as we will see, but they also offer valuable ways of thinking about potential pathways for decarbonization and multiscalar activism.

While there are increasing international efforts to accelerate the transition away from fossil fuels, the pathways for decarbonization are highly contested. Most decarbonization policies rely on "green growth" strategies that frame the climate crisis as an opportunity to redirect economic activities without questioning the uneven global consequences of low-carbon transitions for environmental justice. As many scholars argue, green growth strategies for achieving sustainable transitions have unequal benefits and risks.[7] Benjamin Sovacool and colleagues call this problem "the decarbonization divide," whereby toxic injustices are displaced upstream and downstream along low-carbon supply chains, which are connected to "ecological destruction, gender inequality, child labor, and dispossession."[8] Indeed, environmental justice problems cut across a range of growth-led decarbonization policies, from scaling up renewable energy to controversial carbon offsetting schemes to sweeping center-left Green New Deal proposals. The dominant pathways to net zero are based on market-led solutions, which focus on channeling investments toward green technologies rather than on questioning unsustainable growth.[9] As Jason Hickel says, "'Green growth' is not a thing... Why? Because in a growth-oriented economy, efficiency arguments that *could* help us reduce our impact are harnessed instead to advance the objectives of growth—to pull ever-larger swathes of nature into circuits of extraction and production."[10]

The petrochemical industry is uniquely positioned within decarbonization debates as a hard-to-abate industry with an uncompromising drive for perpetual growth and a monopoly on the technical expertise needed for providing many green technological "solutions." The following analysis examines debates about petrochemical degrowth, decarbonization, and just transitions, focusing on the emblematic case of the petrochemical town of Grangemouth in Scotland. Since the Scottish government introduced its climate change policy in 2019, committing Scotland to net-zero greenhouse emissions by 2045, the petrochemical industry has come under increasing pressure to decarbonize.[11] As a former British Petroleum boomtown, Grangemouth has a strong labor history and identity, and an ambivalent relationship with environmentalism. However, the social contract between the industry and the community, of secure and well-paid employment for factory workers, has gradually eroded since the late 1970s.[12] Amid tremendous gaps between local social and economic deprivation and petrochemical industry profits, residents and workers have started to question their town's dependence on fossil fuels. The language of "just transitions" arose briefly in Grangemouth during 2020 in relation to cuts to oil refinery jobs. While the petrochemical industry still prospers, though, deeper conversations about transitions remain elusive. Rather than considering the need for just transitions only after the loss of industrial jobs, visions for just and sustainable industrial transformations need to be more proactive, speaking to wider degrowth themes of well-being, community participation, and prosperity without extractive growth.

Difficult Decarbonization

If there is any sector in society where there have been widespread calls among powerful stakeholders for degrowth, of sorts, then it is fossil fuels. The reason of course is the climate emergency rather than a philosophical rejection of growth as such, although it is no coincidence that degrowth debates have resurfaced in this era. Decarbonization has become an urgent priority in the global climate race to reach net-zero emissions by 2050. It spells nothing less than the endgame for fossil fuels, which has serious implications for the future of petrochemicals.

Of course, there are reasons to be skeptical about global climate commitments. Yet, just as the age of "king coal" was surpassed by the age of oil, global capitalist elites can envisage the end of the age of oil. While oil has so long seemed synonymous with capitalist interests, it is only one fraction of the capitalist market system, and mainstream economists have warned for years that the end of oil is on the horizon. A special report in the *Economist* on the future of oil argued that "the world needs to face the prospect of an end to the oil era," citing the challenge of climate change, the prospect of viable alternative energy solutions, and the rise of electric vehicles.[13] For decades, the oil industry has funded climate change denial and relied on aggressive lobbying to avoid addressing the issue.[14] However, the industry has been under increasing public pressure to respond to the escalating climate emergency, due to the multiscalar activism of the climate movement, Indigenous land rights struggles, and climate divestment campaigns. Tailing behind the oil and gas majors, which, one after the other, made commitments to become net-zero energy companies between 2019 and 2021, the petrochemical companies have reluctantly joined the race to "net zero." Indeed, Navigating Towards Net Zero was the title of the last World Petrochemical Conference that I observed in March 2022, organized to respond to the COP26 conference in Glasgow, although by then the immediate challenges facing the industry had changed again.[15]

In the years to come, the race to net zero could pose existential threats to the petrochemical industry. In a 2020 report, the International Renewable Energy Agency (IRENA) estimates that with current policies, global petrochemical production (primarily for plastics) could triple by 2050, and related emissions could rise to 2.5 gigatons per year by 2050.[16] The report identified the combined petrochemicals and chemical sector (90 percent of the chemicals sector is in petrochemicals) as one of seven key hard-to-abate sectors, defined as having significant economic, political, and technological hurdles to reaching net zero. Those sectors are the four most energy-intensive industries (iron/steel, cement/lime, chemicals/petrochemicals, and aluminum) and the three transport sectors (road freight, aviation, and shipping). According to the report, the chemicals and petrochemicals sector accounted for nearly 5 percent of total global greenhouse gas emissions in 2017.[17]

It would be naïve to assume that petrochemical corporations have really gotten on board with the transition. They do see decarbonization as a major threat to business, but in the meantime, like their upstream fossil fuel counterparts, they will exploit and profit from what they can before they are forced to quit. Oil, gas, and petrochemical companies received enormous bailouts during the first wave of the COVID-19 pandemic in the aftermath of the crude oil crash of April 2020 and lobbied to roll back environmental regulations where possible. To support their case, they relied on renewed arguments that fossil fuels and petrochemicals are essential industries, providing important energy needs, vital infrastructure and transport, and raw material inputs for making personal protective equipment (PPE).[18] Over the past few years, vertically integrated oil companies have also started to hedge their bets on oil by ramping up their petrochemical investments, in order to serve growing plastic markets.[19] This move has not gone unchallenged by investors. In 2020, the green investment think tank Carbon Tracker issued a report that pointed out that petrochemicals and plastics would become stranded assets in the green transition.[20]

Peter Newell has written about the political challenges of green transformations due to the powerful vested interests of incumbent actors. Newell argues that fossil fuel incumbents deploy Gramscian "trasformismo" strategies of co-optation to "narrow the debate to questions of incremental transition."[21] This dynamic is evident in fossil fuel companies' commitments to net zero, which rely on dubious future technological possibilities for offsetting carbon emissions, on outsourcing carbon emissions to other countries through cap-and-trade programs, on creative accounting of the balance of emissions and offsets, and, ultimately, on kicking the can down the road to the distant time horizon of 2050.[22] To date, most of the social scientific research on green transformations has focused on the energy sector, although there is emerging research in energy-intensive, difficult-to-decarbonize industrial sectors, including petrochemicals.[23]

In the downstream petrochemical industry, the main corporate "trasformismo" strategy in relation to green transformations has been to direct attention, both materially and ideologically, to the industry's expertise in sustainable technological innovation.[24] In the race to net zero, its key decarbonization efforts have focused on developing new "sustainable" and "circular" technologies, including chemical recycling, carbon capture and storage (CCS), and green hydrogen, to name just a few. Many researchers have cast doubt on the ability of these technologies to achieve decarbonization.[25] For example, environmental law researchers have highlighted problems with CCS and green hydrogen related to the lack of economic viability, massive energy requirements, and need for fossil fuel-derived additives in the production process. They contend that "it is fanciful to think that plastic can be 'fossil-free.'"[26]

In another recent article, IRENA researchers examined the challenge of decarbonizing the petrochemical sector and found that it would be extremely difficult to achieve in technical and economic terms, leaving aside the question of politics. Decarbonizing the industry would require the development of many new technologies, each with uncertain potential, and these efforts would need to be "coupled with deep demand reduction and CCS-retrofitted energy recovery."[27] In other words, decarbonizing the petrochemical industry requires both degrowth and offsetting. However, the prospect of *decreasing* the global production of petrochemicals, rather than anticipating *increasing* demand, is not in any market forecast that I have seen. It is time to give serious consideration to degrowth.

Reckoning with Degrowth

Degrowth is a heterogeneous movement, and people arrive at it from different positions, whether from anti-capitalist criticisms of limits to growth and unsustainable development, synergies with autonomous movements in the Global South, or alliances with other forms of environmental justice activism.[28] I have arrived at degrowth laterally, through contemplating the enduring struggles for environmental justice in fenceline petrochemical communities around the world, alongside escalating ecological crisis, which is clearly fueled by the insatiable drive within capitalism for expansion and extraction.

Challenging the dominant economic growth imperative is important not only because of planetary limits related to resource scarcity, waste, and living standards but also because so much of it is destructive, for physical and mental health, and for all forms of life, with vulnerable and marginalized communities being the worst affected. This is particularly the case for petrochemicals. Even Simon Kuznets, who invented the GDP metric in the 1940s, worried that it risked erasing the distinction between "good" and "bad" growth, and toward the end of his career, he felt increasingly uneasy about the promotion of GDP growth at the expense of social well-being.[29]

The idea of degrowth is somewhat misleading since its proponents do not advocate zero growth or negative growth. The term itself is a provocation, firmly rejecting the mantra of growth for growth's sake and GDP growth. Giorgos Kallis and colleagues take aim incisively at the concept of perpetual growth, rather than growth as such, arguing that it is axiomatic that nothing can grow perpetually, yet this expectation has become common sense within mainstream economics.[30] Instead of growth, degrowth scholars promote the "flourishing" of the kinds of economies and practices that they would like to encourage—for example in healthcare, education, and renewable energy.[31]

In fact, degrowth proposals have some similarities with arguments for sustainable growth, including the economist Mariana Mazzucato's thesis that the relentless pursuit of economic growth within capitalism has been fostered by misguided societal narratives about corporate wealth creation. These stories enable corporations to continue apace with value destruction, rather than with value creation, and hence there is a need to reconsider the meaning of value within societies and economies.[32] In other words, it is a question not only of growth but of what kind of growth is socially valuable, equitable, and sustainable.

Many critics of the degrowth concept argue that it is too negative due to its semantic implication of rejecting all forms of growth.[33] The philosopher Kate Soper and the ecological economist Tim Jackson refer instead to "post-growth" to convey more positive aspects of the idea.[34] The degrowth movement has been particularly controversial because of the economic disparities between the Global North and South. Rodríguez-Labajosa and coauthors argue that the concept of degrowth has little appeal for people who are living in poverty in the Global South and who want to see some growth in opportunities and welfare.[35] Indeed, after decades of economic stagnation, exacerbated by the 2008 recession and deepened by the pandemic, degrowth is a hard sell for poor and deindustrialized communities around the world.[36]

In *The Coming of the Postindustrial Society*, Daniel Bell famously predicted the decline of manufacturing and the rise of the knowledge and information economy.[37] However, Bell's thesis has not delivered on its promise. Nothing has replaced the industrial growth engine of manufacturing on a global scale, and the knowledge and service economy is full of precarious and insecure jobs. Over the past half century, deindustrialization has continued to ravage working-class communities, starting in North America and Europe in the 1970s and 1980s, and extending to South America, Africa, China, and other parts of Asia in later decades. The political economist Aaron Benanav argues that we have witnessed global labor deindustrialization, which he attributes to rising industrial overcapacity rather than automation, leading to a global slowdown of industrial output since the 1970s.[38] As global industrial production has slowed down and stagnated, Benanav contends, the global labor population has grown, resulting in a lower proportion of manufacturing as a share of total employment. The petrochemical industry has experienced deindustrialization over the years, but much of it has been labor deindustrialization, involving a declining number of manufacturing jobs due to technological changes and outsourcing.

Degrowth scholars recognize that periods of decline and economic stagnation within capitalism result in increasing workforce exploitation.[39] However, they often fall short of answering how to change capitalism itself, and their proposals are anti-capitalist, or postcapitalist, but are fuzzy on questions of revolution or transformation. Mazzucato's analysis of value extraction versus value creation in the global economy is more useful for examining the failures of capitalism and how it might be reformed, but then again, according to Philip Collins, Mazzucato is "the sort of critical friend capitalism needs."[40] For many degrowth scholars, "sustainable growth" under capitalism is a contradiction in terms.[41] However, on a pragmatic level, it important to engage with tensions between reformist and radical proposals for transformations.

The Dilemmas of Degrowth

Making the case for degrowth during the COVID-19 pandemic, Anitra Nelson and Vincent Liegey write: "Degrowth is about a democratic and serene transition toward new models of society where infinite growth on a finite planet is recognized as neither possible nor desirable."[42] The ease of this kind of vision is what I am uncomfortable with. Given all that we know about capitalism and colonialism, and after centuries of struggles for equality and justice, how could such a transition threatening to overturn the status quo be serene? Many proposals for degrowth envisage similarly smooth democratic transitions toward "convivial societies who live simply, in common and with less."[43] Yet importantly for the global petrochemical industry, degrowth visions of cooperatives, commons, urban gardening, and caring communities, as inspiring as they are, seem oddly detached from the politics of industrial capitalism.

There is a conscious reason for this omission. Instead of aiming to change the dominant world, the aim of many degrowth movements is to create new worlds on the periphery of capitalism, postcapitalist islands that eventually affect continents.[44] In an overview of the concept and keywords of degrowth, Giacomo D'Alisa, Federico Demaria, and Giorgos Kallis propose an analogy for explaining how degrowth is not about less of the same but about something different altogether: "The objective is not to make an elephant leaner, but to turn an elephant into a snail."[45] This begs the question: From whose perspective is it possible or desirable to turn an elephant into a snail?

Ekaterina Chertkovskaya and colleagues argue that the weakest spot of the degrowth political project is that it is "perceived to be ideationally driven, that is, not based on the material interests of any particular social constituency."[46] This is what needs to change. Without imagining the practical realities, dilemmas, and stakes of transformation, radical alternative imaginaries of degrowth seem only fantastical. Degrowth proposals sit most comfortably in postcapitalist alternative economies, but they tend to skirt around the juggernaut of capitalist industrial economies, where the reigning paradigm of economic growth is in full force and desperately in need of stronger countervailing paradigms.

Some degrowth proposals have focused on changing the existing capitalist system, alongside creating new systems. For example, Giuseppe Feola argues that the "unmaking of capitalism" through degrowth requires acts of refusal, resistance, and sacrifice that must arise from within the capitalist system, since "there is 'no out there' from which to impose change."[47] More concretely, Jason Hickel outlines key degrowth pathways to a postcapitalist world, including to end planned obsolescence; cut advertising; shift from ownership to usership; end food waste; and scale down ecologically destructive industries. Hickel singles out the fossil fuel industry as the most obvious example of an ecologically destructive industry, but he also extends this logic to the beef, arms, and private jet industries, and to the reduction of single-use plastics production.[48] In a recent systemic review of degrowth policy proposals, ecological economists Ines Cosme and coauthors found that out of 128 peer-reviewed articles, 54 included proposals for action. The majority of these degrowth policy proposals advocated national top-down approaches, focusing on government as a major driver of change as opposed to local bottom-up approaches, which are typically advocated by degrowth proponents. Hickel's degrowth pathways fit into the top-down category, whereas Feola's methods are more focused on anti-capitalist imaginaries and everyday practices.

Some degrowth scholars and activists "take issue with fossil fuels not only because of peak oil or climate change, but because a high use of energy supports complex technological systems. Complex systems call for specialized experts and bureaucracies to manage them. They unavoidably lead to non-egalitarian and undemocratic hierarchies."[49] On many levels, I agree, but this also seems like an easy get-out. Hubristic faith in technological progress is another prevailing mantra of capitalism, and complex technological systems are undoubtedly a feature of fossil fuel-based economies. However, they are also a feature of all modern industrial systems, including clean energy technologies and systems, healthcare systems, information technology, transportation networks, logistical supply chains, and countless other industries. Is the answer to all modern industries that are embedded within capitalism simply a matter of wishing them away, or forcing their extinction?

On first blush, there appears to be a critical disjuncture within degrowth approaches to action between top-down approaches that rely on capitalist states to drive radical post-growth transformation, and bottom-up approaches that focus on postcapitalist alternatives and avoid confronting the issue of conflict. Yet there is another way of looking at the contradictions of degrowth: as a multipronged approach to advancing planetary just transitions.[50]

Petrochemical Just Transitions

The concept of "just transitions" has its origins in the US labor movement in the 1970s and 1980s, as noted in chapter 2, which aimed to overcome the jobs versus environment dilemma by offering protections to displaced workers when polluting industries were closed. The term "just transition" was coined by Tony Mazzocchi of the Oil, Chemical, and Atomic Workers' Union, who proposed a "superfund for workers" to compensate and retrain those who moved out of environmentally hazardous jobs.[51] The ecologist and activist Barry Commoner also supported the idea of a just transition away from toxic and ecologically destructive industries.[52] In the 1990s, the international trade union movement adapted the concept of just transition as a response to climate change policies and the promotion of new green jobs. Since the 2010s, the just transition concept has expanded and diversified across a wide range of environmental and social movements linked to concepts of environmental racism, zero waste, energy democracy, mass incarceration, and Indigenous rights. In practice, however, just transition debates have been the most prevalent in coal communities in the United States, Europe, and Australia.[53]

The just transition concept has also gained official recognition, inscribed in official UN climate change discussions at the Katowice climate conference (COP24), held in 2018 in Polish coal country and which was dubbed the "Just Transition COP." Although the idea of just transitions has growing support among governments, scholars, and activists, it is also a contested concept. Critics argue that most just transition plans are aligned with green growth narratives and fail to address tensions between different values and interests. For example, David Ciplet and Jill Harrison observe that "scholars have treated 'just transitions' in an aspirational and uncritical way, neglecting to address the conflicts that do or could arise between sustainability and justice goals or among justice goals themselves in planning and activism."[54] Similarly, Linda Clarke and Carla Lipsig-Mummé contend that most proposals for just transitions within the labor movement are confined to variants of ecological modernization aligning with green growth narratives. Yet they also suggest that "a more proactive transformative strategy opening up an alternative eco-socialist vision for the future is emerging," pointing to the example of construction workers in Glasgow opposing building for building's sake.[55] Echoing criticisms of just transitions, scholars and activists have also drawn attention to the problem that Green New Deals in the United States, the United Kingdom, and Europe promise green jobs for workers in their own countries, while ignoring the toxic consequences of green energy supply chains for precarious workers and marginalized communities in the Global South, which are compounded by climate injustices. To overcome these difficulties, Dimitris Stevis and Romain Felli make a case for a "planetary just transition" that aims for greater inclusiveness and justice across different scales and temporalities.[56]

While the principle of a just transition can be traced to antitoxic struggles among unionized petrochemical workers in the 1970s and 1980s, debates about just transitions are relatively absent in the petrochemical industry, as compared with coal, oil, and other heavy industries. There are, of course, some notable exceptions. For example, Lorenzo Feltrin details labor struggles over just transitions in Porto Marghera's "chlorine cycle" in the 2000s, in which some workers campaigned for just transitions away from chlorine-based production, and others campaigned for a just transition within it. The workers managed to make some gains in environmental, social, and health protections, but the plant was eventually shut down, without a just transition in terms of remediation or compensation.[57] Indeed, there are long traditions of labor and environmental alliances over toxic petrochemical exposures, some of which are still active and others that are emerging, even if job blackmail has eroded solidarities. However, it is one thing for workers to demand toxic-free work environments and another to call for the end of their industry. Despite the expanding resonance of the just transition concept among policymakers, scholars, and activists, in practice, just transition debates tend to happen only in the context of industrial closures. Moreover, historically, around the world, most of the transitions from coal and other heavy polluting industries have been unjust.[58]

Multiscalar battles over how to transform the polluting and yet "essential" petrochemical industry have started to emerge, as we saw in chapter 3, combining long-standing concerns about unjust toxic exposures with broader questions of climate justice, Indigenous land rights, plastic pollution, and toxic colonialism. However, decarbonization remains an elusive objective, despite increasing institutional targets and commitments to reach net-zero carbon emissions by 2050. Furthermore, given the primacy of economic growth within mainstream policy, degrowth is not really on the table. Yet there have been signs of change, with rising pressures for all government, cities, and institutions to commit to emissions reduction targets, and for just transition policies to secure the livelihoods of workers and communities in the shift to sustainable production. Within this context, alongside the erosion of industrial relations in places where industry has long had a strong relationship with workers and communities, such as the case of Grangemouth in Scotland, a local politics of fossil fuel refusal has started to emerge.

"Who Benefits?": The Turn against Fossil Fuel Expansion in Grangemouth

In spring 2019, I met with an environmental activist in Grangemouth, who took me on a walking tour past the former BP social club and along the "dirty oil road" that runs through the INEOS refinery and petrochemical complex and includes several of the top polluters in Scotland (figure 5.1).[59]

Figure 5.1. Petrochemical complex and former BP social club in Grangemouth, Scotland, April 2019. Photograph by the author.

The activist had brought hundreds of people on this tour over the past ten years, usually by bicycle or car, including diplomats, members of the Green Party and Scottish Parliament, journalists, and filmmakers. He saw these tours as educational, showing people the connections that were all present along one road. The activist said there were long-standing tensions between trade unions and environmentalists in the area, but he noted that they found common cause in their opposition to fracking in Scotland. He recalled one shop steward at a fracking public meeting who said, "'You're told of all these promises, but it's not a good working environment, it's not a good community environment.' He was prepared to say that as well, so there was the sort of thought like, all right, they're probably on our side as well."[60]

Grangemouth was formerly an oil and petrochemical boomtown dominated by British Petroleum (BP). At its peak of employment in the 1960s, the petrochemical and refinery complex employed over 5,500 people, compared with 1,300 employees today, and the town and company enjoyed a positive reputation.[61] In the 1970s and 1980s, the industry went into decline, and the jobs and benefits for the community began to dwindle. In 2005, the petrochemical newcomer INEOS, owned by entrepreneur Jim Ratcliffe, bought the Grangemouth refinery and petrochemical complex from BP. The new owners brought in a new style of corporate governance, further eroding the social contract with the community that had been slowly declining with BP.[62] Since then, INEOS has grown to become one of the top ten global petrochemical companies, building its fortune by buying "unloved" petrochemical assets from major oil and gas companies and rejuvenating them.[63]

In autumn 2019, the Toxic Expertise research team conducted research in Grangemouth that included three focus groups and ten semi-structured interviews with local workers, residents, local authority representatives, and environmental activists.[64] Residents described their increasing frustration of living with noxious smells, flaring, noise pollution, and the ever-present risk of a major industrial disaster in the shadow of a behemoth industry with no benefits to the community. At the time of our research, Grangemouth included five areas located in the most deprived 10 percent of Scotland, while INEOS CEO Jim Ratcliffe was the UK's richest person, with a wealth of more than £21 billion.[65] The gap between such extreme wealth and local deprivation has been exacerbated by a lack of employment opportunities for local people at the plant. The town has experienced significant labor deindustrialization despite the continuing expansion of industry. Rather than direct, unionized employees, many of the jobs in manufacturing are outsourced to agency and contract workers, and much of the work involves higher levels of qualification than in the past, including work with computers, sophisticated machinery, and complex supply chains.[66]

The case of Grangemouth illustrates the changing role of organized labor and industrial towns in challenging new modes of petrochemical expansion in the twenty-first century. From the outset, Ratcliffe's plans for aggressive industrial restructuring were met with resistance from organized labor. In 2008, as discussed in chapter 2, the unionized Unite workers at Grangemouth went on strike for two days to protect their pensions, and INEOS backed down to avert the disruption. However, Ratcliffe soon began planning for another confrontation. As Ratcliffe and INEOS communications specialist Ursula Heath wrote in their corporate autobiographical book about the first twenty years of INEOS: "It would be a war with more battles before victory. While waiting for what he [Ratcliffe] knew would be an inevitable second confrontation, he went about quietly putting mechanisms in place to reduce the union's power."[67]

In October 2013, oil and petrochemical workers at Grangemouth went on strike again over pay, conditions, and pensions. Within two days, the union was forced to retreat after INEOS threatened to close the plant, resulting in a wage freeze, an end to workers' final-salary pensions, job cuts, and no strikes for three years.[68] At the end of the no-strike period in 2016, INEOS announced that it would withdraw official recognition of Unite at Grangemouth, ending their collective-bargaining agreement. The 2013 strike was a crushing defeat for the union, but in 2018 union recognition was restored at Grangemouth following a workers' vote, and unionized workers have continued to campaign for better pay and conditions.[69]

Mark Lyon, the Unite trade union convener who was sacked after the strike in 2013, wrote a book titled *The Battle of Grangemouth*, detailing workers' accounts of the struggle.[70] In an interview, Lyon reflected that the most likely reason that INEOS decided to "derecognize" Unite was that "the union was calling for the Scottish government to intervene in the proposed sale of the BP Forties Pipeline to INEOS, on the grounds that it was irresponsible to allow the pipeline to be controlled by INEOS after all that had happened."[71] Historically, the position of oil and petrochemical workers on environmental issues in Grangemouth has been ambivalent, given the town's dependence on the industry. As Lyon explained: "You find yourself very conflicted. It's harder to be an ecowarrior when you are defending jobs, wages and conditions in an oil refinery. . . . There are the times when you really have to hold your nose—like when you go to the government and ask them to look again at the carbon floor tax."[72] Another worker we interviewed echoed this point, with a sense of bitterness: "There was stuff that we [Unite workers] did, so a policy conference on emissions and . . . we did stuff with the taxation of fuel and even British Ports. Effectively, we lobbied on behalf of the companies and the industry, and it suited the company for us to do that."[73]

Workers' attitudes toward oil and gas have started to shift, especially in relation to future extraction. Partly, this relates to the sense of betrayal and mistrust after the crushing defeat of the union in 2013. However, Lyon argues that the union's opposition to fracking relates to wider concerns about the risks:

> People have said to us, "Do you think that if industrial relations were still alright, and none of those problems had happened, you would be looking at fracking in a different way—in the way you have looked at other difficult issues in the past?" Is this a vindictive stand, and if things had been different you would have supported the company? These kinds of issues are faced by workers in other industries where there are debates

over environmental issues versus jobs, and they are always difficult. But I think this is different. Having seen it at first hand I know that it is a terrible process. On some days in Pennsylvania, they have had to close down roads because lethal gas leaks have made whole areas unsafe.[74]

A key part of the INEOS vision has been based on the prospect of fracking shale gas in the United Kingdom, as a cheap raw material feedstock, motivated by the success of the US shale gas boom and by declining North Sea reserves. The largest holder of UK fracking licenses, INEOS has lobbied local and national governments extensively to open up fracking exploration. While fracking has gone ahead in England, the Scottish government announced a moratorium on fracking in 2015. Thus in 2016, INEOS took the pioneering step of shipping US shale gas (liquified ethane gas) to Europe, in the world's largest multi-gas carrier, with the support of an £8 million Scottish government grant and a £230 million UK government loan guarantee.[75] In addition, INEOS challenged the Scottish government in court over their anti-fracking policy decision, but they lost the case in 2018.[76]

Most workers and residents who we spoke with in Grangemouth were opposed to fracking, saying that fracking risked contaminating water supplies and causing earth tremors, and that fracking licenses brought additional house insurance costs (even with the moratorium on fracking in Scotland, which could be reversed in the future since there is no legislative ban).

One retired worker said that he would support fracking if there were a "100 percent cast iron guarantee that nothing would go wrong," but the problem was that there is no such assurance. However, most agreed that the risks were not worth taking because there would be no benefits to the community. This perspective was evident in the following discussion about fracking with a petrochemical worker:

> WORKER There is massive financial benefit to come from it in terms of gas, but who is going to benefit? That's another question. I mean if the benefit is going to go to INEOS and the Scottish government and nothing is going to come to the public then to hell with it.
> INTERVIEWER Yeah, they should keep it in the ground?
> WORKER Keep it in the ground, yeah. Because the day is coming anyway, the day is fast approaching when they're going to stop using fossil fuels.

An older local resident echoed this view, recognizing that the time was running out for fossil fuels, but that none of the benefit would flow to the local community:

> And you cannot have an electric [air]plane for any long distance, so all I'm saying is that oil and gas is not going to go away in any of our lifetimes. So, that place [the refinery complex] I think will be okay for fifteen years, and my own view is that you can only get benefits to Grangemouth if we have some political representation, which we do not have.[77]

Amid fragmented trust in industry and government, and uncertainty about the future of the petrochemical industry in Grangemouth, many local people have started to question the town's longstanding dependence on oil and gas. When we asked residents about what they hoped for the future of Grangemouth, the most common theme was that there needed to be social and economic benefits and political representation for the community, because they had none. As one resident with a passion for local parks put it:

> So, [INEOS has] benefitted, and we've actually just slowly declined, and something needs to be put right, and it takes money. So the biggest thing that needs to happen in my view is that we need to be able to create a source of money for the benefit of the community, not for the benefit of industry, but for the benefit in the community to start making the areas, the housing in the town, and the green spaces of the town a higher quality than they are, to compensate for the negativity that the industry will continue to bring.[78]

The resident highlighted the importance of green spaces and housing for the community, which resonates—at least on some levels—with prioritizing well-being rather than economic development for its own sake. However, several residents were also nostalgic about the postwar era of growth and stressed the barriers to finding alternative sources of income beyond the petrochemical industry. One resident, for example, commented: "I think this is a fear of: if INEOS moves out, if this guy decides to shut his plant, then Grangemouth is stuffed. Well, we're not getting much benefit now, so if they're moving away, I don't know if a lot of people would be employed in this area because they're working further afield."[79] This fear relates to the observation by Dimitri D'Andrea that the "most powerful obstacle on the way to a new climate regime . . . is the unimaginability of a different economic system, or even just a new balance between market and society, and between humanity and the environment."[80] A local environmental campaigner summarized the dilemma of confronting this as follows:

> The young voices that are coming through are saying, "Actually, that's not the kind of work we want to be working in. That's not the future that we want for us, never mind our children." There are a lot of grandparents on

the streets as well saying, "This isn't the future we want for our grandchildren. We need to start changing now." But industry is so locked in, and we are so locked into that industry.[81]

Net-Zero Petrochemical Growth Contradictions

Undeterred by the fracking setbacks, INEOS has pushed into conventional fossil fuel expansion. In 2017, INEOS bought the North Sea Pipeline from BP for £200 million, and then acquired the Dong Oil and Gas (North Sea) business for $1.05 billion and revealed ambitious plans for the first large-scale petrochemical investments in Europe in twenty years.[82] Two years later, INEOS invested $2 billion in Saudi Aramco Jubail 2, the world's largest petrochemical project. The company has since come under increasing pressure to decarbonize in the wake of the climate divestment movement and the crude oil crash in 2020.[83] However, as the country's largest polluter, INEOS poses a major hurdle for the Scottish government's 2019 commitment to reach net-zero carbon emissions by 2045. It has been a laggard in the push for net-zero emissions commitments across the industry, at first making only vague commitments, such as launching a new hydrogen business "in support of the drive towards a zero-carbon future."[84] In July 2021, in the lead-up to COP26, INEOS announced its "roadmap to net zero," emphasizing the journey rather than the destination, and stating, "We will not make pledges that we cannot support with real world action plans." As part of its roadmap to net zero, the company stated, "INEOS is aiming to contribute by not only decarbonizing energy for its existing operations, but also by providing hydrogen that will help other businesses and sectors do the same."[85] It was repositioning itself, in other words, as the provider of green technological solutions.

In October 2021, INEOS announced that it would invest more than €2 billion in green hydrogen production, which it announced was "Europe's largest ever investment in electrolysis projects to make green hydrogen with the potential to transform zero carbon hydrogen production across Europe."[86] But INEOS has a track record of aiming for grandiose projects, including its supersized multi-gas carriers, as noted in chapter 3, and its ten-day construction of hand sanitizer plants at the beginning of the COVID-19 pandemic. Green hydrogen, classified as "green" on alleged low-carbon credentials, would be made through the electrolysis of water and used for power generation, transportation, and industrial processes.

As part of their commitment to net zero, the Scottish and UK governments announced a £90 million Growth Deal package for the Falkirk-Grangemouth Investment Zone in July 2020, focusing on innovative technology toward addressing climate change and sustainability, the eleventh such package offered to local regions in the UK since they were launched in 2014.[87] We spoke with an economic development officer in Falkirk who had worked on putting together the bid. She explained that the Growth Deal is like a town's version of a city deal, and one of the focuses of the bid would be looking toward net-zero carbon in Grangemouth. The flagship project would be a center of excellence in biotechnology:

> This is about the proof of concept and taking the technology to the next stage. We have the opportunity to do those sorts of things in Grangemouth. There are a lot of chemical industry processes you wouldn't want to do within a university campus, but you can do it right in the middle of industry and particularly industry that has been established, so that's probably going to be co-allocated with INEOS or the chemical plants, or somewhere like that.[88]

The center for excellence would involve spinoff industries as well as a separate campus within INEOS to explore carbon capture and utilization technologies, which would "diversify the industry into cleaner technologies." She cited a recent INEOS announcement that the company planned to produce a new type of plastic that would be made from 50 percent renewable raw materials, and that they were also investing in more efficient waste recycling. Meanwhile, they would conduct a feasibility study for community energy based on solar power. As the name "Growth Deal" suggests, these government-funded plans are about investing in green technological solutions in partnership with industry rather than in more radical transformation involving shifting away from fossil fuel dependence. The terminology of the Growth Deal, and the inclusion of a focus on achieving growth-driven net-zero carbon emissions, sounds like a watered-down version of proposals for a Green New Deal. A local environmentalist had this to say about it:

> The Scottish government still wants it to be oil driven, but it can't be for our future, so we can invest in that center of excellence for the last bit of oil, or we could put that investment into the transition to renewables.... Ultimately, that plant will have to go, but the thing is, we should be planning for that transition now, rather than trying to make that a center of excellence that then becomes—well, actually nobody wants

to work there because there is no future in jobs in oil and gas, but they want to get the last bit out of it.[89]

In fact, the Scottish government has started to plan for a green transition, but as the Growth Deal suggests, it sees the petrochemical industry, at least in part, as a provider of technological solutions. It does anticipate that there will be future impacts, however, on petrochemical workers. To help achieve its climate change goals, the Scottish government established the Just Transition Commission in 2018, which identified oil, gas, and petrochemical workers as specific groups of employees that would be directly affected by a green transition.[90] In November 2020, the oil refinery Petroineos in Grangemouth, jointly owned by PetroChina and INEOS, announced that 200 jobs were at risk, which would reduce the workforce from 650 down to 450 workers, due to low demand for crude oil. The Scottish government and the Scottish Green Party called for a just transition to support the redundant workers, but the trade union Unite opposed the job cuts, calling them "premature."[91] Calls for a just transition in such cases are necessary to protect, assist, and reskill workers through difficult times, but they offer little consolation when there is no clear alternative vision of the future.

In many ways, the question of a just transition for Grangemouth has already been bypassed, as the community has already witnessed decades of labor deindustrialization and social and economic decline, but without new green jobs or another basis for employment. Another problem at the local level in Grangemouth is that the idea of the "just transition" is not yet a topic of discussion while the petrochemical industry is still prospering, even if there are few jobs in the industry for local people. Unlike the refinery, which followed in the footsteps of several other refinery closures around the world after the crude oil crash and decarbonization drive in 2020, the petrochemical complex is positioned more favorably to weather economic storms, and poised for growth in plastics markets and green technological developments.

Toward Petrochemical Just Transformations

Just transitions are important to protect workers and livelihoods around the world, but these need to offer meaningful visions of alternative futures for local communities as well as for workers. How will deprived petrochemical communities like Grangemouth, already stripped of so many community resources, capacities, and solidarities, fare in green transitions, and what kind of future can they practically hope for, especially with such low trust in public authorities? Rather than considering the need for just transitions only after the loss of industrial jobs, visions for just transitions need to be more proactive, speaking to wider concerns about well-being, commons, community participation, and prosperity without extractive growth. They also need to consider the interconnected planetary scale of ecological crisis, and the consequences of shifting toxic pollution, industrial hazards, and dangerous jobs to other marginalized communities around the world. In this respect, the idea of "just transformations" rather than "just transitions" is more expansive, suggesting radical rather than incremental change, although there is value in working with "just transitions" as an evolving concept.[92]

The global momentum behind decarbonization is critical for tackling the climate emergency, driving far-reaching targets, actions, and investments in renewables. However, decarbonization risks deflection and co-option by corporate incumbents and relies too heavily on growth-driven investments in green technologies with environmental justice consequences, rather than on the difficult work of tackling the problem of perpetual petrochemical expansion. Degrowth offers an important but neglected perspective on debates about decarbonization and just transitions, which both remain premised on GDP growth. Yet many degrowth visions of a smooth and democratic green transition away from dependency on growth avoid confronting practical dilemmas and conflicts of radical industrial transformation. Just transition policies and debates address some of these issues, aiming to resolve conflicts between jobs and the environment by safeguarding the livelihoods of workers and communities, but remain constrained by green growth contradictions. To confront the climate emergency, these perspectives should be brought together to counterbalance their respective limitations, but they should also be extended to address the multiscalar implications of industrial transformations, particularly the consequences of displacing harm to disadvantaged populations around the world.

Some scholars of just transitions have started to make these connections by reconciling more radical perspectives with the practical challenges of deep industrial transformation. For instance, Erik Kojola and Julian Agyeman "locate the need for an active just transition in a broader analysis of just sustainabilities and how interrelated systems of capitalism, racism, colonialism, and patriarchy can (re)produce injustices in a less carbon and resource intensive economy."[93] Similarly, Damian White notes convergences between "just transitions" and "designs for transitions," including degrowth and pluriverse perspectives, suggesting that "convergences between these currents might facilitate modes of anti-racist, feminist and ecosocialist design futuring that can get us to think beyond degrowth/Left ecomodern binaries and toward a design politics that can support a Green New Deal."[94] These perspectives offer important insights into potential ways of reconciling competing visions of sustainability and justice in deep industrial transformations.

Degrowth proposals for alternative ways of living and working have gained traction among many activists and communities, particularly during the first wave of the COVID-19 pandemic, but they remain marginal in mainstream and everyday discourses. While degrowth has its limitations and detractors, it also has incredible strength in offering a vision of well-being that does not rely on the endless pursuit of growth. The task ahead is to extend the political project of degrowth more tangibly and practically within struggles over decarbonization and just transitions (or transformations) across multiple scales. To link this to multiscalar activism, this will mean seeking alliances and common ground across differences, and possibly finding new kinds of language that redefine growth. There are considerable risks to underestimating the dangers of unchecked capitalist expansion and the co-option and rollback of decarbonization agendas. The dilemma between different courses of action, and its resolution, lies in the gap between dominant and alternative narratives, and between highly unequal social and ecological consequences of industrial transformations.

6

Toward an Alternative Planetary Petrochemical Politics

When it comes to levers for change, the insight into the calculated war mentality of the petrochemical industry, on a strategic level, offers cold comfort. If the industry will change only due to external factors, such as war or legislation, then there needs to be more external pressure to stop the toxic petrochemical build-out. To be drawn into the same battleground over the stakes of petrochemical transformation entails—at least on some level—accepting the rules of the game. The petrochemical game is one based on military strategy, involving proactive and defensive strategies, conflicts, and escalation. Its prevailing worldviews stem from racial capitalism, toxic colonialism, and technological prowess. Yet to avoid conflict—to have faith in the dialogical rhythms of liberal democracy—risks relinquishing more and more territories to be used as sinks for pollution, waste, and colonial violence. The corporate dynamics of deception, oppression, and co-optation have a long-standing and constantly evolving history. Invariably, planetary petrochemical proliferation continues, smoothing over the paths of resistance.

Multiscalar activism against petrochemical injustice offers hope because it extends the politics of resistance beyond specific places, communities, and issues, reflecting the expanding resonance of environmental justice. It puts increasing pressure on the industry to change, from taking direct action against fossil fuel infrastructure to waging legal battles with polluters and campaigning for stronger regulations. Rather than having a unitary identity, it is more of a patchwork of different actions, some coordinated, others separate, operating at multiple spatial and temporal points of articulation in a planetary collective struggle. Despite having different strategies and issues, each movement strives, in different ways, for related goals. Yet toxic injustice endures.

There is a real risk that decisive planetary action to address toxic petrochemical injustice will not happen until it is too late, when toxic disaster expands viscerally to affect most people on the planet, overlapping with climate breakdown. This echoes the point that Dina Gilio-Whitaker makes about the climate crisis: "If what the preeminent Indian law scholar Felix Cohen said was true, that Indians are the United States' miner's canary that signals the poison gas of the political atmosphere, to extend the metaphor, then in the larger world dominated by the fossil fuel industry all humans have become the miner's canary."[1]

This chapter offers some reflections about how to transform the complex, adaptive, and destructive petrochemical industry. First, it unpacks the industry's idea of the "essential," particularly in light of the COVID-19 pandemic, in contrast with the critical environmental justice studies idea of the "indispensable."[2] Then, it examines the multiscalar problem of petrochemical lock-in, which is one of the biggest complex systems-level obstacles to radical industrial transformation. To conclude, the chapter outlines some possible critical interventions toward an alternative planetary petrochemical politics.

Essential versus Indispensable

Within the lifespan of one generation, petrochemicals have grown exponentially to saturate nearly everything in modern life. Petrochemicals are so ubiquitous that they seem almost invisible. The industry never tires of pointing out just how essential it is. As one petrochemical executive told me: "Helmets, made of plastics, how many lives have they saved? Are they polluting? Is there anybody who is against a helmet? The same industry in which we use the helmet is producing the plastic bags."[3]

Throughout my research, I have questioned the extent to which the industry really is essential, weighing up the products that benefit society—the windmill blades, the hospital equipment, the shatterproof glass—and the harmful ones—the single-use plastic sachets filling shorelines in Southeast Asia and Africa; the half a trillion plastic bottles that are produced every year; the abundance of cheap plastic toys; and the thousands of consumer products that leach toxic substances. I wonder, though, whether this is the right question. Material dependence does not mean essential, at least not indefinitely. It is a manufactured need.

Petrochemicals and plastics are modern inventions that replaced (or were combined with) other materials, such as wool, glass, metal, and paper. People managed to live without them before. Part of the problem is how enmeshed petrochemicals are with scientific and technological developments, including modern medicine, high-speed transport, fertilizers and pesticides, the built environment, information technology, and digital cultures. Another problem is the lack of straightforward substitutions with the same levels of material versatility as petrochemicals and plastics, but without the environmental and health hazards. Material substitution does not address many underlying sustainability and environmental justice issues with overconsumption, caused by further extraction of metals and minerals, deforestation, biodiversity loss, and greenhouse gas emissions. Furthermore, some plastic products were created specifically with their versatile properties in mind, making them less amenable to substitution.[4] Before asking about material substitution for hazardous products, we should first ask whether we need these products at all. The key question is: Do they benefit society and the environment in meaningful ways?

Yet the industry's "essential" narrative is a powerful obstacle to change. Just as the public was starting to question this narrative, the COVID-19 pandemic began. The petrochemical industry was deemed "essential" in the "invisible war" against the virus. This was despite its historic contributions to the loss of biodiversity, which increased the probability of animal-to-human virus transmission in the first place.[5] In March 2020, INEOS announced that it would build the third largest hand sanitizer plant in Europe within just ten days, and then deliver free sanitizer to hospitals. They relished their new heroic role as being "critical to national resilience" by producing the petrochemicals used in drugs, testing kits, ventilators, and protective clothing.[6] The same month, the Plastics Industry Association wrote a letter to the US Department of Health and Human Services requesting a public statement about the health and safety benefits of single-use plastics "to educate the general public and elected officials that single-use plastic products are the most sanitary choice."[7] Many plastic bag bans and other single-use plastics bans were lifted or delayed out of fears about the spread of the virus.[8] Meanwhile, the crude oil crash rendered markets for recycled plastics uncompetitive, and demand rocketed for plastics in facemasks, food and medical packaging, and other pandemic-related plastics.[9]

The COVID-19 crisis raised deep questions about what is "essential" or "expendable" in society. Around the world, certain workers were classified as "essential," "key," and "critical" for fighting the virus, many on the frontlines of risk and exposure, including healthcare workers, delivery drivers, grocery store workers, teachers, and waste collectors, among others. Nonessential workers stayed home during lockdowns, many cast out of work. Whole industries were also classified as "essential," necessary to keeping society and the economy running, including the "critical infrastructure" of supply chain logistics, energy systems, and the manufacture of essential goods and products.

Despite a narrative early in the pandemic that the virus did not discriminate, research soon emerged showing its disproportionate health effects on racial and ethnic minority groups around the world.[10] The disparity of vulnerabilities to the virus across different groups was a case of environmental racism, with higher rates of COVID-19 infection and mortality in areas with higher air pollution, including in fenceline communities.[11] Indeed, as critical environmental justice scholarship highlights, whole populations were treated as expendable long before the pandemic.[12] Before the wave of protests following the police murder of George Floyd on May 26, 2020, David Pellow wrote that the Black Lives Matter movement that started in 2014 represented an environmental justice issue that was connected to the problem of state-sanctioned racial violence.[13] The pandemic magnified existing inequalities and injustices, acutely highlighting the importance of challenging systemic social and environmental inequalities, particularly the problem of "expendability."[14]

Throughout its history, the petrochemical industry has always operated on the assumption that some lives and environments are expendable.[15] Through manufacturing petrochemical needs, denying toxic risks, and pursuing petrochemical expansion through whatever means possible, the industry has spent decades creating a toxic and tentacular system upon which economies and societies depend. This system has both life-sustaining and life-destroying attributes, given its complex material interdependencies.

Instead of using the term "essential" to describe the petrochemical industry, I propose evaluating it in terms of an ethics of "indispensability," the principle in critical environmental justice studies that "the wellbeing of all people, species, and ecosystems is indispensable."[16] Taking indispensability into account in the petrochemical industry would involve centering issues of environmental justice rather than corporate profit. Ultimately, it would require scaling back the industry dramatically: stripping away the reliance on fossil fuels, the production of toxic chemicals, and the wasteful consumer markets, and leaving only those parts that genuinely protect health, wellbeing, and the environment. There could be a role in the future for the industry in the innovation and production of new green technologies, but only if it would be possible to avoid false solutions, and to ensure that it is done in ways that are both sustainable and socially just. There is no way, of course, that the industry would voluntarily facilitate its own diminution, or reorient its priorities away from profit. At least not under the current global capitalist system. This raises the political question of how to challenge the dominant power structures that enable the destructive aspects of the petrochemical industry.

Multiscalar Petrochemical Lock-In

One of the key political, economic, and ideological barriers to addressing the planetary petrochemical crisis, across multiple scales, is lock-in. It is both material and cultural. On a global scale, the world is locked into a system driven by the imperative for expansion and consumption of plastics, which are ubiquitous in modern life. The industry is based on long investment cycles, large scales of operations, major investments, and incremental process innovation.[17] Across different regional scales, petrochemical production is locked into vast infrastructures of integrated petrochemical and refinery complexes, oil and gas pipelines, and logistical networks.[18] On local scales, many cities and communities around the world have developed economies that are dependent on oil and petrochemical production. This has resulted in a different kind of petrochemical lock-in that is embedded in local contexts, evident in conflicts over the jobs-versus-environment dilemma, and in bitter struggles for environmental justice in polluted fenceline communities.

The idea of petrochemical lock-in relates to Gregory Uhruh's idea of "carbon lock-in," which accounts for how "industrial economies have become locked into fossil fuel-based technological systems through a path-dependent process driven by technological and institutional increasing returns to scale."[19] Fred Bauer and Germain Fontenit extend the analysis of "carbon lock-in" to the petrochemical sector, which they contend has been willfully created by large multinational corporations involved in plastics manufacturing.[20] The carbon lock-in of the petrochemical industry is based on infrastructural and technological lock-in, which is reinforced by modern consumer lifestyles and by new investments in petrochemicals as the future of oil. The consumption side of petrochemical lock-in relates to what the ecological economist Tim Jackson calls the "iron cage of consumerism": a self-reinforcing system of destructive mass consumption, which is a product of powerful social forces and modern institutions.[21]

Even for environmental activists working in fenceline communities, where people live in the shadow of polluting industries, few people would advocate the destruction of the industry itself. For some workers, as we discussed in previous chapters, it is because the petrochemical industry remains an important, if increasingly precarious, source of employment and identity. Even for those who are deeply critical of the industry's capacity for self-transformation, it seems inconceivable to propose plant closures as a practical possibility. The following exchange that I had with a long-time environmental health scientist working with people living in Cancer Alley was revealing of these practical local constraints:

> AM Given your criticisms of the petrochemical industry in Louisiana, do you think that a solution would be to get the industry to move?
>
> SCIENTIST You are not going to have that, because the infrastructure is there. The solution is to get people out of harm's way, reduce the exposure. That improves their quality of life. They feel that they were there first, and they should be able to stay there, and the industry should operate properly and at no risk to them. That is not going to happen, so we need to get them out of harm's way.
>
> AM Okay, so it's sort of a realistic approach.

SCIENTIST   Yes. The infrastructure is there. I mean, they need the ship access up the river. They have the resources. We have the salt that they need to make chlorine for the petrochemicals. We have the natural gas. We have the oil. We have the water, and so that is why they are there. Then they built all the pipeline infrastructure, so they are not going anywhere.[22]

Infrastructural lock-in is not unique to Louisiana. In the case of the petrochemical industry in Nanjing, Qiyan Wu and colleagues draw on Unruh's analysis of carbon lock-in alongside a critique of economic growth (that is, the "pro-growth model") to examine "why an industry that causes unaffordable pollution and hazards can continue to resist the pressure of public and local authorities and grow to be the second largest petrochemical industry cluster in China over the past two decades."[23] In addition to infrastructural and technological lock-in, the authors argue that powerful networks of political elites in the local political economy create a "petrochemical-led pro-growth politics lock-in."[24]

Is there any escape from petrochemical lock-in? Large parts of the petrochemical planet are, and will continue to be, enmeshed in petrochemicals, or what Liboiron calls "plastics as Land." Liboiron and Lepawsky discuss the myth of purity in societal quests to eliminate waste and other discards, as contrasted with the ethical practice of cleanup and care. Following the influential work of Mary Douglas on dirt as "matter out of place," they argue that the myth of purity can reinforce social inequalities: "Purity is about eradicating, striking down, destroying, assimilating, and abolishing differences that might threaten the core of the social order. . . . For example, understanding all single-use plastics as one type of thing—they should all be banned!—erases single-use medical waste that we probably don't want to replace with reusables."[25] This is an important reminder of the importance of considering the complexities and ethical implications of any course of action, including the politics of resistance and refusal. Instead of the purity of cleanup or the "solutionism that treats waste and pollution as technical problems," Liboiron and Lepawsky advocate an ethics of intervention into systems, "a relational approach to determine which factors are the most important to focus on; the answer isn't always or even often the final objects of trash or pollution."[26] Let us consider, then, some possible critical interventions that could lead to moving toward an alternative planetary petrochemical politics.

Critical Interventions

First, a caveat: I do not know what the best course of planetary collective action might be, nor do I have a concrete proposal for how to resolve the tensions between different movements. What is needed, an attentive reader might conclude, is a planetary counter-hegemonic project that combines environmental justice with visions of degrowth, forging connections between different kinds of politics and transcending national boundaries. But in truth, I do not see such a project happening, at least not in the ways that might be anticipated, and not in the short to medium term. I am not even sure that it would be possible. An ethics of intervention requires a relational approach, which attends to diverse contexts and does not assume that solutions can scale up. However, I do think that reaching agreement on some common goals is within the realms of possibility.

While there are deeply divided views about the petrochemical industry, there are some basic points of agreement: the petrochemical industry is difficult to decarbonize, difficult to detoxify, and difficult to disembed from the consumption-driven global capitalist system. The industry itself is willing to admit these "difficulties," which effectively serve as obstacles to change because they are inherent to the "essential" industry. However, these difficulties start to look different when they are no longer counterbalanced by the narrative of what is deemed to be essential. Increasingly, many researchers, policymakers, activists, and communities are realizing that the petrochemical industry, whatever its claim to the contrary, is fundamentally toxic and unsustainable. In the context of ecological crisis, the industry's difficulties offer important starting points for critical intervention: achieving a global mandate to decarbonize, detoxify, and disembed from (that is, reduce material dependence on) the industry.

The real difficulty is that the industry holds the keys to its own technological transformation, not only discursively but materially. The industry benefits from its infrastructural and market lock-in, its monopoly over complex technological systems, and its enormous political and economic influence. And despite the problem with market-led technological fixes, there is no getting around the fact that, barring unforeseen circumstances, technologies will play an important role in deep industrial transformations. Recognizing this challenge, Damian White proposes the idea of "designing" just transitions out of "the sense that it may well be more productive now to acknowledge that all conceivable programs for just transition are going to be socio-technical in nature, multiscalar and, by definition, concerned with designing low-carbon futures."[27] For White, this is a compromise position, in the context of climate breakdown, which will occur in "circumstances not of our choosing."

However, the grip of the petrochemical industry on technological solutions is only as tight as its hold over political, economic, and discursive power. Investigative journalists, researchers, and NGOs have done important work criticizing the flaws in the forecasts of the International Energy Agency, outlining the loopholes in oil and gas companies' net-zero pledges, researching the problems with voluntary corporate sustainability standards, and exposing the false solutions (from chemical recycling to carbon capture and storage, and green hydrogen, to name just a few). There is much work to be done in this rapidly moving field, particularly considering the growth of ESG (environmental, social, and governance) risk assessments and investments, the voluntary use of science-based targets to back up corporate sustainability claims, and the constant stream of new industry scenarios, roadmaps, and forecasts.

The global momentum behind climate action could be a significant dominant policy lever for transforming the petrochemical industry if governments, investors, and policymakers wake up to the fact that petrochemicals are not an exception in the transition away from fossil fuels. Another major policy lever could be the development of legally binding international measures to prevent toxic petrochemical pollution and production. In March 2022, as noted in previous chapters, the UN Environment Assembly in Nairobi agreed on a landmark mandate for a new global treaty to address problems across the full lifecycle of plastics. Negotiating this complex agreement will involve intense political struggle for years to come, with vested business interests determined to keep the regulations focused on waste rather than production. Similarly, Europe's roadmap to ban more than 12,000 household and industrial chemicals, unveiled in April 2022, represents a major step toward binding regulations that protect the environment and health, rather than corporate profits. Of course, there has been pushback, which can be expected to continue. This underlines the importance of keeping up the pressure to develop stricter, legally binding regulations.

Will there be a defining moment when ecological and political tipping points converge? The planetary boundary for chemical and plastic pollution, after all, has already been crossed. There is no global mandate for scaling back the industry, not yet—but multiple forms of resistance are gathering pace. In *Facing the Planetary*, William Connolly envisages a "politics of swarming" emerging organically in response to the ecological crisis, which resembles a swarm of birds, "composed of multiple constituencies, regions, levels, and modes of action, each carrying some potential to augment and intensify the others with which it becomes associated."[28] Perhaps this is how an alternative planetary petrochemical politics might come together, through synchronicity, which occurs naturally in complex systems, such as when fireflies light up with others at the same time.[29]

Perhaps the convergence of tipping points has already begun, but we have not realized it yet. Instead of happening in one synchronic moment or series of moments, it might happen slowly and unevenly, over decades, centuries, or even millennia, with many setbacks along the way. It is possible to imagine an end to the reign of racial capitalism, toxic colonialism, and technological solutionism, what might later become known as the "Darkest Ages." Much as I try though, I do not think it will be possible to avoid ecological catastrophe and untold suffering, which is already unfolding and growing exponentially. It is more of a question of fighting battles on multiple fronts to end the destructive system and to protect livelihoods, communities, and ecosystems through difficult processes of transformation—while recognizing that there is no "purity" option in a toxic, interdependent world.

The tension between urgency and justice in responding to ecological crisis is a sobering reminder of the extent of the damages. To quote Kyle Powys Whyte again: "The relational tipping point got crossed long ago thanks to systems of colonialism, capitalism, and industrialization."[30] If there is to be a planetary transformation, ushering in a new era of social and ecological relations, then it may take many generations to do the necessary work of learning and unlearning, repairing, and reconnecting, and the many other efforts required for healing to take place.

Changing the dominant narratives—of petrochemical lock-in, technological solutionism, and endless growth—is a crucial step toward healing collective planetary histories and futures. But so too is staying open to new possibilities and perspectives. Sometimes, a perspective that you never fully appreciated begins to make sense. At a certain point in my journey researching toxic pollution and environmental justice, I came to degrowth: challenging the perpetual pursuit of extractive GDP growth, reducing consumption, living well with less, and fostering new modes of living, working, and being. Degrowth has its detractors, but it seems to be the only perspective that simultaneously addresses the crises of out of control greenhouse gas emissions, overconsumption, pollution, and waste. Perhaps degrowth is too much of a purity position, though, as a final objective without a specified pathway. That is why I argued, in chapter 5, that it should be combined with multiscalar environmental justice movements and debates about planetary just transitions.[31] Recently, I have come around to pluriverse politics and related ideas around designs for transitions, which Arturo Escobar suggests are compatible with degrowth. While most of the focus of pluriverse politics, like degrowth, is on nurturing anti-capitalist alternatives, Escobar addresses the challenge of transformation within industrial capitalist heartlands as follows:

> For those of us who live in the delocalized and intensely liberal worlds of middle-class urban modernity, the historical imperative is clearly that of recommunalizing and reterritoralizing. New territories of existence and novel forms of being communal need to be imagined, many of them unprecedented, appropriate to the age of unsettlement. For those of us without an ancestral mandate to help our worlds persevere, the question becomes, how do we create and recommunalize our worlds?[32]

As a common goal, "recommunalizing and reterritoralizing our worlds" makes a lot of sense. Multiscalar struggles over petrochemical injustice attest to some convergence around this theme.

However, there can be no linear or singular journey toward just and sustainable industrial transformations. There are multiple points of articulation in the struggle, as this book suggests, including militant as well as reflexive and conciliatory modes of action.

Some days, I loop back to where I started, confronted by the edifice of the petrochemical planet, unable to imagine the possibility of systemic change. Other days, I discover something new that I had not seen before. It is important to keep trying with the tools that you have.

The petrochemical planet is on a path of profound transformation across multiple scales, industries, and places, but its trajectory remains uncertain. There is no way to move backward in time, to unravel the histories of oil, petrochemical, and plastics entanglement. Nor is there a way to predict the future. For its part, the industry never ceases to try, with its constant quest for control of the planet. Yet it is faltering, and more and more people are waking up to the planetary petrochemical crisis. There is the risk that toxic injustice will persist, however, unless we address the roots of systemic inequality. To do so requires multiscalar forms of resistance to the destructive forces of colonialism, capitalism, and fossil fuel expansion, but also regenerating petrochemical communities and ecologies for the sake of past, present, and future generations.

NOTES

Preface

1 Interview with petrochemical industry representative, Brussels, May 3, 2016.
2 The use of chemical dispersants in oil spills is controversial, including those used in the BP oil spill, and some scientists believe that they can do more harm than good. See Danielle M. DeLeo, "Dispersants Sprayed in Wake of Deepwater Horizon Oil Spill More Toxic Than Oil Alone," *The Conversation*, April 21, 2015. For a further discussion of toxic issues related to 2-BE, see Wylie, *Fractivism*, 38–39.
3 Davies, "Slow Violence."
4 McCreary, *Shared Histories*.
5 Lou, "Art of Unnoticing."

Introduction

1 United Nations, "Race to Zero Campaign," accessed September 1, 2022, https://unfccc.int/climate-action/race-to-zero-campaign.
2 Environmental justice activists use different key terms to describe the common features of polluted industrial-residential areas, including "fenceline communities," "frontline communities," "environmental justice communities," and "sacrifice zones," among others. See Bullard, *Dumping in Dixie*; Lerner, *Sacrifice Zones*.
3 Pellow, *What Is Critical Environmental Justice*?

4   Bullard, *Dumping in Dixie*.
5   Polanyi, *Great Transformation*.
6   Gramsci, *Selections from the Prison Notebooks*; Hall, "Gramsci's Relevance"; Hall, "Race, Articulation and Societies."
7   Field notes, various petrochemical industry events, 2016 to 2021.
8   Spivak, *Aesthetic Education*, 338.
9   Spivak, *Aesthetic Education*, 338.
10 Chakrabarty, *Climate of History*.
11 Connolly, *Facing the Planetary*.
12 Liboiron, *Pollution Is Colonialism*.
13 Liboiron, *Pollution Is Colonialism*, 106–9.
14 Petrochemicals Europe, "About Petrochemistry: A Young Industry," accessed September 1, 2022, https://www.petrochemistry.eu/about-petrochemistry.
15 Hamilton et al., *Plastic and Climate*; Azoulay et al., *Plastic and Health*.
16 Unruh, "Understanding Carbon Lock-In"; Pales and Levi, *Future of Petrochemicals*.
17 Hamilton et al., *Plastic and Climate*.
18 Chandler, *Shaping the Industrial Century*; Reubold, Milmo, and Todd, *Petrochemicals and EPCA*.
19 Charles, Kimman, and Saran, *Plastic Waste Makers Index*; Laura Parker, "The Facts about Plastic Pollution," *National Geographic*, December 20, 2018.
20 Pales and Levi, *Future of Petrochemicals*.
21 Field notes, various petrochemical industry events, 2016 to 2021.
22 Newell, *Power Shift*, 78–79.
23 Fredric Bauer and Tobias Nielson, "Oil Companies Are Ploughing Money into Fossil-Fuelled Plastics Production at a Record Rate—New Research," *The Conversation*, November 2, 2021.
24 Pew Charitable Trusts and SYSTEMIQ, *Breaking the Plastic Wave*.
25 Persson et al., "Outside the Safe Operating Space."
26 Ialenti, *Deep Time Reckoning*.
27 Azoulay et al., *Plastic and Health*.
28 Matthew Taylor, "Dozens of Academics Shun Science Museum over Fossil Fuel Ties," *Guardian*, November 19, 2021.
29 Petrochemicals Europe, "Flowchart," accessed September 1, 2022, https://www.petrochemistry.eu/about-petrochemistry/flowchart.
30 Platts, "Petrochemical Flowchart," Petrochemical Market Fundamentals Workshop, Rotterdam, February 7, 2018.
31 Mitchell, *Rule of Experts*, 9.
32 Scott, *Seeing Like a State*, 3.
33 Nixon, *Slow Violence*, 2.

34 Scott, *Seeing Like a State*; Ferguson, "Seeing Like an Oil Company."
35 Scott, *Seeing Like a State*, 6.
36 Barrowclough and Birkbeck, "Transforming the Global Plastics Economy."
37 Cowen, *Deadly Life of Logistics*, 9.
38 Cowen, *Deadly Life of Logistics*, 5.
39 Field notes, petrochemical plant tour, Fawley, April 28, 2016.
40 Interview with petrochemical manager, Antwerp, January 17, 2019.
41 Field notes, petrochemical industry training workshops, March 15, 2016, February 7, 2018, and September 26, 2018.
42 Field notes, Global Petrochemicals Summit, Lisbon, November 15, 2016.
43 Stengers, *In Catastrophic Times*, 9.
44 Stengers, *In Catastrophic Times*, 40.
45 Beck, *Risk Society*, 59.
46 See Boudia and Jas, *Powerless Science*; Hecht, *Radiance of France*; Hecht, *Being Nuclear*; Irwin, *Citizen Science*; Jasanoff and Kim, *Dreamscapes of Modernity*; Petryna, *Life Exposed*.
47 Ferguson, "Seeing Like an Oil Company," 381.
48 See Gilio-Whitaker, *As Long as Grass Grows*; Kojola and Pellow, "New Directions in Environmental Justice Studies"; Liboiron, *Pollution Is Colonialism*; Pellow, *What Is Critical Environmental Justice?*; Schlosberg and Carrothers, "Indigenous Struggles"; Whyte, "Indigenous Experience."
49 Sze, *Environmental Justice*, 5.
50 Bullard, "Race and Environmental Justice"; Taylor, *Toxic Communities*; Walker and Bulkeley, "Geographies of Environmental Justice."
51 Carson, *Silent Spring*.
52 See Commoner, *Closing Circle*; Alice Mah, "The US Love Canal Disaster and Its Legacy," *China Dialogue*, April 27, 2016.
53 See Beck, *Risk Society*; Commoner, *Closing Circle*.
54 For histories of the early development of the petrochemical industry, see Chandler, *Shaping the Industrial Century*; Galambos, Hikino, and Zamagni, *Global Chemical Industry*; Geiser, *Materials Matter*.
55 Estes, *Our History Is the Future*; Gilio-Whitaker, *As Long as Grass Grows*; Whyte, "Indigenous Climate Change Studies."
56 Gilio-Whitaker, *As Long as Grass Grows*, 25.
57 Yusoff, *A Billion Black Anthropocenes*, 49; Myles, "Decolonizing Energy," 24.
58 Pellow, *What Is Critical Environmental Justice?*, 8–19.
59 Pellow, *What Is Critical Environmental Justice?*, 20–21.
60 Kojola and Pellow, "New Directions in Environmental Justice Studies," 3–4.
61 See Escobar, *Pluriversal Politics*; Estes, *Our History Is the Future*; Gilio-Whitaker, *As Long as Grass Grows*; Kimmerer, "Mishkos Kenomagwen"; Povinelli, *Geontologies*; Whyte, "Indigenous Experience."

62 Escobar, *Pluriversal Politics*, xii.
63 Escobar, *Pluriversal Politics*, xii.
64 Rowe and Tuck, "Settler Colonialism."
65 Ho, "Embedded Activism."
66 Liboiron, *Pollution Is Colonialism*; Pellow, *Resisting Global Toxics*; Pratt, "Decreasing Dirty Dumping."
67 See Mah, *Plastic Unlimited*, 60–62.
68 Max Liboiron, "Waste Colonialism," *Discard Studies*, November 1, 2018.
69 See Givens, Huang, and Jorgenson, "Ecologically Unequal Exchange"; Malm, *Corona, Climate, Chronic Emergency*, 52–54.
70 See Mah, *Plastic Unlimited*.
71 Ciplet and Harrison, "Transition Tensions"; Morena, Krause, and Stevis, *Just Transitions*.
72 Agyeman, Bullard, and Evans, *Just Sustainabilities*, 5.
73 Morena, Krause, and Stevis, *Just Transitions*.
74 For more on the challenge of "petrochemical lock-in," see chapter 6.
75 Rittel and Webber, "Dilemmas in a General Theory of Planning."
76 Newell, "Trasformismo or Transformation?"
77 Cox, "Gramsci," 162.
78 See Mah, "Future-Proofing Capitalism"; Tilsted et al., "Petrochemical Transition Narratives."
79 The main conceptual and empirical discussion of multiscalar activism is in chapter 3, but it is also a key theme throughout the book.
80 Vasilis Kostakis and Chris Giotitsas, "Small and Local Are Not Only Beautiful, They Can Be Powerful," *Antipode Online*, April 2, 2020, https://antipodeonline.org/2020/04/02/small-and-local/; Robra, Pazaitis, and Latoufis, "Counter-Hegemonic Decision Premises."
81 Tsing, *Mushroom at the End of the World*, 38.
82 Liboiron and Lepawsky, *Discard Studies*, 39.
83 Liboiron and Lepawsky, *Discard Studies*, 40.
84 Liboiron and Lepawsky, *Discard Studies*, 44.
85 European Research Council, "Toxic Expertise: Environmental Justice and the Global Petrochemical Industry—Results in Brief," *CORDIS Magazine*, May 6, 2021.
86 See Appel, Mason, and Watts, *Subterranean Estates*.
87 Mitchell, "Carbon Democracy."
88 Barry, *Material Politics*.
89 Appel, *Licit Life of Capitalism*.
90 See, for example, Aftalion, *History of the International Chemical Industry*; Chandler, *Shaping the Industrial Century*; Galambos, Hikino, and Zamagni,

Global Chemical Industry; Reubold, Milmo, and Todd, *Petrochemicals and EPCA*.

91 See Burawoy, "Extended Case Method."

92 All the events that I attended were quasi-public, quasi-private events, which were open for a fee to representatives from business, academia, the media, government, and other industry stakeholders. All interviews were conducted with informed consent, and all names of participants are pseudonyms unless their statements are matters of public record. For examples of similar methods of research in other industries, see Leivestad and Nyqvist, *Ethnographies of Conferences and Trade Fairs*; Müftüoglu et al., "Rethinking Access"; Smith, "Ethics of Material Provisioning."

93 Environmental justice and case-study-based Toxic Expertise project publications include: Brown, Mah, and Walker, "Tenacity of Trust"; Davies, "Slow Violence"; Davies, "Toxic Space and Time"; Feltrin, "Situating Class"; Feltrin, Mah, and Brown, "Noxious Deindustrialization"; Feltrin and Sacchetto, "Work-Technology Nexus"; Lou, "Art of Unnoticing"; Mah and Wang, "Accumulated Injuries"; Mah and Wang, "Research on Environmental Justice"; Verbeek, "Explaining Public Risk Acceptance."

94 Jephcote et al., "Systematic Review"; Jephcote and Mah, "Regional Inequalities"; Verbeek and Mah, "Integration and Isolation."

95 The Global Petrochemical Map is hosted by Mapping for Change, a London-based organization that specializes in participatory mapping services for voluntary and community groups. See "Global Petrochemical Map," accessed September 2, 2022, https://globalpetrochemicalmap.communitymaps.org.uk. The map was developed as an online public resource for the Toxic Expertise research project between 2017 and 2019. Our aim in creating this online participatory resource was to enable further comparison and dialogue between fenceline petrochemical communities, while recognizing that any attempt to map such an extensive industry would be necessarily partial. The Global Petrochemical Map draws inspiration from the Environmental Justice Atlas (EJAtlas), an online resource mapping more than 3,200 cases of environmental justice around the world (https://ejatlas.org). The EJAtlas focuses on "ecological distribution conflicts" and the uneven distribution of ecological harms and benefits, and it includes many different types of conflict, including several related to the petrochemical industry. See Temper, Del Bene, and Martínez-Alier. "Mapping the Frontiers"; Leah Temper et al., "Global Environmental Justice Atlas." Rather than following conflicts, the Global Petrochemical Map follows major sites of petrochemical production and fenceline local communities, including seventy-five case studies across North America, Europe, Asia, the Middle East, South America, Africa, and Australasia. The locations were selected from a judgment sample of major petrochemical sites operating in different countries and regions. While researchers consulted references in multiple languages, the resource itself is available only in English, due to resource and capacity limitations, as a pilot project. See David Brown and

Lorenzo Feltrin, "The Global Petrochemical Map: Drawing the Political-Spatial Nexus of Petrochemical Production," *Toxic News*, August 29, 2019.
96 Nader, "Up the Anthropologist."
97 See the discussion on corporate strategy in chapter 1.
98 Luhmann, Baecker, and Gilgen, *Introduction to Systems Theory*; Connolly, *Fragility of Things*.
99 Luhmann, Baecker, and Gilgen, *Introduction to Systems Theory*; Connolly, *Fragility of Things*.
100 Escobar, *Designs for the Pluriverse*.
101 Raworth, *Doughnut Economics*.
102 Cote and Nightingale, "Resilience Thinking."
103 Hayek, *Fatal Conceit*.
104 Walker and Cooper, "Genealogies of Resilience."
105 Walker and Cooper, "Genealogies of Resilience," 154.
106 Connolly, *World of Becoming*, 10.
107 Connolly, *Fragility of Things*.
108 Hall, "Gramsci's Relevance," 19.
109 Hall, "Gramsci's Relevance," 19.

Chapter 1. The Petrochemical Game of War

1 See the discussion of corporate ethnography at industry events in the methodology section in the introduction.
2 Field notes, European Petrochemicals Conference, Amsterdam, March 3, 2016.
3 Field notes, Future of Polyolefins Conference, Antwerp, January 16, 2019.
4 Field notes, European Petrochemicals Conference, Amsterdam, March 3, 2016.
5 This echoes the findings of Müftüoglu et al., "Rethinking Access," 256, who observed rituals of corporate confession among oil company representatives in multi-stakeholder corporate social responsibility events.
6 Field notes, virtual World Petrochemical Conference, March 12, 2021.
7 These titles are from presentations at petrochemical conferences that I attended (some virtually), a selection from the period from 2016 to 2020, including the World Petrochemical Conference, Global Petrochemical Summit, and European Petrochemicals Conference.
8 The phrase "see like the petrochemical industry" builds on Scott, *Seeing Like a State*; and Ferguson, "Seeing Like an Oil Company."
9 See Gramsci, *Selections from the Prison Notebooks*; Newell, *Power Shift*.
10 Buch-Hansen and Henriksen, "Toxic Ties."
11 Ingram, "Great Britain's Great Game"; Chamberlain, *Scramble for Africa*; Gregory, *Colonial Present*; Mitchell, "Carbon Democracy."

12 Grove, *Savage Ecology*.
13 Grove, *Savage Ecology*, 61.
14 Phosgene, used primarily in the production of foams, is so deadly that it has the highest barriers to entry within the industry. Some 70 percent of its producers include just a few companies, including BASF and Bayer, both successors to the notorious IG Farben corporation. Hydrogen cyanide is used in nail polish, nylon, and gold mining. Field notes, petrochemical markets workshops, March 15, 2016, February 7, 2018, and September 26, 2018. See also Chandler, *Shaping the Industrial Century*; Hanieh, "Petrochemical Empire," 29.
15 Chandler, *Shaping the Industrial Century*.
16 Abelshauser et al., *German Industry and Global Enterprise*; Borkin, *Crime and Punishment*; Jeffreys, *Hell's Cartel*.
17 Okonta and Douglas, *Where Vultures Feast*; Ako and Olawuyi, "Environmental Justice."
18 Matthew Taylor, "'Grotesque Greed': Immoral Fossil Fuel Profits Must Be Taxed, Says UN Chief," *Guardian*, August 3, 2022.
19 Markowitz and Rosner, *Deceit and Denial*; Michaels, *Doubt Is Their Product*.
20 See Buch-Hansen and Henriksen, "Toxic Ties"; Chandler, *Shaping the Industrial Century*; Markowitz and Rosner, *Deceit and Denial*.
21 Mack et al., *Managing in a VUCA World*.
22 See European Research Council, "Toxic Expertise: Environmental Justice and the Global Petrochemical Industry—Results in Brief," *CORDIS Magazine*, May 6, 2021; Alice Mah, "Lessons from Love Canal: Toxic Expertise and Environmental Justice," *openDemocracy*, August 7, 2013.
23 Scott, *Seeing Like a State*, 6.
24 Gómez-Barris, *Extractive Zone*, 6–7.
25 Gómez-Barris, *Extractive Zone*, 3.
26 See Ferguson, "Seeing Like an Oil Company."
27 See Walker and Cooper, "Genealogies of Resilience."
28 Clews, *Project Finance*; Galambos, Hikino, and Zamagni, *Global Chemical Industry*.
29 For fascinating histories of the early development of synthetic plastics, see Altman, "Myth of Historical Bio-Based Plastics"; Rebecca Altman, "Time-Bombing the Future," *Aeon*, January 2, 2019, https://aeon.co/essays/how-20th-century-synthetics-altered-the-very-fabric-of-us-all; Geiser, *Materials Matter*; Tully, *Devil's Milk*.
30 Chandler, *Shaping the Industrial Century*, 147.
31 Buch-Hansen and Henriksen, "Toxic Ties," 25; Edwards, "International Cartels."
32 See Spitz, *Chemical Industry at the Millennium*; Spitz, *Petrochemicals*; Spitz, *Primed for Success*.
33 Spitz, *Primed for Success*, 9.
34 Spitz, *Primed for Success*, x.

35 Jessberger, "On the Origins of Individual Criminal Responsibility."
36 Jessberger, "On the Origins of Individual Criminal Responsibility," 788.
37 Jessberger, "On the Origins of Individual Criminal Responsibility."
38 Spitz, *Primed for Success*, x.
39 Krammer, "Technology Transfer," 97; Hanieh, "Petrochemical Empire," 38.
40 Spitz, *Primed for Success*, 34–35.
41 Spitz's work has been widely cited in business histories, including Chandler, *Shaping the Industrial Century*; and Reubold et al., *Petrochemicals and EPCA*.
42 Jeffreys, *Hell's Cartel*, 232.
43 Jeffreys, *Hell's Cartel*, 232.
44 Abelshauser et al., *German Industry and Global Enterprise*.
45 Buch-Hansen and Henriksen, "Toxic Ties," 25; Spitz, *Primed for Success*, 3.
46 Hanieh, "Petrochemical Empire," 38.
47 Markowitz and Rosner, *Deceit and Denial*, 139.
48 Reubold et al., *Petrochemicals and EPCA*, 17.
49 Hanieh, "Petrochemical Empire," 41.
50 Reubold et al., *Petrochemicals and EPCA*, 29.
51 Reubold et al., *Petrochemicals and EPCA*, 29.
52 Commoner, "Once and Future Threat," 5.
53 Markowitz and Rosner, *Deceit and Denial*.
54 Galambos, Hikino, and Zamagni, *Global Chemical Industry*.
55 Throughout the 1980s and 1990s, the European chemical industry continued to exercise market control during periods of uncertainty through forming within-industry corporate board interlocks and mergers. See Buch-Hansen and Henriksen, "Toxic Ties," 25.
56 Geiser, *Materials Matter*, 47.
57 De Marchi, "Seveso"; Fortun, *Advocacy after Bhopal*; Gibbs, *Love Canal*.
58 Chandler, *Shaping the Industrial Century*, 76.
59 Reubold et al., *Petrochemicals and EPCA*, 36. See also Mah, *Plastic Unlimited*.
60 Buch-Hansen and Henriksen, "Toxic Ties," 24.
61 Clews, *Project Finance*; Chandler *Shaping the Industrial Century*.
62 Verbeek and Mah, "Integration and Isolation."
63 Verbeek and Mah, "Isolation and Integration," 383.
64 De Graaff, "Global Energy Network"; Heemskerk and Takes, "Corporate Elite Community Structure."
65 Verbeek and Mah, "Isolation and Integration," 383.
66 Reams of corporate history detail the specific developments in each company, each marked by technological developments and achievements, as well as by scandals. Just to take one example, BP has its own archive, housed at the University of Warwick, where I work, and much has been written detailing its

early imperial history and development as a national oil company. See Ferrier, *History of the British Petroleum Company*; Bamberg, *History of the British Petroleum Company*; Bamberg, *British Petroleum and Global Oil*.

67 Several incidents of corporate crime and negligence will be discussed in this book, but to catalogue even a fraction of the toxic petrochemical injustices worldwide would fill a whole library.

68 "Vertical integration" means combining different stages of production across the value chain in one company. A "pure-play" company is one that invests in a single line of business, in this case petrochemicals.

69 Chandler, *Shaping the Industrial Century*.

70 Interview with a petrochemical company representative, London, September 27, 2018.

71 Field notes, IP Week, London, February 25, 2020.

72 Field notes, IP Week, London, February 25, 2020.

73 Field notes, IP Week, London, February 25, 2020.

74 See Barry, *Material Politics*; Mitchell, "Carbon Democracy."

75 Field notes, petrochemical markets workshop, London, September 26, 2018.

76 Inkpen and Ramaswamy, "Breaking Up Global Value Chains."

77 Sabrina Valle, "Exxon Posts Record-Breaking Second Quarter Profit," *Bloomberg*, July 29, 2022.

78 See Duane Dickson, Andrew Slaughter, and Anshu Mittal, "One Downstream: Strategic Imperatives for the Evolving Refining and Chemical Sectors," *Deloitte Insights*, June 25, 2019.

79 Chandler, *Shaping the Industry Century*; Inkpen and Ramaswamy, "Breaking up Global Value Chains."

80 Arns, "Chemical Raw Materials."

81 Field notes, petrochemical markets workshop, London, September 26, 2018.

82 Field notes, petrochemical markets workshop, London, September 26, 2018.

83 Çetinkaya et al., "Petrochemicals 2030."

84 Chandler, *Shaping the Industry Century*.

85 Spitz, *Primed for Success*, 9. See also Pettigrew, *Awakening Giant*; Owen and Harrison, "Why ICI Chose to Demerge."

86 Interview with a former ICI chemical engineer, Manchester, December 21, 2017. This discussion emerged without any prompting, during a general discussion about the interviewee's perspectives on the chemical industry.

87 Interview with a polymer scientist, University of Warwick, May 10, 2019.

88 Chandler, *Shaping the Industrial Century*, 18.

89 Field notes, Future of Polyolefins Conference, Antwerp, January 16, 2019.

90 For example, the industry scientists were aiming to make mono-material rather than multi-material packaging (the latter is difficult to reduce), reduce or eliminate contamination from inks and other additives, develop recycling com-

patibilizers to "upcycle" instead of "downcycle," and all the while try to ensure performance, quality, cost-effectiveness, and efficient waste streams.

91 See chapter 4. See also Mah, "Future-Proofing Capitalism."
92 Blue chip companies are stable, profitable, and reputable corporations on the stock market that are relatively safe investments. The term "blue chip" originates from the game of poker, as the blue chips are the highest value pieces. See Steven Nickolas, "What Qualifies a Company as a Blue Chip Company?" Investopedia, December 17, 2021.
93 In 2020, Chinese Sinopec became the second largest petrochemical company in the world, up from third place after the breakup of DowDuPont in 2019, a position that it retained in 2021. See Chemical and Engineering News, "Global Top 50 Chemical Industries in 2021," accessed April 3, 2022, https://cen.acs.org/sections/global-top-50.html.
94 Chemical and Engineering News, "C&EN's Top 50 Chemical Producers for 2022," accessed December 30, 2022, https://cen.acs.org/business/finance/CENs-Global-Top-50-2022/100/i26.
95 Mark Eramo, "Global Chemical Industry Outlook: Assessing Today's Strong Markets and Preparing for the 2020s," IHS Markit, August 3, 2018, https://ihsmarkit.com/research-analysis/global-chemical-industry-outlook-2020.html.
96 Çetinkaya et al., "Petrochemicals 2030."
97 Escobar, *Designs for the Pluriverse*, 91.
98 Johnson et al., *Exploring Strategy*.
99 Shaw, "Strategy and Social Process."
100 Shaw, "Strategy and Social Process," 469.
101 Shaw, "Strategy and Social Process."
102 Shaw, "Strategy and Social Process," 466–67.
103 Cowen, *Deadly Life of Logistics*.
104 On oil and armed conflict, see Le Billon, *Wars of Plunder*; Appel, Mason, and Watts, *Subterranean Estates*.
105 Wylie, *Fractivism*.
106 Field notes, petrochemical markets workshops, March 15, 2016, February 7, 2018, and September 26, 2018.
107 The Brazilian petrochemical industry uses sugar as a feedstock, which it promotes as "green" despite producing the same toxic petrochemicals. See da Rocha et al., "Map of Conflicts"; Fiorentino, Ripa, and Ulgiati, "Chemicals from Biomass."
108 Johnson et al., *Exploring Strategy*, 227.
109 Walker and Cooper, "Genealogies of Resilience"; Johnson et al., *Exploring Strategy*, 227.
110 Johnson et al., *Exploring Strategy*, 8.
111 Ratcliffe and Heath, *Alchemists*.

112 Ratcliffe and Heath, *Alchemists*, preface.
113 Reubold et al., *Petrochemicals and EPCA*.
114 Field notes, petrochemical markets workshops, March 15, 2016, February 7, 2018, and September 26, 2018.
115 For example, in the case of BTX chemicals, the problem of producing too much toluene, but not enough benzene or xylene, would be resolved through three different chemical processes: toluene disproportionation, toluene transalkylation, and toluene hydrodealkylation. Field notes, petrochemical markets workshop, September 26, 2018.
116 Interview with a petrochemical executive, Brussels, May 31, 2016.
117 Escobar, *Designs for the Pluriverse*, 220; Von Werlhof, "Using, Producing, and Replacing Life?"
118 Bear, "Capitalist Divination," 416.
119 Markowitz and Rosner, *Deceit and Denial*, 139.
120 Markowitz and Rosner, *Deceit and Denial*, 168–94.
121 Markowitz and Rosner, *Deceit and Denial*, 168–94.
122 Markowitz and Rosner, *Deceit and Denial*, 168–94.
123 The phrase "strategic ignorance" is taken from McGoey, *Unknowers*. See also Michaels, *Doubt Is Their Product*; Markowitz and Rosner, *Deceit and Denial*; Proctor and Schiebinger, *Agnotology*.
124 Hoffman, "Institutional Evolution."
125 Hoffman, "Institutional Evolution"; Mol, *Refinement of Production*.
126 Dauvergne, *Will Big Business Destroy Our Planet?*, 40.
127 See Mah, *Plastic Unlimited*; Mah, "Future-Proofing Capitalism." See also chapter 4.
128 This is discussed in chapter 6.
129 Field notes, European Petrochemical Conference, Rotterdam, February 7, 2018.
130 Interview with an environmental law campaigner, Brussels, January 24, 2017.
131 The acronym REACH stands for "registration, evaluation, authorisation and restriction of chemicals."
132 Field notes, European Petrochemical Conference, Rotterdam, February 7, 2018.
133 Mack et al., *Managing in a VUCA World*.
134 Field notes, European Petrochemical Conference, Rotterdam, February 7, 2018.
135 Mack et al., *Managing in a VUCA World*, 6.
136 Johnson et al., *Exploring Strategy*, 36.

Chapter 2. Enduring Toxic Injustice and Fenceline Mobilizations

1 The opening quotes for this chapter are from qualitative interviews that were conducted between 2016 and 2019 by researchers for the Toxic Expertise project, in accordance with ethical standards of informed consent and confidentiality.

My idea for including an extended montage of quotes to open this chapter was inspired by Karida L. Brown's evocative use of oral history montages in Brown, *Gone Home*.

2   Bullard, *Dumping in Dixie*; Lerner, *Sacrifice Zones*.

3   See Barca, "Work, Bodies, Militancy"; Feltrin, Mah, and Brown, "Noxious Deindustrialization"; Steinhardt and Wu, "In the Name of the Public"; Wright, "Race, Politics, and Pollution."

4   "The Global Petrochemical Map," accessed September 2, 2022, https://globalpetrochemicalmap.communitymaps.org.uk. Most studies of fenceline petrochemical communities are based on single case studies, while existing comparative studies rely on a small number of cases. There are so many case studies that it is not possible to reference all of the literature, but notable studies of single cases include Adams et al., "Petrochemical Pollution"; Allen, *Uneasy Alchemy*; Auyero and Swistun, *Flammable*; Barca, "Work, Bodies, Militancy"; Jobin, "Our 'Good Neighbor' Formosa Plastics"; López-Navarro, "Legitimating Confrontational Discourses"; Ottinger, *Refining Expertise*; Steinhardt and Wu, "In the Name of the Public"; Wiebe, *Everyday Exposure*; and Wright, "Race, Politics, and Pollution." See also the publications of the Toxic Expertise team: Brown, Mah, and Walker, "Tenacity of Trust"; Davies, "Slow Violence"; Davies, "Toxic Space and Time"; Feltrin, "Situating Class"; Feltrin, Mah, and Brown, "Noxious Deindustrialization"; Feltrin and Sacchetto, "Work-Technology Nexus"; Lou, "Art of Unnoticing"; Mah and Wang, "Accumulated Injuries"; Mah and Wang, "Concept of Environmental Justice"; Verbeek, "Explaining Public Risk Acceptance." Some comparative examples include Allen, "Tale of Two Lawsuits"; Kemberling and Roberts, "When Time Is on Their Side"; Siqueira, *Dependent Convergence*.

5   Morena, Krause, and Stevis, *Just Transitions*.

6   Gottlieb, *Forcing the Spring*; Barca, "On Working-Class Environmentalism"; Gordon, "'Shell No!'"

7   Cf. Hess, *Good Green Jobs*; Mayer, *Blue-Green Coalitions*; Estabrook, Levenstein, and Wooding, *Labor-Environmental Coalitions*.

8   See Brown, Mah, and Gordon, "Tenacity of Trust"; Feltrin, "Situating Class"; Verbeek, "Explaining Public Risk Acceptance."

9   Boudia et al., *Residues*; Boudia and Jas, *Powerless Science*; Brown, *Toxic Exposures*; Davies and Mah, *Toxic Truths*; Wylie, *Fractivism*; Tesh, *Uncertain Hazards*.

10 Mudu, Terracini, and Martuzzi, *Human Health*.

11 According to many scientists and epidemiologists, there are in fact no safe limits for exposure to vinyl chloride, benzene, or other petrochemicals with carcinogenic or mutagenic properties. Debates on environmental exposure limits relate to concentrations, length of time, and how to measure these. See Brown, *Toxic Exposures*; Joyce and Senior, "Why Environmental Exposures?"; Michaels, *Doubt Is Their Product*; Tesh, *Uncertain Hazards*.

12 Markowitz and Rosner, *Deceit and Denial*; Michaels, *Doubt Is Their Product*.
13 Pellow, *What Is Critical Environmental Justice?*
14 For example, the fenceline community of Convent in St. James Parish, Louisiana, successfully protested against the siting of a new petrochemical plant (Shintech) in 1996, and the proposed plant moved instead to Plaquemine, Louisiana, twenty-five miles north of the original site. Similarly, after the anti-PX protests against a petrochemical project in Xiamen, China, in 2007, the petrochemical plant was relocated to Zhangzhou in Fujian Province. See Hines, "African Americans' Struggle"; Steinhardt and Wu, "In the Name of the Public."
15 Lerner, *Sacrifice Zones*; Bullard, *Dumping in Dixie*.
16 Pellow, *What Is Critical Environmental Justice?*, 17; original emphasis.
17 Tuck, "Suspending Damage."
18 Tuck, "Suspending Damage," 415; original emphasis.
19 Tuck, "Suspending Damage," 422.
20 Hoover, *River Is in Us*, 276; Liboiron, Tironi, and Calvillo, "Toxic Politics," 342; Murphy, "Alterlife," 496.
21 See Estes, *Our History Is the Future*; Gilio-Whitaker, *As Long as Grass Grows*.
22 Jarrige and Le Roux, *Contamination of the Earth*, 232–33.
23 Jas and Boudia, *Toxicants, Health and Regulation*.
24 De Marchi, "Seveso"; Fortun, *Advocacy after Bhopal*; Gibbs, *Love Canal*.
25 De Marchi, "Seveso"; Barca, "On Working-Class Environmentalism."
26 Gibbs, *Love Canal*.
27 Zavestoski, "Struggle for Justice"; Fortun, *Advocacy after Bhopal*.
28 Bullard, *Dumping in Dixie*, 1–20. See also Taylor, *Toxic Communities*, 6–7.
29 This contrasted with the case of Love Canal, where residents were relocated, and many received compensation. See Murdoch, "History of Environmental Justice," 7.
30 United Church of Christ Commission for Racial Justice, *Toxic Wastes and Race*.
31 Bullard, *Dumping in Dixie*, 149, 152.
32 Markowitz and Rosner, *Deceit and Denial*, 245.
33 See Gottlieb, *Forcing the Spring*, 376–79; Markowitz and Rosner, *Deceit and Denial*, 246–47.
34 Markowitz and Rosner, *Deceit and Denial*, 247.
35 Allen, *Uneasy Alchemy*; Brown, "When the Public Knows Better."
36 Lerner, *Diamond*; Ottinger, *Refining Expertise*.
37 Scott and Barnett, "Something in the Air"; Leonard and Pelling, "Mobilisation and Protest."
38 In 2010, a lawsuit over chronic pollution in Chemical Valley was filed against the Province of Ontario's Ministry of Environment and Suncor Energy Products, on behalf of two members of the Aamjiwnaang community. The lawsuit, filed by Macdonald and Rang, was ultimately withdrawn, but it nonetheless

highlighted the need for the government to take action about chronic pollution in Chemical Valley. See Margot Venton, Kaitlyn Mitchell, Elaine MacDonald, and Ian Miron, "Changing Course in Chemical Valley," *Ecojustice Blog*, April 16, 2016; Wiebe, *Everyday Exposure*.

39 Allen, "Strongly Participatory Science"; López-Navarro, "Legitimating Confrontational Discourses."
40 Valenzuela Pérez, "Coppered Lives," 13–14.
41 Valenzuela Pérez, "Coppered Lives."
42 Efren Legaspi, "'El aire está malo': Living with Toxics in a Chilean Sacrifice Zone," *Toxic News*, February 28, 2020, https://toxicnews.org/2020/02/28/el-aire-esta-malo-living-with-toxics-in-a-chilean-sacrifice-zone/.
43 Legaspi, "'El aire está malo.'"
44 Patton et al., *Formosa Plastics Group*, 42.
45 Coalition against Death Alley, "Coalition against Death Alley," accessed September 2, 2022, https://www.enddeathalley.org.
46 Interview with environmental activist, St. James Parish, Louisiana, June 16, 2018.
47 O'Brien and Li, *Rightful Resistance*.
48 Lora-Wainwright, *Resigned Activism*.
49 Guha and Martínez-Alier, *Varieties of Environmentalism*; Guha, *Environmentalism*; Martínez-Alier, "Environmentalism of the Poor."
50 Martínez-Alier, "Environmentalism of the Poor," 240.
51 Foster and Holleman, "Theory of Unequal Ecological Exchange."
52 Adeola, "Cross-National Environmental Injustice"; Ako and Olawuyi, "Environmental Justice."
53 Daniel Leader, "Supreme Court to Hear Nigerian Communities' Pollution Claims against Shell," Leigh Day, June 15, 2020, https://www.leighday.co.uk/latest-updates/news/2020-news/supreme-court-to-hear-nigerian-communities-pollution-claims-against-shell.
54 Sandra Laville and Emmanuel Akinwotu, "Nigerians Can Bring Claims against Shell in UK, Supreme Court Rules," *Guardian*, February 12, 2021.
55 Gottlieb, "Where We Live."
56 Energy Justice Network, "Principles of Environmental Justice," last modified April 6, 1996, https://www.ejnet.org/ej/principles.html. See also United Church of Christ Commission for Racial Justice, *Proceedings of the First National People of Color Environmental Leadership Summit*.
57 Gottlieb, *Forcing the Spring*; Markowitz and Rosner, *Deceit and Denial*.
58 Gottlieb, *Forcing the Spring*.
59 Barca, "On Working-Class Environmentalism."
60 Gottlieb, *Forcing the Spring*. The Occupational Safety and Health Administration and the Environmental Protection Agency came into being at the time of the accompanying acts of 1970.

61 Morena, Krause, and Stevis, *Just Transitions*.
62 Barca, "On Working-Class Environmentalism."
63 Barca, "On Working-Class Environmentalism," 71, 73.
64 Feltrin, Mah, and Brown, "Noxious Deindustrialization."
65 This claim is based on a review of data from the Global Petrochemical Map. See also Brown and Feltrin, "The Global Petrochemical Map"; Lorenzo Feltrin, "Mapping and Making Petrochemical Connections on a Global Level," *Toxic News*, November 18, 2019.
66 See also Morena, Krause, and Stevis, *Just Transitions*; Ciplet and Harrison, "Transition Tensions."
67 ILO, "Chemical Industries," accessed September 2, 2022, https://www.ilo.org/global/industries-and-sectors/chemical-industries/lang--en/index.htm.
68 See Feltrin, "Situating Class."
69 MFA (Migrant Forum in Asia), "Reform of the Kafala (Sponsorship) System." See also Kali Robinson, "What Is the Kafala System?" Council on Foreign Relations, March 23, 2021, https://www.cfr.org/backgrounder/what-kafala-system.
70 Adham, "Political Economy of Work," 76.
71 According to ILO figures from 2015, the average monthly salary for petrochemical workers was US$3,547 for Saudis compared with US$1,289 for migrant workers. Adham, "Political Economy of Work," 69–70.
72 "Saudi Arabia Announces Changes to Kafala System," *Al Jazeera News*, March 14, 2021; Amnesty International, *"They Think That We're Machines"*; Human Rights Watch, "Saudi Arabia: Labor Reforms Insufficient," March 25, 2021, https://www.hrw.org/news/2021/03/25/saudi-arabia-labor-reforms-insufficient; Immenkamp, "2022 FIFA World Cup."
73 Adham, "Political Economy of Work," 145, 212.
74 For example, in 2010, a group of Yanbu residents voiced concerns over odors from sulfuric compounds emanating from the petrochemical complex, fearing that they could be dangerous for their health. Muhammad Al-Sulami, "Yanbu, Badr Residents Worried about Health Due to Gas Smell," *Arab News*, June 5, 2010. See also Abdel-Moneim et al., "Monitoring Metal Levels"; Jawad and Ibrahim, "Environmental Oil Pollution"; "Mangaluru: Fire Tragedy at Saudi Refinery—6 from DK among Dead," *Daijiworld News*, April 18, 2016; "8 Workers Injured in Ras Tanura Fire," *Arab News*, September 20, 2016.
75 "Workers Strike at Gas Expansion Project," *Arabian Business*, July 20, 2007; Conrad Egbert, "300 Workers Walk Off Ruwais HGCE Project," *Arabian Business*, July 27, 2007.
76 Egbert, "300 Workers."
77 "Saudi Police Fires at Angry Workers Protesting over Unpaid Salaries," *The Peninsula*, October 4, 2018.
78 Mahnoor Sheikh, "Saudi Police Opens Fire at Pakistanis Protesting over Unpaid Wages," *UrduPoint*, January 24, 2019.

79 William T. Vollmann, "I Am Here Only for Working: Conversations with the Petroleum Brotherhood in UAE." *Harper's Magazine*, December 2017.
80 Vollmann, "I Am Here Only for Working."
81 Vollmann, "I Am Here Only for Working."
82 Mah and Wang, "Accumulated Injuries."
83 Mah and Wang, "Accumulated Injuries," 13, 15.
84 Pai, *Scattered Sand*, 87.
85 Field notes, interviews with petrochemical village residents, Nanjing, September 2016.
86 Interview with petrochemical village resident, Nanjing, September 29, 2016.
87 Becker, *Social Ties*, 2.
88 Pai, *Scattered Sand*.
89 Pai, *Scattered Sand*; Becker, *Social Ties*; Pun, *Migrant Labor*; Adham, "Political Economy of Work."
90 On workers as "expendable," see Pellow, *What Is Critical Environmental Justice?* In China, some migrant workers are viewed as more "expendable" than others—as exemplified by the racially motivated murder of two Uighur migrants at a toy factory in Shaoguan in 2009, which sparked the July 2009 Ürümqi riots in the Muslim province of Xinjiang in western China. See Pai, *Scattered Sand*, 282–83. The closing quotation comes from Robinson, *Black Marxism*, 9.
91 Rebitzer, "Job Safety"; Huber, *Lifeblood*; Feltrin, Mah, and Brown, "Noxious Deindustrialization."
92 Rebitzer, "Job Safety."
93 Bluestone and Harrison, *Deindustrialization of America*.
94 Feltrin, Mah, and Brown, "Noxious Deindustrialization."
95 Ratcliffe and Heath, *Alchemists*.
96 Lyon, *Battle of Grangemouth*.
97 Interview with a retired contract worker, Grangemouth, October 23, 2019.
98 Mah and Wang, "Accumulated Injuries."
99 Gottlieb and Ng, *Global Cities*; cf. Pablo Unzueta, "In the Shadows of Industry: LA County's Port Communities," *Cal Matters*, February 2, 2022.
100 Hess and Satcher, "Conditions."
101 Tuck, "Suspending Damage," 415.
102 Sze, *Environmental Justice in a Time of Danger*, 3–4, 9.

Chapter 3. Multiscalar Activism and Petrochemical Proliferation

1 Estes, *Our History Is the Future*.
2 Estes, *Our History Is the Future*.

3   Break Free from Plastic, "Who We Are," accessed September 2, 2022, https://www.breakfreefromplastic.org/about.
4   Masson-Delmotte et al., *Global Warming of 1.5°C*.
5   Hall, "Race, Articulation and Societies."
6   Liboiron and Lepawksy, *Discard Studies*, 31.
7   On "scaling wide" across open and diverse networks, see Kostakis and Giotitsas, "Small and Local"; Robra, Pazaitis, and Latoufis, "Counter-Hegemonic Decision Premises."
8   Klein, *This Changes Everything*, 294–95.
9   See Hamilton et al., *Plastic and Climate*.
10 Hamilton et al., *Plastic and Climate*.
11 Dewey Johnson and R. J. Chang, "Crude Oil-to-Chemicals Projects Presage a New Era in Global Petrochemical Industry," S&P Global, August 6, 2018; Mark Thomas, "Crude Oil-to-Chemicals: A Game Changer for the Chemical Industry," *Chemical Week*, November 29, 2019.
12 "Q&A with Head of Petrochemicals Europe," *Chemical Week*, October 1, 2018.
13 Pales and Levi, *Future of Petrochemicals*.
14 Barret et al., *Oil 2021*.
15 Yergin, *New Map*.
16 Bill McKibben, "'He Can't Quite Recognise the Urgency': Yergin's New Book Seems to Miss Some Realities of the Climate Crisis," *Independent*, October 2, 2020.
17 Newell, *Power Shift*, 77–78.
18 Coutard and Shove, "Infrastructures," 14.
19 See, for example, Carbon Tracker, *Future's Not in Plastics*.
20 Fiona Harvey, "IPCC Issues 'Bleakest Warning Yet' on Impacts of Climate Breakdown," *Guardian*, February 28, 2022.
21 Helen Briggs, "Plastic Pollution: Green Light for 'Historic' Treaty," BBC News, March 2, 2022.
22 Somini Sengupta, "Suddenly, Oil Companies Are Upbeat Again," *New York Times*, March 8, 2022.
23 Hamilton Nolan, "The World Is Ablaze and the Oil Industry Just Posted Record Profits: It's Us or Them," *Guardian*, August 2, 2022.
24 See Hess and Satcher, "Conditions for Successful Environmental Justice Mobilizations."
25 Estes, *Our History Is the Future*.
26 Black et al., *Line in the Tar Sands*.
27 Temper, "Blocking Pipelines," 103–4.
28 McCreary and Turner, "Contested Scales," 233; see also Temper, "Blocking Pipelines."
29 Black, "Petro-chemical Legacies."

30 Kristina Marusic, "This Is What Indigenous Resistance to Fracking Looks Like in Pennsylvania," *Environmental Health News*, October 25, 2018.

31 Aviena Shen, "Louisiana's Floating Pipeline Protest Camp Prepares to Take On 'the Black Snake,'" *Climate Progress*, September 15, 2017; Davies, "Slow Violence," 10.

32 See Lauren Zanolli, "'Cancer Alley' Residents Say Industry Is Hurting Town: 'We're Collateral Damage.'" *Guardian*, June 6, 2017.

33 Lauren Zanolli, "'They're Billin' Us for Killin' Us': Activists Fight Dakota Pipeline's Final Stretch," *Guardian*, October 17, 2018; Mary Annette Pember, "Inside the Long Hard Fight to Stop the Bayou Bridge Pipeline," *Colorlines*, January 9, 2019.

34 Estes, *Our History Is the Future*, 21.

35 Adam Eisenberg, "Pipeline Protesters Challenge Law That Makes Trespassing at 'Critical Infrastructures' a Felony," *Louisiana Record*, August 23, 2019.

36 Crepelle, "Standing Rock," 142–43.

37 Cherri Foytlin, quoted in *L'eau est la vie (Water Is Life): From Standing Rock to the Swamp*, dir. Sam Vinal, Mutual Aid Media, 2019.

38 For further details about the Toxic Expertise research in Louisiana, see Davies, "Slow Violence"; and Davies, "Toxic Time and Space."

39 Field notes, Louisiana, September 28, 2017. See also Strauss, "Pipeline Resistance," 93–97.

40 Gilio-Whitaker, *As Long as Grass Grows*.

41 Davies, "Slow Violence," 9.

42 Field notes, Louisiana, September 16, 2017.

43 Nina Lakhani, "Cancer Alley Campaigner Wins Goldman Prize for Environmental Defenders," *Guardian*, June 15, 2021; Oliver Laughland, "Louisiana Greenlights Huge Pollution-Causing Plastics Facility in 'Cancer Alley,'" *Guardian*, January 8, 2020.

44 Patton et al., *Formosa Plastics Group*, 58.

45 Center for Biological Diversity, "Army Corps Suspends Permit for Formosa Plastics' Controversial Louisiana Plant," press release, November 4, 2020, https://biologicaldiversity.org/w/news/press-releases/army-corps-suspends-permit-for-formosa-plastics-controversial-louisiana-plant-2020-11-04.

46 Sharon Lavigne, quoted in Julie Dermansky, "After a Legal Battle, Juneteenth Ceremony Honors Enslaved Ancestors at Gravesite on Formosa Plastics Land," *DeSmog*, June 19, 2020.

47 Lavigne, quoted in Dermansky, "After a Legal Battle."

48 Denise Chow, "Why 'I Can't Breathe' Is Resonating with Environmental Justice Activists," NBC News, June 10, 2020.

49 Robert Bullard, quoted in Rick Mullen, "The Rise of Environmental Justice," *Chemical and Engineering News*, August 24, 2020, original emphasis.

50 Tristan Baurick, "Biden Utters the Words 'Cancer Alley,' But Will He Help Louisiana's Chemical Corridor?" NOLA.com, January 28, 2021.

51 Baurick, "Biden Utters the Words 'Cancer Alley.'"

52 United Nations, "Environmental Racism in Louisiana's 'Cancer Alley' Must End, Say UN Human Rights Experts," *UN News*, March 2, 2021.

53 David J. Mitchell, "US Army Corps of Engineers Announced That They Would Commission a Full Environmental Impact Review of the Planned Expansion," *The Advocate*, November 1, 2021,

54 "China Enters into Largest and Longest LNG Import Deal with US," *Maritime Executive*, December 21, 2021.

55 Chen Aizhu and Marwa Rashad, "US Supplies Give China Muscle to Become Major Force in Global LNG Trade," Reuters, February 13, 2022.

56 See Gürsan and de Gooyert, "Systemic Impact."

57 Azoulay et al., *Plastic and Health*; Gabrys, "Citizen Sensing"; Howarth, "Methane Emissions"; Sicotte, "From Cheap Ethane to a Plastic Planet"; Wylie, *Fractivism*.

58 Robert Rapier, "Is Fracking a Threat to Water Supplies?" *Forbes*, December 9, 2021.

59 INEOS, "World's Largest Ethane Carrier Named Pacific INEOS Belstaff at Ceremony in Texas," press release, February 10, 2022, https://www.ineos.com/news/shared-news/worlds-largest-ethane-carrier-named--pacific-ineos-belstaff-at-ceremony-in-texas.

60 Sheela Tobben, "Asia Pushes US Supertanker Ports to New Record," *Bloomberg*, February 2, 2021.

61 Joel Morales, quoted in Megan Quinn, "Plastic Supply Pressures Create Market Challenges and Opportunities for Recycled Resins, Analysts Say," *Waste Dive*, March 8, 2022.

62 David J. Mitchell, "Months after Bad Faith Claims in St. James Project, Chemical Companies Inch toward Startup," *Advocate*, January 26, 2021; Xinhua/Wang Ying, "Chinese, U.S. Companies Jointly Building Mega Methanol Plant in Louisiana," *Xinhuanet.com*, March 27, 2019.

63 Sheng Hong, Yifan Jie, Xiaosong Li, and Nathan Liu, "China's Chemical Industry: New Strategies for a New Era," McKinsey and Company, March 20, 2019, https://www.mckinsey.com/industries/chemicals/our-insights/chinas-chemical-industry-new-strategies-for-a-new-era.

64 Bella Weetch, "Global Date: China to Lead Global Petrochemical Capacity Additions by 2030," *Hydrocarbon Engineering*, January 4, 2022.

65 Li and Shapiro, *China Goes Green*, 6.

66 Li and Shapiro, *China Goes Green*, 10–11.

67 Ho, "Embedded Activism"; O'Brien and Li, *Rightful Resistance*; Wang and Wang, "Soft Confrontation."

68 Lora-Wainwright, *Resigned Activism*.

69 See Mah and Wang, "Research on Environmental Justice in China."
70 Rootes, *Environmental Movements*.
71 Voulvouli, "Transenvironmental Protest," 863.
72 Hongyan, "Nimbyism in China."
73 Steinhardt and Wu, "In the Name of the Public," 69.
74 Mah and Wang, "Accumulated Injuries," 14.
75 Liu, "Digital Media."
76 Chen, "Environmental Disputes."
77 Sun, Huang, and Yip, "Dynamic Political Opportunities."
78 Chen, "Environmental Disputes."
79 Lee and Ho, "Maoming Anti-PX Protest," 39.
80 Lee and Ho, "Maoming Anti-PX Protest," 35.
81 Lee and Ho, "Maoming Anti-PX Protest," 37.
82 Tom Hancock, "Xi's China: Smothering Dissent," *Financial Times*, July 27, 2016; Qian Zhecheng, "Environmental Whistleblower Sues Police for Unlawful Detention," *Sixth Tone*, March 31, 2018.
83 Benjamin Hass, "China Riot Police Seal Off City Centre after Smog Protesters Put Masks on Statues," *Guardian*, December 12, 2016.
84 Gerry Shih, "'Nothing Ever Changes': Life after One of China's Deadliest Chemical Disasters," *Independent*, April 10, 2019.
85 See Mah and Wang, "Accumulated Injuries."
86 Steinhardt and Wu, "In the Name of the Public."
87 Interview with environmental NGO representative, Nanjing, November 12, 2018.
88 Interview with environmental NGO representative, Nanjing, November 12, 2018.
89 Estes, *Our History Is the Future*, 18–19.
90 See Hamilton et al., *Plastic and Climate*; Azoulay et al., *Plastic and Health*; Mah, *Plastic Unlimited*.
91 Clapp, "Rising Tide."
92 Clapp and Swanston, "Doing Away with Plastic Shopping Bags."
93 Liamson et al., *Sachet Economy*; Pellow, *Resisting Global Toxics*; Max Liboiron, "Waste Colonialism," in Liboiron and Lepawsky, *Discard Studies*.
94 O'Neill, *Waste*, 156–59.
95 Laura Parker, "China's Ban on Trash Imports Shifts Waste Crisis to Southeast Asia," *National Geographic*, November 16, 2018; Cheryl Katz, "Piling Up: How China's Ban on Importing Waste Has Stalled Global Recycling," *Yale Environment 360*, March 7, 2019.
96 Kate O'Neill, "Can the World Win the War on Plastic?" *World Politics Review*, March 10, 2020.
97 Break Free from Plastic, "Who We Are."
98 Von Hernandez, quoted in Rebecca Gao, "The Changing Story of Plastic: A Q&A with Von Hernandez," *Asparagus Magazine*, November 27, 2020.

99 See Mah, "Future-Proofing Capitalism."

100 Graham Hamilton, "EPA: Regulate 'Chemical Recycling' for What It Is—Incineration," Break Free from Plastic, March 9, 2022, https://www.breakfreefromplastic.org/2022/03/09/epa-regulate-chemical-recycling-for-what-it-is-incineration.

101 Marissa Heffernan, "Ocean Conservancy Withdraws 2015 Ocean Plastics Report," *Plastics Recycling Update*, July 19, 2022.

102 Megan Quinn, "Break Free from Plastic Pollution Act Reintroduced, Plastics Industry Ramps Up Opposition," *Waste Dive*, March 25, 2021.

103 Karen McVeigh, "Coca-Cola, Pepsi and Nestlé Named Top Plastic Polluters for Third Year in a Row," *Guardian*, Dec 7, 2020.

104 See Break Free from Plastic, "Toxic Tours," accessed November 9, 2022, https://www.toxictours.org/.

105 Klein, *This Changes Everything*, 298.

106 Estes, *Our History Is the Future*.

107 McCreary and Turner, "Contested Scales," 233.

Chapter 4. The Competing Stakes of the Planetary Petrochemical Crisis

1 Cavicchioli et al., "Scientists' Warning to Humanity"; Pierrehumbert, "There Is No Plan B"; Raymond, Matthews, and Horton, "Emergence of Heat and Humidity"; Ripple et al., "World Scientists' Warning."

2 Nina Lakhanai, "'A Death Sentence': Indigenous Climate Activists Denounce COP26 Deal," *Guardian*, November 16, 2021; Centre for International Environmental Law, "At COP26, a Failure of Vision, Action, Equity and Urgency," press release, November 13, 2021, https://www.ciel.org/news/at-cop26-a-failure-of-vision-action-equity-and-urgency; Michael Sheldrick, "COP26: A Failure for the Planet and the World's Poor," *Forbes*, November 15, 2021.

3 Persson et al., "Outside the Safe Operating Space."

4 Oreskes and Conway, *Merchants of Doubt*.

5 On Exxon, see the website of #exxonknew (https://exxonknew.org) and Banerjee et al., *Exxon*. For Break Free from Plastic's brand audit, see "The Coca-Cola Company and PepsiCo Named Top Plastic Polluters for the Fourth Year in a Row," October 25, 2021, https://www.breakfreefromplastic.org/2021/10/25/the-coca-cola-company-and-pepsico-named-top-plastic-polluters-for-the-fourth-year-in-a-row.

6 Azoulay et al., *Plastic and Health*; Charles et al., *Plastic Waste Makers Index*; Hamilton et al., *Plastic and Climate*; Barrowclough and Birkbeck, "Transforming the Global Plastics Economy"; Patton et al., *Formosa Plastics Group*.

7 Whyte, "Too Late for Indigenous Climate Justice," 2.

8 Stengers, *In Catastrophic Times*, 18.

9 Stengers, *In Catastrophic Times*, 29.
10 Stengers, *In Catastrophic Times*, 33.
11 Stengers, *In Catastrophic Times*, 9.
12 Whyte, "Indigenous Climate Change Studies,"159.
13 Plumwood, *Feminism and the Mastery of Nature*.
14 Barca, *Forces of Reproduction*, 18.
15 Moore, *Anthropocene or Capitalocene*; Armiero, *Wasteocene*; Haraway, "Anthropocene."
16 Chakrabarty, *Climate of History*, 42.
17 Chakrabarty, *Climate of History*, 42.
18 Latour, *Down to Earth*
19 For example, see Bennett, *Vibrant Matter*; Coole and Frost, *New Materialisms*.
20 Kimmerer, "Mishkos Kenomagwen," 27.
21 Liboiron, *Pollution Is Colonialism*, 53.
22 Todd, "Indigenous Feminist's Take on the Ontological Turn."
23 Malm, *Corona, Climate, Chronic Emergency*, 105.
24 Malm, *Corona, Climate, Chronic Emergency*, 121; see also Malm, *How to Blow Up a Pipeline*.
25 Bill McKibben, "'It Cannot Be Activism as Usual': Kumi Naidoo and Luisa Neubauer on the Way Forward for Climate Justice," *Guardian*, June 17, 2022.
26 O'Connor, "Capitalism, Nature, Socialism."
27 Stengers, *In Catastrophic Times*, 9.
28 Unruh, "Understanding Carbon Lock-In."
29 Falzon and Batur, "Lost and Damaged"; Sealey-Huggins, "1.5°C to Stay Alive"; Kiara Worth, "COP27 Closes with Deal on Loss and Damage: 'A Step Towards Justice,' Says UN Chief," *UN News*, November 20, 2022.
30 See Newell, "Trasformismo or Transformation?"
31 See Sovacool et al., "Decarbonisation Divide."
32 Azoulay et al., *Plastic and Health*; Commoner, "Once and Future Threat"; Hamilton et al., *Plastic and Climate*; Tickner, Geiser, and Baima, "Transitioning the Chemical Industry."
33 Colborn, "Fossil Fuel Connection."
34 Azoulay et al., *Plastic and Health*; Hamilton et al., *Plastic and Climate*.
35 Hamilton et al., *Plastic and Climate*, 2.
36 Azoulay et al., *Plastic and Health*, 1.
37 Susan Shaw, quoted in David A. Taylor, "We're Facing an Uncertain Plastic Future," *Discover Magazine*, May 1, 2021. The phrase "ecological overshoot" is taken from Bradshaw et al., "Underestimating the Challenges."
38 Bradshaw et al., "Underestimating the Challenges," 6.
39 Pales and Levi, *Future of Petrochemicals*, 11.

40 Commoner, "Once and Future Threat."
41 Commoner, "Once and Future Threat," 6.
42 Commoner, "Once and Future Threat," 2.
43 Geiser, *Materials Matter*, 54.
44 Wylie, *Fractivism*; Black et al., *Line in the Tar Sands*.
45 See Mah, *Plastic Unlimited*.
46 Azoulay et al., *Plastic and Health*.
47 Field notes, petrochemical markets workshop, London, September 26, 2018.
48 Jephcote and Mah, "Regional Inequalities."
49 See Brown, De La Rosa, and Cordner, "Toxic Trespass."
50 Environment Working Group (EWG), "DuPont, Chemours and Corteva Reach $4 Billion Settlement on 'Forever Chemicals' Lawsuits," January 22, 2022, https://www.ewg.org/news-insights/news-release/dupont-chemours-and-corteva-reach-4-billion-settlement-forever-chemicals.
51 EWG, "DuPont, Chemours and Corteva"; Business and Human Rights Resource Centre, "DuPont Lawsuits (Re PFOA Pollution in USA)," accessed November 10, 2022, https://www.business-humanrights.org/en/latest-news/dupont-lawsuits-re-pfoa-pollution-in-usa/.
52 Arthur Nelson, "EU Unveils Plan for 'Largest Ever Ban' on Dangerous Chemicals," *Guardian*, April 25, 2022.
53 Wilder and Brown, "Environmental Factors."
54 Botos, Graham, and Illés, "Industrial Chemical Regulation."
55 Interview with an environmental law campaigner, January 24, 2017.
56 Meghani and Kuzma, "Revolving Door"; Ferrara, "Revolving Doors"; Novotny, "Glyphosate"; Dialer and Richter, *Lobbying*.
57 European Commission, "REACH," accessed September 6, 2022, https://ec.europa.eu/environment/chemicals/reach/reach_en.htm.
58 Nelson, "EU Unveils Plan."
59 Nelson, "EU Unveils Plan."
60 Dino Grandoni, "EPA Finally Move to Label Some 'Forever Chemicals' as Hazardous," *Washington Post*, August 26, 2022.
61 Tickner, Geiser, and Baima, "Transitioning the Chemical Industry."
62 Tickner, Geiser, and Baima, "Transitioning the Chemical Industry," 5.
63 Tickner, Geiser, and Baima, "Transitioning the Chemical Industry," 13.
64 Rob Westervelt, quoted in "WPC 2022 Preview," *Chemical Week* podcast, March 17, 2022, https://soundcloud.com/chemweek/2022-wpc-preview.
65 Field notes, virtual World Petrochemical Conference, April 7–14, 2020.
66 European Petrochemical Association (EPCA), Report of the 2013 47th EPCA Annual Meeting, Global Leadership and the Chemical Industry, Berlin, October 2013, https://silo.tips/download/epca-annual-report-2013.

67 EPCA, Report of the 2016 50th EPCA Anniversary Annual Meeting, 50 Years of Global Chemical Industrial Evolution: What Next?, Budapest, October 2016, https://www.nadinedereza.com/wp-content/uploads/AM2016ReportFull.pdf.

68 EPCA, Report of the 2016 50th EPCA Anniversary Annual Meeting.

69 Interview with a policy director for an environmental health charity, April 27, 2016.

70 Field notes, virtual World Petrochemical Conference, March 8–12, 2021.

71 Hoffman, "Institutional Evolution"; Mah, *Plastic Unlimited*; Markowitz and Rosner, *Deceit and Denial*.

72 UK Chemical Stakeholders Forum (UKCSF), *Fourteenth Annual Report*; field notes, UKCSF meetings, 2016–17.

73 Interview with a retired chemical consultant, London, October 24, 2018.

74 Field notes, Future of Polyolefins Conference, Antwerp, January 16, 2019.

75 Pales and Levi, *Future of Petrochemicals*; Pew Charitable Trusts and SYSTEMIQ, *Breaking the Plastic Wave*.

76 MacBride, *Recycling Reconsidered*.

77 See Rebecca Altman, "On Wishcycling," *Discard Studies*, February 15, 2021, https://discardstudies.com/2021/02/15/on-wishcycling/; Freinkel, *Plastic*, 162.

78 See Mah, "Future-Proofing Capitalism."

79 Tim Sykes, "Chemical Recycling 101," *Packaging Europe*, February 28, 2018; Kaushik Mitra and Mark Morgan, "Is Chemical Recycling a Game Changer?" IHS Markit, April 23, 2020, https://cdn.ihsmarkit.com/www/pdf/0820/Is-chemical-recycling-a-game-changer.pdf.

80 Ragaert, Delva, and Van Geem, "Mechanical and Chemical Recycling"; Huggett and Levin, "Toxicity."

81 Graham Hamilton, "EPA: Regulate 'Chemical Recycling' for What It Is—Incineration," Break Free from Plastic, March 9, 2022, https://www.breakfreefromplastic.org/2022/03/09/epa-regulate-chemical-recycling-for-what-it-is-incineration/.

82 Laura Parker, "Fast Facts about Plastic Pollution," *National Geographic*, December 20, 2018.

83 Laura Sullivan, "Transcript: Plastic Wars," *Frontline* and NPR, March 2020, https://www.pbs.org/wgbh/frontline/documentary/plastic-wars/transcript/.

84 Joseph Winters, "The Petrochemical Industry Is Convincing States to Deregulate Plastic Incineration," *Grist*, August 18, 2022.

85 Global Alliances for Incinerator Alternatives (GAIA), "Legislative Alert 2022."

86 See Mah, *Plastic Unlimited*, 46–71.

87 Stafford and Jones, "Ocean Plastic Pollution."

88 Marine biologist, personal communication, February 2, 2020.

89 Pales and Levi, *Future of Petrochemicals*; field notes, European Petrochemical Conference, Rotterdam, February 6–7, 2018.

90   Meikle, *American Plastic*, 272.
91   Field notes, petrochemical markets workshop, London, September 26, 2018.
92   Field notes, European Petrochemicals Conference, Amsterdam, March 3, 2016.
93   Field notes, Global Petrochemical Summit, Lisbon, November 15, 2016.
94   Eskander, Fankhauser, and Setzer, "Global Lessons."
95   Braungardt, van den Bergh, and Dunlop, "Fossil Fuel Divestment"; Baines and Hager, "From Passive Owners to Planet Savers."
96   United Nations, "Race to Zero Campaign," accessed September 1, 2022, https://unfccc.int/climate-action/race-to-zero-campaign.
97   World Business Council for Sustainable Development, "WBCSD Raises the Bar for Sustainable Business Leadership," October 26, 2020, https://www.wbcsd.org/Overview/News-Insights/General/News/New-membership-criteria.
98   Nicholas Kusnetz, "What Does Net Zero Emissions Mean for Big Oil? Not What You'd Think," *Inside Climate News*, July 16, 2020; Mike Coffin, "Net-Zero Goals for Oil Companies Do Not Tell the Whole Story," *Financial Times*, June 25, 2020.
99   See, for example, BASF, "BASF Presents Roadmap to Climate Neutrality," March 2021, https://www.basf.com/global/en/media/news-releases/2021/03/p-21-166.html; INEOS, "Our Journey to Net Zero," 2021, https://www.ineos.com/inch-magazine/articles/issue-22/our-journey-to-net-zero.
100 Field notes, COP26 observer, Glasgow, November 1–12, 2021.
101 Matthew Taylor, "No Formal COP26 Role for Big Oil amid Doubts over Firms' Net Zero Plans," *Guardian*, October 21, 2021.
102 Matt McGrath, "COP26: Fossil Fuel Industry Has Largest Delegation at Climate Summit," BBC News, November 8, 2021.
103 Field notes, European Petrochemicals Virtual Conference, November 22, 2021.
104 Field notes, European Petrochemicals Virtual Conference, November 22, 2021.
105 Markowitz and Rosner, *Deceit and Denial*.
106 Cordner, *Toxic Safety*; Ottinger, *Refining Expertise*.
107 Interview with a petrochemical company manager, Nanjing, November 9, 2018.
108 Interview with a petrochemical executive, Brussels, May 31, 2016.
109 McGoey, "Logic of Strategic Ignorance," 555.
110 Merry and Bacani, *Unwrapping the Risks*, 27.
111 Reubold et al., *Petrochemicals and EPCA*, 3.
112 Field notes, World Petrochemical Conference, April 2021.
113 Mark Eramo, quoted in Mark Thomas, "WPC 2022: Chemical Earnings Outlook Upbeat on Tight Markets, Supply Disruptions, Demand Growth," *Chemical Week*, March 23, 2022.
114 Milkoreit et al., "Defining Tipping Points," 11.
115 Persson et al., "Outside the Safe Operating Space."
116 Meadows, Meadows, and Randers, *Beyond the Limits*; Meadows, Randers, and Meadows, *Limits to Growth*.

117 Whyte, "Too Late for Indigenous Climate Justice," 5.
118 Moore et al., "Studying the Complexity of Change"; Blythe et al., "Dark Side of Transformation."
119 Escobar, *Designs for the Pluriverse*; White, "Just Transitions."

Chapter 5. Petrochemical Degrowth, Decarbonization, and Just Transformations

This chapter is a revised and extended version of an article that was originally published as "Ecological Crisis, Decarbonisation, and Degrowth: The Dilemmas of Just Petrochemical Transformations," *Stato e Mercato*, no. 121 (2021): 51–78.

1 Bradshaw et al., "Underestimating the Challenges"; Meadows, Meadows, and Randers, *Beyond the Limits*.
2 Hickel, *Less Is More*.
3 D'Alisa, Demaria, and Kallis, *Degrowth*, 3.
4 The phrase "case for degrowth" is taken from Kallis et al., *Case for Degrowth*.
5 For example, the Index of Sustainable Economic Welfare, the Genuine Progress Indicator, and the OECD Better Life Index. See Hickel, *Less Is More*, 202–3.
6 Morena, Krause, and Stevis, *Just Transitions*.
7 Hickel and Kallis, "Is Green Growth Possible?"; Paul, "Green New Deal."
8 Sovacool, et al., "Decarbonisation Divide."
9 Newell, "Trasformismo or Transformation?"; Hickel, *Less Is More*; Shiva, *Soil Not Oil*.
10 Hickel, *Less Is More*, 23; original emphasis.
11 For Scottish government policy, see Scottish Government, "Reducing Greenhouse Gas Emissions," accessed March 19, 2023, https://www.gov.scot/policies/climate-change/reducing-emissions/.
12 Feltrin, Mah, and Brown, "Noxious Deindustrialization."
13 " Breaking the Habit: The Future of Oil," *Economist*, November 24, 2016.
14 Oreskes and Conway, *Merchants of Doubt*; Klein, *This Changes Everything*.
15 Field notes as COP26 observer, Glasgow, November 1–12, 2021.
16 Estimates vary between reports, which use different models. The IRENA estimate in Durrant et al., *Reaching Zero with Renewables*, 73, is more conservative than Hamilton et al., *Plastic and Climate*, cited in chapter 4, which estimated 2.8 gigatons of petrochemical greenhouse gas emissions by 2050.
17 Durrant et al., *Reaching Zero with Renewables*, 73.
18 Beth Gardiner, "In Pandemic Recovery Efforts, Polluting Industries Are Winning Big," *Yale Environment 360*, June 23, 2020.
19 Frederic Bauer and Tobias Dan Nielson, "Oil Companies Are Ploughing Money into Fossil-Fuelled Plastics Production at a Record Rate," *The Conversation*, November 2, 2021.

20 Carbon Tracker, *Future's Not in Plastics*.
21 Newell, "Trasformismo or Transformation?," 28.
22 Coffin, "Net-Zero Gfoals for Oil Companies Do Not Tell the Whole Story," *Financial Times*, June 25, 2020; Kusnetz, "What Does Net Zero Emissions Mean?"
23 Wesseling et al., "Transition of Energy Intensive Processing Industries"; Nilsson et al., "Industrial Policy Framework"; Bauer and Fuenfschilling, "Local Initiatives;" Tilsted et al., "Petrochemical Transition Narratives"; Geels, "Conflicts between Economic and Low-Carbon Reorientation."
24 See Tilsted et al., "Petrochemical Transition Narratives."
25 Bauer and Fontenit, "Plastic Dinosaurs"; Mah, "Future-Proofing Capitalism."
26 Centre for International Environmental Law, *Plastic Is Carbon*.
27 Saygin and Gielen, "Zero-Emission Pathway," 16.
28 D'Alisa et al., *Degrowth*; Kallis et al., *Case for Degrowth*; Martínez-Alier et al., "Sustainable De-growth."
29 Various degrowth and post-growth scholars mention this story about Kuznetz. See, for example, Barca, Chertkovskaya, and Paulsson, "End of Political Economy"; Hickel, *Less Is More*; Raworth, *Doughnut Economics*.
30 Kallis et al., *Case for Degrowth*, 11–12.
31 D'Alisa et al., *Degrowth*, 5.
32 Mazzucato, *Value of Everything*.
33 Drews and Antal, "Degrowth"; Rodríguez-Labajos et al., "Not So Natural an Alliance."
34 Jackson, *Post Growth*; Soper, *Post-growth Living*.
35 Rodríguez-Labajos et al., "Not So Natural an Alliance."
36 See Huber, "Ecological Politics."
37 Bell, *Coming of Post-industrial Society*.
38 Benanav, *Automation*.
39 Blauwhof, "Overcoming Accumulation."
40 Philip Collins, "The Value of Everything by Mariana Mazzucato—How to Save Capitalism," *The Times*, April 18, 2018.
41 See D'Alisa et al., *Degrowth*.
42 Anitra Nelson and Vincent Liegey, "Limit Growth: Liberate Degrowth," *openDemocracy*, May 18, 2020.
43 D'Alisa et al., *Degrowth*, 15.
44 Escobar, *Designs for the Pluriverse*, 174.
45 D'Alisa et al., *Degrowth*, p. 4.
46 Barca, Chertkovskaya, and Paulsson, "End of Political Economy," 6.
47 Feola, "Degrowth."
48 Hickel, *Less Is More*.

49 D'Alisa et al., *Degrowth*, 8.
50 Stevis and Felli, "Planetary Just Transition?"
51 Morena, Krause, and Stevis, *Just Transitions*.
52 White, "Just Transitions," 22.
53 Morena, Krause, and Stevis, *Just Transitions*.
54 Ciplet and Harrison, "Transition Tensions."
55 Clarke and Lipsig-Mummé, "Future Conditional," 351.
56 Stevis and Felli, "Planetary Just Transition."
57 Feltrin, "Situating Class."
58 Kojola and Agyeman, "Just Transitions."
59 Interview with environmental activist, Grangemouth, April 3, 2019.
60 Interview with environmental activist, Grangemouth, April 3, 2019.
61 Phillimore et al., "Residents, Regulators, and Risk"; INEOS, "Careers," accessed September 2, 2022, https://www.ineos.com/sites/grangemouth/careers.
62 Lyon, *Battle of Grangemouth*; Feltrin, Mah, and Brown, "Noxious Deindustrialization."
63 Ratcliffe and Heath, *Alchemists*.
64 Feltrin, Mah, and Brown, "Noxious Deindustrialization."
65 Scottish Government, *Scottish Index of Multiple Deprivation 2020*; Ian Smith, "INEOS Founder Jim Ratcliffe Tops UK Rich List," *Financial Times*, May 13, 2018.
66 Feltrin, Mah, and Brown, "Noxious Deindustrialization."
67 Ratcliffe and Heath, *Alchemists*, 176.
68 Richard Seymour, "How INEOS Humiliated Unite in Grangemouth," *Guardian*, November 9, 2013.
69 Allister Thomas, "Workers Vote to Restore Union Recognition at Grangemouth Refinery," *Energy Voice*, October 24, 2018; Joanna Partridge, "Workers Block Road at Ineos Grangemouth Oil Refinery in Pay Dispute," *Guardian*, August 10, 2022.
70 Lyon, *Battle of Grangemouth*.
71 Lyon, "Continuing Battle of Grangemouth," 67.
72 Lyon, "Continuing Battle of Grangemouth," 70.
73 Interview with a petrochemical worker, Grangemouth, October 22, 2019.
74 Lyon, "Continuing Battle of Grangemouth," 69.
75 INEOS, "Government Support Was Crucial, Says INEOS," December 2016, https://www.ineos.com/inch-magazine/articles/issue-11/government-support-was-crucial-says-ineos.
76 "INEOS Loses Its Legal Challenge to Scottish Government Fracking 'Ban,'" *Scotsman*, June 19, 2018.
77 Focus-group interview, Grangemouth, October 22, 2019.

78 Focus-group interview, Grangemouth, October 22, 2019.
79 Focus-group interview, Grangemouth, October 22, 2019.
80 D'Andrea, "We Are Still Modern," 12.
81 Focus-group interview, Grangemouth, October 22, 2019.
82 Adam Vaughan, "Ineos Buys Dong Energy's Oil and Gas Business in £1bn Deal," *Guardian*, May 25, 2017.
83 INEOS, "INEOS to Invest $2bn in Saudi Arabia," June 3, 2019, https://www.ineos.com/news/shared-news/ineos-to-invest-2bn-in-saudi-arabia/.
84 INEOS, "INEOS Launches a New Clean Hydrogen Business to Accelerate the Drive to Net Zero Carbon Emissions," November 9, 2020, https://www.ineos.com/news/ineos-group/ineos-launches-a-new-clean-hydrogen-business-to-accelerate-the-drive-to-net-zero-carbon-emissions.
85 INEOS, "Net Zero by 2050," July 2022, accessed September 3, 2022, https://www.ineos.com/sustainability.
86 INEOS, "INEOS Announces over €2 Billion Investment in Green Hydrogen Production," press release, October 18, 2021, https://www.ineos.com/news/ineos-group/ineos-announces-over-2-billion-investment-in-green-hydrogen-production.
87 Falkirk Council, "Falkirk Growth Deal," accessed November 15, 2022, https://www.falkirk.gov.uk/services/business-investment/falkirk-grangemouth.aspx.
88 Interview with an economic development officer, Falkirk, October 2019.
89 Focus-group interview, Grangemouth, October 22, 2019.
90 Scottish Government, "Just Transition Commission," accessed September 6, 2022, https://www.gov.scot/groups/just-transition-commission.
91 James Trimble, "Union Brands Petroineos' Grangemouth Job Cut Proposals 'Premature,'" *Falkirk Herald*, November 10, 2020.
92 Clarke and Lipsig-Mummé, "Future Conditional"; Stevis and Felli, "Planetary Just Transition."
93 Kojola and Agyeman, "Just Transitions," 132.
94 White, "Just Transitions," 20.

Chapter 6. Toward an Alternative Planetary Petrochemical Politics

1 Gilio-Whitaker, *As Long as Grass Grows*, ix.
2 Pellow, *What Is Critical Environmental Justice?*
3 Interview with a petrochemical executive, Brussels, May 31, 2016.
4 See Freinkel, *Plastic*.
5 Malm, *Corona, Climate, Chronic Emergency*.
6 INEOS, "INEOS Keeps Its Commitments and Starts to Deliver Free Hand Sanitiser to Hospitals in Southern France," press release, April 15, 2022,

https://www.ineos.com/news/ineos-group/ineos-keeps-its-commitments-and-start-to-deliver-new-hand-sanitiser-to-hospitals-in-southern-france/.

7. See Samantha Maldonado and Marie J. French, "Plastics Industry Goes After Bag Bans during Pandemic," *Politico*, April 24, 2020; Schlegel and Gibson, "Making of an Echo Chamber."

8. Tridibesh Dey and Mike Michael, "Driving Home 'Single-Use': Plastic Politics in the Times of the COVID-19," *Discover Society*, April 30, 2020.

9. See Joe Brock, "Plastic Pandemic: Covid-19 Trashed the Recycling Dream," Reuters, October 5, 2020; Beth Gardiner, "In Pandemic Recovery Efforts, Polluting Industries Are Winning Big," *Yale Environment 360*, June 23, 2020; Mah, *Plastic Unlimited*, 94–111.

10. On the narrative that COVID-19 does not discriminate, see Jason Farrell, "Coronavirus Doesn't Discriminate between People—But the Lockdown Does," *Sky News*, April 1, 2020; Blake Farmer, "The Coronavirus Doesn't Discriminate: US Health Care May Be a Different Story," podcast, NPR, April 1, 2020, https://www.npr.org/2020/04/01/825499515/the-coronavirus-doesnt-discriminate-u-s-health-care-may-be-a-different-story. For the virus's disproportionate health effects, see Njoku, "COVID-19"; Rodrigues and Lowan-Trudeau, "Global Politics."

11. Njoku, "COVID-19"; Rodrigues and Lowan-Trudeau, "Global Politics."

12. Pellow, "Toward a Critical Environmental Justice Studies."

13. Pellow, "Toward a Critical Environmental Justice Studies."

14. Handal et al., "'Essential but Expendable'"; Pellow, "Toward a Critical Environmental Justice Studies."

15. There are many revealing histories of the industry, including Markowitz and Rosner, *Deceit and Denial*; Freinkel, *Plastic*; Geiser, *Materials Matter*; and Rebecca Altman, "Time-Bombing the Future," *Aeon*, January 2, 2019, https://aeon.co/essays/how-20th-century-synthetics-altered-the-very-fabric-of-us-all.

16. Andrews et al., "No Body Is Expendable"; Edwards, "Racial Capitalism"; Handal et al., "'Essential' but Expendable."

17. Wesseling et al., "Transition of Energy Intensive Processing Industries."

18. Murphy, "Chemical Infrastructures"; Wylie, Shapiro, and Liboiron, "Making and Doing Politics."

19. Unruh, "Understanding Carbon Lock-In," 217.

20. Bauer and Fontenit, "Plastic Dinosaurs," 2.

21. Jackson, *Prosperity without Growth*, 116.

22. Interview with an environmental health scientist, Louisiana, December 14, 2013. The interview was conducted as part of a research project about port cities and social and environment movements. See Mah, *Port Cities*.

23. Wu et al., "Pro-growth Giant Business," 327.

24. Wu et al., "Pro-growth Giant Business," 330.

25. Liboiron and Lepawsky, *Discard Studies*, 122.

26 Liboiron and Lepawsky, *Discard Studies*, 41.
27 White, "Just Transitions," 21.
28 Connolly, *Facing the Planetary*, 125.
29 Yuen Yiu, "How to Synchronize Like Fireflies," *Inside Science*, June 2, 2017.
30 Whyte, "Too Late for Indigenous Climate Justice," 5.
31 Stevis and Felli. "Planetary Just Transition."
32 Escobar, *Designs for the Pluriverse*, 200.

BIBLIOGRAPHY

Abdel-Moneim, Ashraf M., Mohamed A. Al-Kahtani, Omar M. Elmenshawy, Hany El-sawy, Aly M. Hafez, and Marwa A. Genena. "Monitoring Metal Levels in Water and Multiple Biomarkers in the Grouper (*Epinephelus tauvina*) to Assess Environmental Stressors on the Arabian Gulf Coast of Saudi Arabia." *Toxicology and Industrial Health* 34, no. 5 (2018): 301–14.

Abelshauser, Werner, Wolfgang Von Hippel, Jeffrey Allan Johnson, and Raymond G. Stokes. *German Industry and Global Enterprise: BASF; The History of a Company*. Cambridge: Cambridge University Press, 2003.

Adams, Alison E., Thomas E. Shriver, Laura A. Bray, and Chris M. Messer. "Petrochemical Pollution and the Suppression of Environmental Protest." *Sociological Inquiry* 90, no. 3 (2020): 646–68.

Adeola, Francis O. "Cross-National Environmental Injustice and Human Rights Issues: A Review of Evidence in the Developing World." *American Behavioral Scientist* 43, no. 4 (2000): 686–706.

Adham, Ayman. "The Political Economy of Work in Saudi Arabia: A Comparative Labour Process Analysis in Two Firms." PhD diss., De Montfort University, 2018.

Aftalion, Fred. *The History of the International Petrochemical Industry: From the "Early Days" to 2000*. 2nd ed. Philadelphia: Chemical Heritage Foundation, 2005.

Agyeman, Julian, Robert Doyle Bullard, and Bob Evans, eds. *Just Sustainabilities: Development in an Unequal World*. Cambridge, MA: MIT Press, 2003.

Ako, Rhuks T., and Damilola S. Olawuyi. "Environmental Justice in Nigeria: Divergent Tales, Paradoxes and Future Prospects." In *The Routledge Handbook of Environmental Justice*, edited by Ryan Holifeld, Jayajit Chakraborty, and Gordon Walker, 567–77. London: Routledge, 2017.

Allen, Barbara L. "Strongly Participatory Science and Knowledge Justice in an Environmentally Contested Region." *Science, Technology, and Human Values* 43, no. 6 (2018): 947–97.

Allen, Barbara L. "A Tale of Two Lawsuits: Making Policy/Relevant Environmental Health Knowledge in Italian and US Chemical Regions." In *Dangerous Trade: Histories of Industrial Hazards across a Globalizing World*, edited by Christopher Sellers and Joseph Melling, 154–167. Philadelphia: Temple University Press, 2012.

Allen, Barbara L. *Uneasy Alchemy: Citizens and Experts in Louisiana's Chemical Corridor Disputes*. Cambridge, MA: MIT Press, 2003.

Altman, Rebecca. "The Myth of Historical Bio-based Plastics." *Science* 373 (2021): 47–49.

Amnesty International. *"They Think That We're Machines": Forced Labour and Other Abuse of Migrant Workers in Qatar's Private Security Sector*. London: Amnesty International, Ltd., 2022. https://www.amnesty.org/en/documents/mde22/5388/2022/en/.

Andrews, Erin E., Kara B. Ayers, Kathleen S. Brown, Dana S. Dunn, and Carrie R. Pilarski. "No Body is Expendable: Medical Rationing and Disability Justice During the COVID-19 Pandemic." *American Psychologist* 76, no. 3 (2021): 451–61.

Appel, Hannah. *The Licit Life of Capitalism: US Oil in Equatorial Guinea*. Durham, NC: Duke University Press, 2019.

Appel, Hannah, Arthur Mason, and Michael Watts, eds. *Subterranean Estates: Life Worlds of Oil and Gas*. Ithaca, NY: Cornell University Press, 2015.

Armiero, Marco. *Wasteocene: Stories from the Global Dump*. Cambridge: Cambridge University Press, 2021.

Arns, Dorothee. "Chemical Raw Materials in Europe: Trends and Challenges." Petrochemicals Europe, 2018.

Auyero, Javier, and Débora Alejandra Swistun. *Flammable: Environmental Suffering in an Argentine Shantytown*. Oxford: Oxford University Press, 2009.

Azoulay, David, Priscilla Villa, Yvette Arellano, Miriam Gordon, Doun Moon, Kathryn Miller, and Kristen Thompson. *Plastic and Health: The Hidden Cost of a Plastic Planet*. Report, Center for International Environmental Law, 2019. https://www.ciel.org/wp-content/uploads/2019/02/Plastic-and-Health-The-Hidden-Costs-of-a-Plastic-Planet-February-2019.pdf.

Baines, Joseph, and Sandy Brian Hager. "From Passive Owners to Planet Savers? Asset Managers, Carbon Majors and the Limits of Sustainable Finance." CITYPERC Working Paper No. 2022–04, City University of London, 2022. https://www.econstor.eu/bitstream/10419/249674/1/20220200-baines-hager-from-passive-owners-to-planet-savers.pdf.

Bamberg, James. *British Petroleum and Global Oil 1950–1975: The Challenge of Nationalism*. Cambridge: Cambridge University Press, 2000.

Bamberg, James. *The History of the British Petroleum Company, Vol. 2: The Anglo-Iranian Years 1928–1954*. Cambridge: Cambridge University Press, 1994.

Banerjee, Neela, John H. Cushman Jr., David Hasemyer, and Lisa Song, *Exxon: The Road Not Taken*. Scotts Valley, CA: CreateSpace, 2015.

Barca, Stefania. *Forces of Reproduction: Notes for a Counter-Hegemonic Anthropocene*. Cambridge: Cambridge University Press, 2020.

Barca, Stefania. "On Working-Class Environmentalism: A Historical and Transnational Overview." *Interface: A Journal for and about Social Movements* 4, no. 2 (2012): 61–80.

Barca, Stefania. "Work, Bodies, Militancy: The 'Class Ecology' Debate in 1970s Italy." In *Powerless Science? Science and Politics in a Toxic World*, edited by Soraya Boudia and Nathalie Jas, 115–33. Oxford: Berghahn Books, 2014.

Barca, Stefania, Ekaterina Chertkovskaya, and Alexander Paulsson. "The End of Political Economy as We Knew It? From Growth Realism to Nomadic Utopianism." In *Towards a Political Economy of Degrowth*, edited by Ekaterina Chertkovskaya, Alexander Paulsson, and Stefania Barca, 1–18. Lanham, MD: Rowman and Littlefield, 2019.

Barret, Christophe, Olivier Lejeune, Peg Mackey, Toril Bosoni, Anne Kloss, Kristine Petrosyan, Masataka Yarita, and Jeremy Moorhouse. *Oil 2021*. Report, International Energy Agency, 2021. https://iea.blob.core.windows.net/assets/1fa45234-bac5-4d89-a532-768960f99d07/Oil_2021-PDF.pdf.

Barrowclough, Diana, and Carolyn Deere Birkbeck. "Transforming the Global Plastics Economy: The Political Economy and Governance of Plastics Production and Pollution." Global Economic Governance Programme Working Paper No. 142, University of Oxford, 2020. https://www.geg.ox.ac.uk/sites/default/files/2020-07/GEG%20WP%20142%20Transforming%20the%20Global%20Plastics%20Economy.pdf.

Barry, Andrew. *Material Politics: Disputes along the Pipeline*. Chichester, UK: Wiley-Blackwell, 2013.

Bauer, Fredric, and Germain Fontenit. "Plastic Dinosaurs: Digging Deep into the Accelerating Carbon Lock-In of Plastics." *Energy Policy* 156 (2021): 112418.

Bauer, Fredric, and Lea Fuenfschilling. "Local Initiatives and Global Regimes: Multi-Scalar Transition Dynamics in the Chemical Industry." *Journal of Cleaner Production* 216 (2019): 172–83.

Bear, Laura. "Capitalist Divination: Popularist Speculators and Technologies of Imagination on the Hooghly River." *Comparative Studies of South Asia, Africa and the Middle East* 35, no. 3 (2015): 408–23.

Beck, Ulrich. *Risk Society: Towards a New Modernity*. London: Sage, 1992.

Becker, Jeffrey. *Social Ties, Resources, and Migrant Labor Contention in Contemporary China: From Peasants to Protesters*. Lanham, MD: Lexington Books, 2014.

Bell, Daniel. *The Coming of Post-industrial Society: A Venture in Social Forecasting*. New York: Basic Books, 1973.

Benanav, Aaron. *Automation and the Future of Work*. London: Verso Books, 2020.

Bennett, Jane. *Vibrant Matter: A Political Ecology of Things*. Durham, NC: Duke University Press, 2010.

Black, Toban. "Petro-chemical Legacies and Tar Sands Frontiers: Chemical Valley versus Environmental Justice." In *A Line in the Tar Sands: Struggles for Environmental Justice*, edited by Toban Black, Stephen D'Arcy, Tony Weis, and Joshua Kahn Russell, 134–45. Oakland, CA: PM Press, 2014.

Black, Toban, Stephen D'Arcy, Tony Weis, and Joshua Kahn Russell, eds. *A Line in the Tar Sands: Struggles for Environmental Justice*. Oakland, CA: PM Press, 2014.

Blauwhof, Frederik Berend. "Overcoming Accumulation: Is a Capitalist Steady-State Economy Possible?" *Ecological Economics* 84 (2012): 254–61.

Bluestone, Barry, and Bennett Harrison. *The Deindustrialization of America: Plant Closings, Community Abandonment, and the Dismantling of Basic Industry*. New York: Basic Books, 1982.

Blythe, Jessica, Jennifer Silver, Louisa Evans, Derek Armitage, Nathan J. Bennett, Michele-Lee Moore, Tiffany H. Morrison, and Katrina Brown. "The Dark Side of Transformation: Latent Risks in Contemporary Sustainability Discourse." *Antipode* 50, no. 5 (2018): 1206–23.

Borkin, Joseph. *The Crime and Punishment of IG Farben*. New York: Free Press, 1978.

Botos, Ágnes, John D. Graham, and Zoltán Illés. "Industrial Chemical Regulation in the European Union and the United States: A Comparison of REACH and the Amended TSCA." *Journal of Risk Research* 22, no. 10 (2019): 1187–1204.

Boudia, Soraya, Angela N. H. Creager, Scott Frickel, Emmanuel Henry, Nathalie Jas, Carsten Reinhardt, and Jody A. Roberts. *Residues: Thinking through Chemical Environments*. New Brunswick, NJ: Rutgers University Press, 2021.

Boudia, Soraya, and Nathalie Jas, eds. *Powerless Science? Science and Politics in a Toxic World*. Oxford: Berghahn Books, 2014.

Bradshaw, Corey J. A., Paul R. Ehrlich, Andrew Beattie, Gerardo Ceballos, Eileen Crist, Joan Diamond, Rodolfo Dirzo, et al. "Underestimating the Challenges of Avoiding a Ghastly Future." *Frontiers in Conservation Science* 1 (2021): 615419.

Braungardt, Sibylle, Jeroen van den Bergh, and Tessa Dunlop, "Fossil Fuel Divestment and Climate Change: Reviewing Contested Arguments." *Energy Research and Social Science* 50 (2019): 191–200.

Brown, David, Alice Mah, and Gordon Walker. "The Tenacity of Trust in Petrochemical Communities: Reckoning with Risk on the Fawley Waterside (1997–2019)." *Environment and Planning E: Nature and Space* 5, no. 3 (2021): 1207–29.

Brown, Karida L. *Gone Home: Race and Roots through Appalachia*. Chapel Hill: University of North Carolina Press, 2018.

Brown, Phil. *Toxic Exposures: Contested Illnesses and the Environmental Health Movement*. New York: Columbia University Press.

Brown, Phil. "When the Public Knows Better: Popular Epidemiology Challenges the System." *Environment: Science and Policy for Sustainable Development* 35, no. 8 (1993): 16–41.

Brown, Phil, Vanessa De La Rosa, and Alissa Cordner. "Toxic Trespass: Science, Activism, and Policy Concerning Chemicals in Our Bodies." In *Toxic Truths: Environmental Justice and Citizen Science in a Post-truth Age*, edited by Thom Davies and Alice Mah, 34–58. Manchester: Manchester University Press, 2020.

Buch-Hansen, Hubert, and Lasse Folke Henriksen. "Toxic Ties: Corporate Networks of Market Control in the European Chemical Industry, 1960–2000." *Social Networks* 58 (2019): 24–36.

Bullard, Robert D. *Dumping in Dixie: Race, Class, and Environmental Quality*. Boulder, CO: Westview Press, 1990.

Bullard, Robert D. "Race and Environmental Justice in the United States." *Yale Journal of International Law* 18 (1993): 319–35.

Burawoy, Michael. "The Extended Case Method." *Sociological Theory* 16, no. 1 (1998): 4–33.

Carbon Tracker. *The Future's Not in Plastics: Why Plastics Sector Demand Won't Rescue the Oil Sector*. Report, Carbon Tracker, 2020. https://carbontracker.org/reports/the-futures-not-in-plastics/.

Carson, Rachel. *Silent Spring*. Boston, MA: Houghton Mifflin Harcourt, 1962.

Cavicchioli, Ricardo, William J. Ripple, Kenneth N. Timmis, Farooq Azam, Lars R. Bakken, Matthew Baylis, Michael J. Behrenfeld, et al. "Scientists' Warning to Humanity: Microorganisms and Climate Change." *Nature Reviews: Microbiology* 17, no. 9 (2019): 569–86.

CEFIC (European Chemical Industry Council). *Facts and Figures 2020 of the European Chemical Industry*. Report, CEFIC, 2020. https://cefic.org/a-pillar-of-the-european-economy/facts-and-figures-of-the-european-chemical-industry/.

Çetinkaya, Eren, Nathan Liu, Theo Jan Simons, and Jeremy Wallach. "Petrochemicals 2030: Reinventing the Way to Win in a Changing Industry." McKinsey and Company, February 21, 2018. https://www.mckinsey.com/industries/chemicals/our-insights/petrochemicals-2030-reinventing-the-way-to-win-in-a-changing-industry.

Chakrabarty, Dipesh. *The Climate of History in a Planetary Age*. Chicago: University of Chicago Press, 2021.

Chamberlain, Muriel Evelyn. *The Scramble for Africa*. London: Routledge, 2014.

Chandler, Alfred D. *Shaping the Industrial Century: The Remarkable Story of the Modern Chemical and Pharmaceutical Industries*. Cambridge, MA: Harvard University Press, 2005.

Charles, Dominic, Laurent Kimman, and Nakul Saran. *The Plastic Waste Makers Index*. Report, Minderoo Foundation, 2021. https://www.minderoo.org/plastic-waste-makers-index/.

Chen, Sibo. "Environmental Disputes in China: A Case Study of Media Coverage of the 2012 Ningbo Anti-PX Protest." *Global Media and China* 2, nos. 3–4 (2017): 303–16.

CIEL (Centre for International Environmental Law). *Plastic Is Carbon: Unwrapping the "Net Zero" Myth*. Report, CIEL, 2021. https://www.ciel.org/wp-content/uploads/2021/10/Plastic-is-Carbon-Oct2021.pdf.

Ciplet, David, and Jill Lindsey Harrison. "Transition Tensions: Mapping Conflicts in Movements for a Just and Sustainable Transition." *Environmental Politics* 29, no. 3 (2019): 435–56.

Clapp, Jennifer. "The Rising Tide against Plastic Waste: Unpacking Industry Attempts to Influence the Debate." In *Histories of the Dustheap: Waste, Material Cultures, Social Justice*, edited by Stephanie Foote and Elizabeth Mazzolini, 199–225. Cambridge, MA: MIT Press, 2012.

Clapp, Jennifer, and Linda Swanston. "Doing Away with Plastic Shopping Bags: International Patterns of Norm Emergence and Policy Implementation." *Environmental Politics* 18, no. 3 (2007): 315–32.

Clarke, Linda, and Carla Lipsig-Mummé. "Future Conditional: From Just Transition to Radical Transformation?" *European Journal of Industrial Relations* 26, no. 4 (2020): 351–66.

Clews, Robert. *Project Finance for the International Petroleum Industry*. Cambridge, MA: Academic Press, 2016.

Colborn, Theo. "The Fossil Fuel Connection." *EarthFocus*, October 1, 2013. Video, 6 min. Linktv.org/earthfocus.

Commoner, Barry. *The Closing Circle: Nature, Man, and Technology*. New York: Bantam Books, 1971.

Commoner, Barry. "The Once and Future Threat of the Petrochemical Industry to the World of Life." *New Solutions*, 11, no. 1 (2001): 1–12.

Connolly, William E. *Facing the Planetary*. Durham, NC: Duke University Press, 2017.

Connolly, William E. *The Fragility of Things: Self-Organizing Processes, Neoliberal Fantasies, and Democratic Activism*. Durham, NC: Duke University Press, 2013.

Connolly, William E. *A World of Becoming*. Durham, NC: Duke University Press, 2011.

Coole, Diana, and Samantha Frost, eds. *New Materialisms: Ontology, Agency, and Politics*. Durham, NC: Duke University Press, 2010.

Cordner, Alissa. *Toxic Safety: Flame Retardants, Chemical Controversies, and Environmental Health*. New York: Columbia University Press, 2016.

Cote, Muriel, and Andrea J. Nightingale. "Resilience Thinking Meets Social Theory: Situating Social Change in Socio-ecological Systems (SES) Research." *Progress in Human Geography* 36, no. 4 (2012): 475–89.

Coutard, Olivier, and Elizabeth Shove. "Infrastructures, Practices, and the Dynamics of Demand." In *Infrastructures in Practice: The Dynamics of Demand in Networked Societies*, edited by Elizabeth Shove and Frank Trentmann, 10–22. London: Routledge, 2018.

Cowen, Deborah. *The Deadly Life of Logistics: Mapping Violence in Global Trade*. Minneapolis: University of Minnesota Press, 2014.

Cox, Robert. "Gramsci, Hegemony and International Relations: An Essay in Method." *Millennium: Journal of International Studies* 12, no. 2 (1983): 162–75.

Crepelle, Adam. "Standing Rock in the Swamp: Oil, the Environment, and the United Houma Nation's Struggle for Federal Recognition." *Loyola Law Review* 64 (2018): 141–86.

D'Alisa, Giacomo, Federico Demaria, and Giorgos Kallis, eds. *Degrowth: A Vocabulary for a New Era*. London: Routledge, 2014.

D'Andrea, Dimitri. "We Are Still Modern: Cognitive, Anthropological and Institutional Obstacles to the Fight against Climate Change." *Stato e Mercato* 121 (2021): 3–22.

Da Rocha, Diogo Ferreira, Marcelo Firpo Porto, Tania Pacheco, and Jean Pierre Leroy. "The Map of Conflicts Related to Environmental Injustice and Health in Brazil." *Sustainability Science* 13, no. 3 (2018): 709–19.

Dauvergne, Peter. *Will Big Business Destroy Our Planet?* Cambridge: Polity Press, 2018.

Davies, Thom. "Slow Violence and Toxic Geographies: 'Out of Sight' to Whom?" *Environment and Planning C: Politics and Space* 40, no. 2 (2022): 409–27.

Davies, Thom. "Toxic Space and Time: Slow Violence, Necropolitics, and Petrochemical Pollution." *Annals of the American Association of Geographers* 108, no. 6 (2018): 1537–53.

Davies, Thom, and Alice Mah, eds. *Toxic Truths: Environmental Justice and Citizen Science in a Post-truth Age*. Manchester: Manchester University Press, 2020.

De Graaff, Nana. "A Global Energy Network? The Expansion and Integration of Non-Triad National Oil Companies." *Global Networks* 11, no. 2 (2011): 262–83.

De Marchi, Bruna. "Seveso: From Pollution to Regulation." *International Journal of Environment and Pollution* 7, no. 4 (1997): 526–37.

Dialer, Doris, and Margarethe Richter, eds. *Lobbying in the European Union: Strategies, Dynamics and Trends*. Cham, Switzerland: Springer, 2018.

Drews, Stefan, and Miklós Antal. "Degrowth: A 'Missile Word' That Backfires?" *Ecological Economics* 126 (2016): 182–87.

Durrant, Paul, Carlos Ruiz, Padmashree Gehl Sampath, Sean Ratka, Elena Ocenic, Seungwoo Kang, and Paul Komo. *Reaching Zero with Renewables: Eliminating CO_2 Emissions from Industry and Transport in Line with the 1.5°C Climate Goal*. Report, International Renewable Energy Agency, 2020. https://www.irena.org/publications/2020/Sep/Reaching-Zero-with-Renewables.

Edwards, Corwin D. "International Cartels as Obstacles to International Trade." *American Economic Review* 34, no. 1 (1944): 330–39.

Edwards, Zophia. "Racial Capitalism and COVID-19." *Monthly Review* 72, no. 10 (2021): 21–32.

Escobar, Arturo. *Designs for the Pluriverse*. Durham, NC: Duke University Press, 2018.

Escobar, Arturo. *Pluriversal Politics: The Real and the Possible*. Durham, NC: Duke University Press, 2020.

Eskander, Shaikh, Sam Fankhauser, and Joana Setzer. "Global Lessons from Climate Change Legislation and Litigation." *Environmental and Energy Policy and the Economy* 2, no. 1 (2021): 44–82.

Estabrook, Thomas, Charles Levenstein, and John Wooding. *Labor-Environmental Coalitions: Lessons from a Louisiana Petrochemical Region*. London: Routledge, 2018.

Estes, Nick. *Our History Is the Future: Standing Rock versus the Dakota Access Pipeline, and the Long Tradition of Indigenous Resistance*. London: Verso Books, 2019.

Eurostat. "Oil and Petroleum Products: A Statistical Overview." Accessed September 2, 2022. https://ec.europa.eu/eurostat/statistics-explained.

Falzon, Danielle, and Pinar Batur. "Lost and Damaged: Environmental Racism, Climate Justice, and Conflict in the Pacific." In *Handbook of the Sociology of Racial and Ethnic Relations*, edited by Pinar Batur and Joe R. Feagin, 401–12. Cham, Switzerland: Springer, 2018.

Feltrin, Lorenzo. "Situating Class in Workplace and Community Environmentalism: Working-Class Environmentalism and Deindustrialisation in Porto Marghera, Venice." *Sociological Review* 70, no. 6 (2022) 1141–62.

Feltrin, Lorenzo, Alice Mah, and David Brown. "Noxious Deindustrialization: Experiences of Precarity and Pollution in Scotland's Petrochemical Capital." *Environment and Planning C: Politics and Space* 40, no. 3 (2022): 950–69.

Feltrin, Lorenzo, and Devi Sacchetto. "The Work-Technology Nexus and Working-Class Environmentalism: Workerism versus Capitalist Noxiousness in Italy's Long 1968." *Theory and Society* 50 (2021): 815–35.

Feola, Giuseppe. "Degrowth and the Unmaking of Capitalism." *ACME: An International Journal for Critical Geographies* 18, no. 4 (2019): 977–97.

Ferguson, James. "Seeing Like an Oil Company: Space, Security, and Global Capital in Neoliberal Africa." *American Anthropologist* 107, no. 3 (2005): 377–82.

Ferrara, Jennifer. "Revolving Doors: Monsanto and the Regulators." *Ecologist* 28, no. 5 (1998): 280–87.

Ferrier, Ronald W. *The History of the British Petroleum Company, Vol. 1: The Developing Years, 1901–1932.* Cambridge: Cambridge University Press.

Fiorentino, Gabriella, Maddalena Ripa, and Sergio Ulgiati. "Chemicals from Biomass: Technological versus Environmental Feasibility." *Biofuels, Bioproducts and Biorefining* 11, no.1 (2017): 195–214.

Fortun, Kim. *Advocacy after Bhopal: Environmentalism, Disaster, New Global Orders.* Chicago: University of Chicago Press, 2009.

Foster, John Bellamy, and Hannah Holleman. "The Theory of Unequal Ecological Exchange: A Marx-Odum Dialectic." *Journal of Peasant Studies* 41, no. 2 (2014): 199–233.

Freinkel, Susan. 2011. *Plastic: A Toxic Love Story.* Boston: Mariner Books.

Gabrys, Jennifer. "Citizen Sensing, Air Pollution and Fracking: From 'Caring about Your Air' to Speculative Practices of Evidencing Harm." *Sociological Review* 65, no. 2 (2017): 172–92.

Galambos, Louis, Takashi Hikino, and Vera Zamagni, eds. *The Global Chemical Industry in the Age of the Petrochemical Revolution.* Cambridge: Cambridge University Press, 2007.

Geels, Frank W. "Conflicts between Economic and Low-Carbon Reorientation Processes: Insights from a Contextual Analysis of Evolving Company Strategies in the United Kingdom Petrochemical Industry (1970–2021)." *Energy Research and Social Science* 91 (2022): 102729.

Geiser, Kenneth. *Materials Matter: Toward a Sustainable Materials Polity.* Cambridge, MA: MIT Press, 2001.

Geyer, Roland, Jenna R. Jambeck, and Kara Lavender Law. "Production, Use, and Fate of All Plastics Ever Made." *Science Advances* 3, no. 7 (2017): e1700782.

Gibbs, Lois. *Love Canal: The Story Continues.* Rev. ed. Gabriola Island, BC: New Society Publishers, 1998.

Gilio-Whitaker, Dina. *As Long as Grass Grows: The Indigenous Fight for Environmental Justice, from Colonization to Standing Rock.* Boston: Beacon Press, 2019.

Givens, Jennifer E., Xiaorui Huang, and Andrew K. Jorgenson. "Ecologically Unequal Exchange: A Theory of Global Environmental Injustice." *Sociology Compass* 13, no. 5 (2019): e12693.

Gómez-Barris, Macarena. *The Extractive Zone: Social Ecologies and Decolonial Perspectives*. Durham, NC: Duke University Press, 2017.

Gordon, Robert. "'Shell No!': OCAW and the Labor-Environmental Alliance." *Environmental History* 3, no. 2 (1998): 460–87.

Gottlieb, Robert. *Forcing the Spring: The Transformation of the American Environmental Movement*. Rev. ed. Washington, DC: Island Press, 2005.

Gottlieb, Robert. "Where We Live, Work, Play . . . and Eat: Expanding the Environmental Justice Agenda." *Environmental Justice* 2, no. 1 (2009): 7–8.

Gottlieb, Robert, and Simon Ng. *Global Cities: Urban Environments in Los Angeles, Hong Kong, and China*. Cambridge, MA: MIT Press, 2017.

Gramsci, Antonio. *Selections from the Prison Notebooks*. London: Lawrence and Wishart, 1971.

Gregory, Derek. *The Colonial Present: Afghanistan, Palestine, Iraq*. Malden, MA: Blackwell Publishing, 2004.

Grove, Jairus Victor. *Savage Ecology: War and Geopolitics at the End of the World*. Durham, NC: Duke University Press, 2019.

Gu, Hongyan. "Nimbyism in China: Issues and Prospects of Public Participation in Facility Siting." *Land Use Policy* 51 (2015): 527–34.

Guha, Ramachandra. *Environmentalism: A Global History*. London: Pearson, 1999.

Guha, Ramachandra, and Joan Martínez-Alier. *Varieties of Environmentalism: Essays North and South*. London: Routledge, 2013.

Gürsan, Cem, and Vincent de Gooyert. "The Systemic Impact of a Transition Fuel: Does Natural Gas Help or Hinder the Energy Transition?" *Renewable and Sustainable Energy Reviews* 138 (2021): 110552.

Hall, Stuart. "Gramsci's Relevance for the Study of Race and Ethnicity." *Journal of Communication Inquiry* 10, no. 2 (1986): 5–27.

Hall, Stuart. "Race, Articulation and Societies Structured in Dominance." In *Sociological Theories: Race and Colonialism*, edited by United Nations Educational Scientific and Cultural Organisation, 305–45. Paris: UNESCO, 1980.

Hamilton, Lisa A., Steven Feit, Carroll Muffett, Matt Kelso, Samantha Malone Rubright, Courtney Bernhardt, Eric Schaeffer, Doun Moon, Jeffrey Morris, and Rachel Labbé-Bellas. *Plastic and Climate: The Hidden Costs of a Plastic Planet*. Report, Center for International Environmental Law, 2019. https://www.ciel.org/plasticandclimate/.

Handal, Alexis J., Lisbeth Iglesias-Ríos, Paul J. Fleming, Mislael A. Valentín-Cortés, and Marie S. O'Neill. "'Essential' but Expendable: Farmworkers during the COVID-19 Pandemic—the Michigan Farmworker Project." *American Journal of Public Health* 110, no. 12 (2020): 1760–62.

Hanieh, Adam. "Petrochemical Empire: The Geo-politics of Fossil-Fuelled Production." *New Left Review* 130 (2021): 25–51.

Haraway, Donna. "Anthropocene, Capitalocene, Plantationocene, Chthulucene: Making Kin." *Environmental Humanities* 6, no. 1 (2015): 159–65.

Hayek, Friedrich Von. *The Fatal Conceit: The Errors of Socialism*. Chicago: University of Chicago Press, 1988.

Hecht, Gabrielle. *Being Nuclear: Africans and the Global Uranium Trade*. Cambridge, MA: MIT Press, 2014.

Hecht, Gabrielle. *The Radiance of France: Nuclear Power and National Identity after World War II*. Cambridge, MA: MIT Press, 1998.

Heemskerk, Eelke M., and Frank W. Takes. "The Corporate Elite Community Structure of Global Capitalism." *New Political Economy* 21, no. 1 (2016): 90–118.

Hess, David J. *Good Green Jobs in a Global Economy: Making and Keeping New Industries in the United States*. Cambridge, MA: MIT Press, 2012.

Hess, David J., and Lacee A. Satcher. "Conditions for Successful Environmental Justice Mobilizations: An Analysis of 50 Cases." *Environmental Politics* 28, no. 4 (2019): 663–84.

Hickel, Jason. *Less Is More: How Degrowth Will Save the World*. New York: Random House, 2020.

Hickel, Jason, and Giorgos Kallis. "Is Green Growth Possible?" *New Political Economy* 25, no. 4 (2020): 469–86.

Hines, Revathi I. "African Americans' Struggle for Environmental Justice and the Case of the Shintech Plant: Lessons Learned from a War Waged." *Journal of Black Studies* 31, no. 6 (2001): 777–89.

Ho, Peter. "Embedded Activism and Political Change in a Semiauthoritarian Context." *China Information* 21, no. 2 (2007): 187–209.

Hoffman, Andrew J. "Institutional Evolution and Change: Environmentalism and the US Chemical Industry." *Academy of Management Journal* 42, no. 4 (1999): 351–71.

Hong, Sheng, Yifan Jie, Xiaosong Li, and Nathan Liu. "China's Chemical Industry: New Strategies for a New Era." McKinsey and Company, March 20, 2019. https://www.mckinsey.com/industries/chemicals/our-insights/chinas-chemical-industry-new-strategies-for-a-new-era.

Hoover, Elizabeth. *The River Is in Us: Fighting Toxics in a Mohawk Community*. Minneapolis: University of Minnesota Press, 2017.

Howarth, Robert W. "Methane Emissions and Climatic Warming Risk from Hydraulic Fracturing and Shale Gas Development: Implications for Policy." *Energy and Emission Control Technologies* 3 (2015): 45–54.

Huber, Matthew T. "Ecological Politics for the Working Class." *Catalyst* 3, no. 1 (2019). https://catalyst-journal.com/vol3/no1/ecological-politics-for-the-working-class.

Huber, Matthew T. *Lifeblood: Oil, Freedom, and the Forces of Capital*. Minneapolis: University of Minnesota Press, 2013.

Huggett, Clayton, and Barbara C. Levin, "Toxicity of the Pyrolysis and Combustion Products of Poly(Vinyl Chlorides): A Literature Assessment." *Fire and Materials* 11, no. 3 (1987): 131–42.

Ialenti, Vincent. *Deep Time Reckoning: How Future Thinking Can Help Earth Now*. Cambridge, MA: MIT Press, 2020.

Immenkamp, Beatrix. "The 2022 FIFA World Cup in Qatar: Turning the Spotlight on Workers' Rights." European Parliament Briefing, 2021. https://www.europarl.europa.eu/RegData/etudes/BRIE/2021/698856/EPRS_BRI(2021)698856_EN.pdf.

Ingram, Edward. "Great Britain's Great Game: An Introduction." *International History Review* 2, no. 2 (1980): 160–71.

Inkpen, Andrew, and Kannan Ramaswamy. "Breaking Up Global Value Chains: Evidence from the Oil and Gas Industry." *Advances in International Management* 30 (2017): 55–80.

Irwin, Alan. *Citizen Science: A Study of People, Expertise and Sustainable Development*. London: Routledge, 2002.

Jackson, Tim. *Post Growth: Life after Capitalism*. Cambridge: Polity Press, 2021.

Jackson, Tim. *Prosperity without Growth: Foundations for the Economy of Tomorrow*. London: Routledge, 2016.

Jarrige, François, and Thomas Le Roux. *The Contamination of the Earth: A History of Pollutions in the Industrial Age*. Cambridge, MA: MIT Press, 2020.

Jas, Nathalie, and Soraya Boudia, eds. *Toxicants, Health and Regulation Since 1945*. London: Routledge, 2015.

Jasanoff, Sheila, and Sang-Hyun Kim, eds. *Dreamscapes of Modernity: Sociotechnical Imaginaries and the Fabrication of Power*. Chicago: University of Chicago Press, 2015.

Jawad, Laith A., and Mustafa Ibrahim. "Environmental Oil Pollution: A Possible Cause for the Incidence of Ankylosis, Kyphosis, Lordosis and Scoliosis in Five Fish Species Collected from the Vicinity of Jubail City, Saudi Arabia, Arabian Gulf." *International Journal of Environmental Studies* 75, no. 3 (2018): 425–42.

Jeffreys, Diarmuid. *Hell's Cartel: IG Farben and the Making of Hitler's War Machine*. Basingstoke: Macmillan, 2008.

Jephcote, Calvin, David Brown, Thomas Verbeek, and Alice Mah. "A Systematic Review and Meta-analysis of Haematological Malignancies in Residents Living near Petrochemical Facilities." *Environmental Health* 19, no. 1 (2020): 1–18.

Jephcote, Calvin, and Alice Mah. "Regional Inequalities in Benzene Exposures across the European Petrochemical Industry: A Bayesian Multilevel Modelling Approach." *Environment International* 132 (2019): 104812.

Jessberger, Florian. "On the Origins of Individual Criminal Responsibility under International Law for Business Activity: IG Farben on Trial." *Journal of International Criminal Justice* 8, no. 3 (2010): 783–802.

Jobin, Paul. "Our 'Good Neighbor' Formosa Plastics: Petrochemical Damage(s) and the Meanings of Money." *Environmental Sociology* 7, no. 1 (2021): 40–53.

Johnson, Gerry, Richard Whittington, Kevan Scholes, Duncan Angwin, and Patrick Regnér. *Exploring Strategy: Text and Cases*. 11th ed. Harlow: Pearson Education, 2017.

Joyce, Kelly, and Laura Senier. "Why Environmental Exposures?" *Environmental Sociology* 3, no. 2 (2017): 101–6.

Kallis, Giorgos, Susan Paulman, Giacomo D'Alisa, and Federico Demaria. *The Case for Degrowth*. Cambridge: Polity Press, 2020.

Kemberling, Melissa, and J. Timmons Roberts. "When Time Is on Their Side: Determinants of Outcomes in New Siting and Existing Contamination Cases in Louisiana." *Environmental Politics* 18, no. 6 (2009): 851–68.

Kimmerer, Robin Wall. "Mishkos Kenomagwen, the Lessons of Grass: Restoring Reciprocity with the Good Green Earth." In *Traditional Ecological Knowledge:*

Learning from Indigenous Practices for Environmental Sustainability, edited by Melissa K. Nelson and Dan Shilling, 27–56. Cambridge: Cambridge University Press, 2018.

Klein, Naomi. *This Changes Everything: Capitalism vs. the Climate*. New York: Simon and Schuster, 2015.

Kojola, Erik, and Julian Agyeman. "Just Transitions and Labor." In *Handbook of Environmental Sociology*, edited by Beth Schaefer Caniglia, Andrew Jorgenson, Stephanie A. Malin, Lori Peek, and David N. Pellow, 115–38. Cham, Switzerland: Springer, 2021.

Kojola, Erik, and David N. Pellow. "New Directions in Environmental Justice Studies: Examining the State and Violence." *Environmental Politics* 30, nos. 1–2 (2021): 100–18.

Kostakis, Vasilis, and Christos Giotitsas. "Intervention—Small and Local Are Not Only Beautiful; They Can Be Powerful." *Antipode Online*, April 2, 2020. https://antipodeonline.org/2020/04/02/small-and-local/.

Krammer, Arnold. "Technology Transfer as War Booty: The US Technical Oil Mission to Europe, 1945." *Technology and Culture* 22, no. 1 (1981): 68–103.

Kusnetz, Nicholas. "What Does Net Zero Emissions Mean for Big Oil?" *Inside Climate News*, July 16, 2020.

Latour, Bruno. *Down to Earth: Politics in the New Climatic Regime*. Cambridge: Polity, 2018.

Le Billon, Philippe. *Wars of Plunder: Conflicts, Profits, and the Politics of Resources*. Oxford: Oxford University Press, 2014.

Lee, Kingsyhon, and Ming-Sho Ho. "The Maoming Anti-PX Protest of 2014: An Environmental Movement in Contemporary China." *China Perspectives* 3, no. 3 (2014): 33–39.

Leivestad, Hege Høyer, and Anette Nyqvist, eds. *Ethnographies of Conferences and Trade Fairs: Shaping Industries, Creating Professionals*. Berlin: Springer, 2017.

Lennon, Myles. "Decolonizing Energy: Black Lives Matter and Technoscientific Expertise amid Solar Transitions." *Energy Research and Social Science* 30 (2017): 18–27.

Leonard, Llewellyn, and Mark Pelling. "Mobilisation and Protest: Environmental Justice in Durban, South Africa." *Local Environment* 15, no. 2 (2010): 137–51.

Lerner, Steve. *Diamond: A Struggle for Environmental Justice in Louisiana's Chemical Corridor*. Cambridge, MA: MIT Press, 2006.

Lerner, Steve. *Sacrifice Zones: The Front Lines of Toxic Chemical Exposure in the United States*. Cambridge, MA: MIT Press, 2012.

Li, Yifei, and Judith Shapiro, *China Goes Green: Coercive Environmentalism for a Troubled Planet*. Cambridge: Polity Press, 2020.

Liamson, Catherine, Sherma Benosa, Miko Aliño, and Beau Baconguis. *Sachet Economy: Big Problems in Small Packets*. Report, Global Alliance for Incinerator Alternatives, 2020. https://www.no-burn.org/wp-content/uploads/Sachet-Economy_final.pdf.

Liboiron, Max. *Pollution Is Colonialism*. Durham, NC: Duke University Press, 2021.

Liboiron, Max, and Josh Lepawsky. *Discard Studies: Wasting, Systems, and Power*. Cambridge, MA: MIT Press, 2022.

Liboiron, Max, Manuel Tironi, and Nerea Calvillo. "Toxic Politics: Acting in a Permanently Polluted World." *Social Studies of Science* 48, no. 3 (2018): 331–49.

Liu, Jun. "Digital Media, Cycle of Contention, and Sustainability of Environmental Activism: The Case of Anti-PX Protests in China." *Mass Communication and Society* 19, no. 5 (2016): 604–25.

López-Navarro, Miguel A. "Legitimating Confrontational Discourses by Local Environmental Groups: The Case of Air Quality Monitoring in a Spanish Industrial Area." In *Toxic Truths: Environmental Justice and Citizen Science in a Post-truth Age*, edited by Thom Davies and Alice Mah, 182–98. Manchester, UK: Manchester University Press, 2020.

Lora-Wainwright, Anna. *Resigned Activism: Living with Pollution in Rural China*. Rev. ed. Cambridge, MA: MIT Press, 2021.

Lou, Loretta. "The Art of Unnoticing: Contrived Ignorance and Petrochemical Risk Perception in China." *American Ethnologist* 49, no. 4 (2022): 1–15.

Luhmann, Niklas, Dirk Baecker, and Peter Gilgen. *Introduction to Systems Theory*. Cambridge: Polity Press, 2013.

Lyon, Mark. *The Battle of Grangemouth: A Worker's Story*. London: Lawrence and Wishart, 2017.

Lyon, Mark. "The Continuing Battle of Grangemouth." *Soundings* 67 (2017): 62–74.

MacBride, Samantha. *Recycling Reconsidered: The Present Failure and Future Promise of Environmental Action in the United States*. Cambridge, MA: MIT Press, 2011.

Mack, Oliver, Anshuman Khare, Andreas Krämer, and Thomas Burgartz, eds. *Managing in a VUCA World*. Berlin: Springer, 2015.

Mah, Alice. "Future-Proofing Capitalism: The Paradox of the Circular Economy for Plastics." *Global Environmental Politics* 21, no. 2 (2021): 121–42.

Mah, Alice. *Plastic Unlimited: How Corporations Are Fuelling the Ecological Crisis and What We Can Do about It*. Cambridge: Polity Press, 2022.

Mah, Alice. *Port Cities and Global Legacies: Urban Identity, Waterfront Work, and Radicalism*. Basingstoke: Palgrave Macmillan, 2014.

Mah, Alice, and Xinhong Wang. "Accumulated Injuries of Environmental Injustice: Living and Working with Petrochemical Pollution in Nanjing, China." *Annals of the American Association of Geographers* 109, no. 6 (2019): 1961–77.

Mah, Alice, and Xinhong Wang. "Research on Environmental Justice in China: Limitations and Possibilities." *Chinese Journal of Environmental Law* 1, no. 2 (2017): 263–72.

Malik, Divy, Parth Manchanda, Theo Jan Simons, and Jeremy Wallach. "The Impact of COVID-19 on the Global Petrochemical Industry." McKinsey and Company, October 28, 2020. https://www.mckinsey.com/industries/chemicals/our-insights/the-impact-of-covid-19-on-the-global-petrochemical-industry.

Malm, Andreas. *Corona, Climate, Chronic Emergency: War Communism in the Twenty-First Century*. London: Verso Books, 2020.

Malm, Andreas. *How to Blow Up a Pipeline*. London: Verso Books, 2021.

Markowitz, Gerald, and David Rosner. *Deceit and Denial: The Deadly Politics of Industrial Pollution*. Berkeley: University of California Press, 2002.

Martínez-Alier, Joan. "The Environmentalism of the Poor." *Geoforum* 54 (2014): 239–41.

Martínez-Alier, Joan, Unai Pascual, Franck-Dominique Vivien, and Edwin Zaccai. "Sustainable De-growth: Mapping the Context, Criticisms and Future Prospects of an Emergent Paradigm." *Ecological Economics* 69, no. 9 (2010): 1741–47.

Masson-Delmotte, Valérie, Panmao Zhai, Hans-Otto Pörtner, Debra Roberts, Jim Skea, Priyadarshi R. Shukla, Anna Pirani, et al. *Global Warming of 1.5°C: An IPCC Special Report*. Intergovernmental Panel on Climate Change, 2018. https://www.ipcc.ch/sr15/.

Mayer, Brian. *Blue-Green Coalitions: Fighting for Safe Workplaces and Healthy Communities*. Ithaca, NY: Cornell University Press, 2011.

Mazzucato, Mariana. *The Value of Everything: Making and Taking in the Global Economy*. London: Allen Lane, 2018.

McCreary, Tyler. *Shared Histories: Witsuwit'en-Settler Relations in Smithers, British Columbia 1913–1973*. Smithers, BC: Creekstone Press, 2018.

McCreary, Tyler, and Jerome Turner. "The Contested Scales of Indigenous and Settler Jurisdiction: Unist'ot'en Struggles with Canadian Pipeline Governance." *Studies in Political Economy* 99, no. 3 (2018): 223–45.

McGoey, Linsey. "The Logic of Strategic Ignorance." *British Journal of Sociology* 63, no. 3 (2012): 533–76.

McGoey, Linsey. *The Unknowers: How Strategic Ignorance Rules the World*. London: Zed Books, 2019.

Meadows, Donella H., Dennis L. Meadows, and Jørgen Randers. *Beyond the Limits: Global Collapse or a Sustainable Future*. Oxford: Earthscan, 1992.

Meadows, Donella, Jorgen Randers, and Dennis Meadows. *Limits to Growth: The Thirty Year Update*. Chelsea, VT: Chelsea Green Publishing, 2004.

Meghani, Zahra, and Jennifer Kuzma. "The 'Revolving Door' between Regulatory Agencies and Industry: A Problem That Requires Reconceptualizing Objectivity." *Journal of Agricultural and Environmental Ethics* 24, no. 6 (2011): 575–99.

Meikle, Jeffrey. *American Plastic: A Cultural History*. New Brunswick, NJ: Rutgers University Press, 1995.

Merry, Alice, and Butch Bacani. *Unwrapping the Risks of Plastic Pollution to the Insurance Industry*. Report, United Nations Environment Programme, 2019. https://www.unepfi.org/wordpress/wp-content/uploads/2019/11/PSI-unwrapping-the-risks-of-plastic-pollution-to-the-insurance-industry.pdf.

MFA (Migrant Forum in Asia). "Reform of the Kafala (Sponsorship) System." Policy Briefing No. 2, Migrant Forum in Asia, 2012. https://mfasia.org/migrantforumasia/wp-content/uploads/2012/07/reformingkafala_final.pdf.

Michaels, David. *Doubt Is Their Product: How Industry's Assault on Science Threatens Your Health*. Oxford: Oxford University Press, 2008.

Milkoreit, Manjana, Jennifer Hodbod, Jacopo Baggio, Karina Benessaiah, Rafael Calderón-Contreras, Jonathan F. Donges, Jean-Denis Mathias, et al. "Defining Tipping Points for Social-Ecological Systems Scholarship: An Interdisciplinary Literature Review." *Environmental Research Letters* 13, no. 3 (2018): 033005.

Mitchell, Timothy. "Carbon Democracy." *Economy and Society* 38, no. 3 (2009): 399–432.

Mitchell, Timothy. *Rule of Experts*. Berkeley: University of California Press, 2002.

Mol, Arthur P. J. *The Refinement of Production: Ecological Modernisation Theory and the Chemical Industry*. Utrecht: Jan van Arkel/International Books, 1995.

Moore, Jason W., ed. *Anthropocene or Capitalocene? Nature, History, and the Crisis of Capitalism*. Oakland, CA: PM Press, 2016.

Moore, Michele-Lee, Ola Tjornbo, Elin Enfors, Corrie Knapp, Jennifer Hodbod, Jacopo A. Baggio, Albert Norström, et al. "Studying the Complexity of Change: Toward an Analytical Framework for Understanding Deliberate Social-Ecological Transformations." *Ecology and Society* 19, no. 4 (2014): 54.

Morena, Edouard, Dunja Krause, and Dimitris Stevis, eds. *Just Transitions: Social Justice in the Shift Towards a Low-Carbon World*. London: Pluto Press, 2020.

Mudu, Pierpaolo, Benedetto Terracini, and Marco Martuzzi, eds. *Human Health in Areas with Industrial Contamination*. Copenhagen: World Health Organization Regional Office for Europe, 2014.

Müftüoglu, Ingrid Birce, Ståle Knudsen, Ragnhild Freng Dale, Oda Eiken, Dinah Rajak, and Siri Lange. "Rethinking Access: Key Methodological Challenges in Studying Energy Companies." *Energy Research and Social Science* 45 (2018): 250–57.

Murdoch, Esme. "A History of Environmental Justice: Foundations, Narratives, and Perspectives," *Environmental Justice: Key Concepts*, edited by Brendan Coolsaet, 6–17. London: Routledge, 2020.

Murphy, Michelle. "Alterlife and Decolonial Chemical Relations." *Cultural Anthropology* 32, no. 4 (2017): 494–503.

Murphy, Michelle. "Chemical Infrastructures of the St Clair River." In *Toxicants, Health and Regulation since 1945*, edited by Nathalie Jas and Soraya Boudia, 103–15. London: Routledge, 2015.

Nader, Laura. "Up the Anthropologist: Perspectives Gained from Studying Up." In *Reinventing Anthropology*, edited by Dell Hymes, 284–311. New York: Pantheon, 1969.

Newell, Peter. *Power Shift: The Global Political Economy of Energy Transitions*. Cambridge: Cambridge University Press, 2021.

Newell, Peter. "Trasformismo or Transformation? The Global Political Economy of Energy Transitions." *Review of International Political Economy* 26, no. 1 (2019): 25–48.

Nilsson, Lars J., Fredric Bauer, Max Åhman, Fredrik N. G. Andersson, Chris Bataille, Stephane de la Rue du Can, Karin Ericsson, et al. "An Industrial Policy Framework for Transforming Energy and Emissions Intensive Industries towards Zero Emissions," *Climate Policy* 21, no. 8 (2021): 1053–65.

Nixon, Rob. *Slow Violence and the Environmentalism of the Poor*. Cambridge, MA: Harvard University Press, 2011.

Njoku, Anuli U. "COVID-19 and Environmental Racism: Challenges and Recommendations." *European Journal of Environmental Public Health* 5, no. 2 (2021): em0079.

Novotny, Eva. "Glyphosate, Roundup and the Failures of Regulatory Assessment." *Toxics* 10, no. 6 (2022): 321.

O'Brien, Kevin J., and Lianjiang Li. *Rightful Resistance in Rural China*. Cambridge: Cambridge University Press, 2006.

O'Connor, James. "Capitalism, Nature, Socialism: A Theoretical Introduction." *Capitalism, Nature, Socialism* 1, no. 1 (1988): 11–38.

Okonta, Ike, and Oronto Douglas. *Where Vultures Feast: Shell, Human Rights, and Oil in the Niger Delta*. London: Verso, 2003.

O'Neill, Kate. *Waste*. Cambridge: Polity, 2019.

Oreskes, Naomi, and Erik M. Conway. *Merchants of Doubt: How a Handful of Scientists Obscured the Truth on Issues from Tobacco Smoke to Global Warming*. London: Bloomsbury, 2011.

Ottinger, Gwen. *Refining Expertise*. New York: New York University Press, 2013.

Owen, Geoffrey, and Trevor Harrison. "Why ICI Chose to Demerge." *Harvard Business Review* 73, no. 2 (1995): 133–42.

Pai, Hsiao-Hung. *Scattered Sand: The Story of China's Rural Migrants*. London: Verso Books, 2012.

Pales, Araceli Fernandez, and Peter Levi. *The Future of Petrochemicals: Towards More Sustainable Plastics and Fertilisers*. Report, International Energy Agency, 2018. https://iea.blob.core.windows.net/assets/bee4ef3a-8876-4566-98cf-7a130c013805/The_Future_of_Petrochemicals.pdf.

Patton, Jane, Nikki Reisch, Delia Ridge Creamer, and Ethan Buckner. *Formosa Plastics Group: A Serial Offender of Environmental and Human Rights*. Report, Centre for International Environmental Law, 2021. https://www.ciel.org/wp-content/uploads/2021/10/Formosa-Plastics-Group_A-Serial-Offender-of-Environmental-and-Human-Rights.pdf.

Paul, Harpreet Kaur. "The Green New Deal and Global Justice." *Renewal: A Journal of Labour Politics* 28, no. 1 (2020): 61–71.

Pew Charitable Trusts (PCT) and SYSTEMIQ. *Breaking the Plastic Wave: A Comprehensive Assessment of Pathways Towards Stopping Ocean Pollution*. Report, PCT, 2020. https://www.pewtrusts.org/-/media/assets/2020/07/breakingtheplasticwave_report.pdf.

Pellow, David N. *Resisting Global Toxics: Transnational Movements for Environmental Justice*. Cambridge, MA: MIT Press, 2007.

Pellow, David N. "Toward a Critical Environmental Justice Studies: Black Lives Matter as an Environmental Justice Challenge." *Du Bois Review* 13, no. 2 (2016): 221–36.

Pellow, David N. *What Is Critical Environmental Justice?* Cambridge: Polity, 2017.

Peng, Zhou, Theo Jan Simons, Jeremy Wallach, and Adam Youngman. "Petrochemicals 2020: A Year of Resilience and the Road to Recovery." McKinsey and Company, May 21, 2021. https://www.mckinsey.com/industries/chemicals/our-insights/petrochemicals-2020-a-year-of-resilience-and-the-road-to-recovery.

Persson, Linn, Bethanie M. Carney Almroth, Christopher D. Collins, Sarah Cornell, Cynthia A. de Wit, Miriam L. Diamond, Peter Fantke, et al. "Outside the Safe Operating Space of the Planetary Boundary for Novel Entities." *Environmental Science and Technology* 56, no. 3 (2022): 1510–21.

Petryna, Adriana. *Life Exposed: Biological Citizens after Chernobyl*. Princeton, NJ: Princeton University Press, 2013.

Pettigrew, Andrew M. *The Awakening Giant: Continuity and Change in Imperial Chemical Industries*. New York: Basil Blackwell, 1985.

Phillimore, Peter, Alex Schlüter, Tanja Pless-Mulloli, and Patricia Bell. "Residents, Regulators, and Risk in Two Industrial Towns." *Environment and Planning C: Politics and Space* 25, no. 1 (2007): 73–89.

Pierrehumbert, Raymond. "There Is No Plan B for Dealing with the Climate Crisis." *Bulletin of the Atomic Scientists* 75, no. 5 (2019): 215–21.

Plumwood, Val. *Feminism and the Mastery of Nature*. London: Routledge, 2002.

Polanyi, Karl. *The Great Transformation*. Boston: Beacon Press, 1944.

Povinelli, Elizabeth A. *Geonotologies: A Requiem to Late Liberalism*. Durham, NC: Duke University Press, 2016.

Pratt, Laura A. W. "Decreasing Dirty Dumping: A Reevaluation of Toxic Waste Colonialism and the Global Management of Transboundary Hazardous Waste." *William and Mary Environmental Law and Policy Review* 35, no. 2 (2011): 581–623.

Proctor, Robert N., and Londa Schiebinger, eds. *Agnotology: The Making and Unmaking of Ignorance*. Stanford, CA: Stanford University Press, 2008.

Pun, Ngai. *Migrant Labor in China: Post-socialist Transformations*. Cambridge: Polity Press, 2016.

Ragaert, Kim, Laurens Delva, and Kevin Van Geem. "Mechanical and Chemical Recycling of Solid Plastic Waste." *Waste Management* 69 (2017): 24–58.

Ratcliffe, Jim, and Ursula Heath. 2018. *The Alchemists: The INEOS Story—An Industrial Giant Comes of Age*. London: Biteback Publishing.

Raworth, Kate. *Doughnut Economics*. London: Chelsea Green Publishing, 2017.

Raymond, Colin, Tom Matthews, and Radley M. Horton. "The Emergence of Heat and Humidity Too Severe for Human Tolerance." *Science Advances* 6, no. 19 (2020): eaaw1838.

Rebitzer, James B. "Job Safety and Contract Workers in the Petrochemical Industry." *Industrial Relations* 34, no. 1 (1995): 40–57.

Reubold, Michael, Sean Milmo, and Martin Todd. *Petrochemicals and EPCA: A Passionate Journey*. Brussels: European Petrochemical Association, 2016.

Ripple, William J., Christopher Wolf, Thomas M. Newsome, Phoebe Barnard, and William R. Moomaw. "World Scientists' Warning of a Climate Emergency." *BioScience* 70, no. 1 (2020): 8–12.

Rittel, Horst, and Melvin Webber. "Dilemmas in a General Theory of Planning." *Policy Sciences* 4, no. 2 (1973): 155–69.

Robinson, Cedric J. *Black Marxism: The Making of the Black Radical Tradition*. Chapel Hill: University of North Carolina Press, 2000.

Robra, Ben, Alex Pazaitis, and Kostas Latoufis. "Counter-Hegemonic Decision Premises in Commons-Based Peer Production: A Degrowth Case Study." *tripleC: Communication, Capitalism and Critique* 19, no. 2 (2021): 343–70.

Rodrigues, Cae, and Greg Lowan-Trudeau. "Global Politics of the COVID-19 Pandemic, and Other Current Issues of Environmental Justice." *Journal of Environmental Education* 52, no. 5 (2021): 293–302.

Rodríguez-Labajos, Beatriz, Ivonne Yánez, Patrick Bond, Lucie Greyl, Serah Munguti, Godwin Uyi Ojo, and Winfridus Overbeek. "Not So Natural an Alliance? Degrowth and Environmental Justice Movements in the Global South." *Ecological Economics* 157 (2019): 175–84.

Rootes, Christopher. *Environmental Movements: Local, National, and Global*. London: Routledge, 1999.

Rowe, Aimee Carrillo, and Eve Tuck. "Settler Colonialism and Cultural Studies: Ongoing Settlement, Cultural Production, and Resistance." *Cultural Studies, Critical Methodologies* 17, no. 1 (2017): 3–13.

Saygin, Deger, and Dolf Gielen. "Zero-Emission Pathway for the Global Chemical and Petrochemical Sector." *Energies* 14, no. 13 (2021): 3772.

Schlegel, Ian, and Connor Gibson. "The Making of an Echo Chamber: How the Plastic Industry Exploited Anxiety about COVID-19 to Attack Reusable Bags." Research brief, Greenpeace, 2020. https://www.greenpeace.org/usa/wp-content/uploads/2020/03/The-Making-of-an-Echo-Chamber_-How-the-plastic-industry-exploited-anxiety-about-COVID-19-to-attack-reusable-bags-1.pdf.

Schlosberg, David, and David Carruthers. "Indigenous Struggles, Environmental Justice, and Community Capabilities." *Global Environmental Politics* 10, no. 4 (2010): 12–35.

Scott, Dianne, and Clive Barnett. "Something in the Air: Civic Science and Contentious Environmental Politics in Post-apartheid South Africa." *Geoforum* 40, no. 3 (2009): 373–82.

Scott, James C. *Seeing Like a State: How Certain Schemes to Improve the Human Condition Have Failed*. New Haven, CT: Yale University Press, 1998.

Scottish Government. *Scottish Index of Multiple Deprivation 2020*. Report, Scottish Government, 2000. https://www.gov.scot/collections/scottish-index-of-multiple-deprivation-2020.

Sealey-Huggins, Leon. "'1.5° C to Stay Alive': Climate Change, Imperialism and Justice for the Caribbean." *Third World Quarterly* 38, no. 11 (2017): 2444–63.

Shaw, Martin. "Strategy and Social Process: Military Context and Sociological Analysis." *Sociology* 24, no. 3 (1990): 465–73.

Shiva, Vandana. *Soil Not Oil: Environmental Justice in a Time of Climate Crisis*. Boston: South End Press, 2008.

Sicotte, Diane M. "From Cheap Ethane to a Plastic Planet: Regulating an Industrial Global Production Network." *Energy Research and Social Science* 66 (2020): 101479.

Siqueira, Carlos E. *Dependent Convergence: The Struggle to Control Petrochemical Hazards in Brazil and the United States*. London: Routledge, 2003.

Smith, Jessica M. "The Ethics of Material Provisioning: Insiders' Views of Work in the Extractive Industries." *Extractive Industries and Society* 6, no. 3 (2019): 807–14.

Soper, Kate. *Post-growth Living: For an Alternative Hedonism*. London: Verso Books, 2020.

Sovacool, Benjamin K., Andrew Hook, Mari Martiskainen, Andrea Brock, and Bruno Turnheim. "The Decarbonisation Divide: Contextualizing Landscapes of Low-Carbon Exploitation and Toxicity in Africa." *Global Environmental Change* 60 (2020): 102028.

Spitz, Peter H. *The Chemical Industry at the Millennium: Maturity, Restructuring, and Globalization*. Philadelphia, PA: Chemical Heritage Foundation, 2002.

Spitz, Peter H. *Petrochemicals: The Rise of an Industry*. Chichester, UK: Wiley, 1988.

Spitz, Peter H. *Primed for Success: The Story of Scientific Design Company*. New York: Springer, 2019.

Spivak, Gayatri Chakravorty. *An Aesthetic Education in the Era of Globalization*. Cambridge, MA: Harvard University Press, 2013.

Stafford, Richard, and Peter J. S. Jones. "Ocean Plastic Pollution: A Convenient but Distracting Truth?" *Marine Policy* 103 (2019): 187–91.

Steinhardt, H. Christoph, and Fengshi Wu. "In the Name of the Public: Environmental Protest and the Changing Landscape of Popular Contention in China." *China Journal* 75, no. 1 (2016): 61–82.

Stengers, Isabelle. *In Catastrophic Times: Resisting the Coming Barbarism*. London: Open Humanities Press, 2015.

Stevis, Dimitris, and Romain Felli. "Planetary Just Transition? How Inclusive and How Just?" *Earth System Governance* 6 (2020): 100065.

Strauss, Mariya. "Pipeline Resistance Confronts Big Oil in the Bayou." *New Labor Forum* 27, no. 2 (2018): 93–97.

Sun, Xiaoyi, Ronggui Huang, and Ngai-Ming Yip. "Dynamic Political Opportunities and Environmental Forces Linking Up: A Case Study of Anti-PX Contention in Kunming." *Journal of Contemporary China* 26, no. 106 (2017): 536–48.

Sze, Julie. *Environmental Justice in a Moment of Danger*. Berkeley: University of California Press, 2020.

Taylor, Dorceta. *Toxic Communities: Environmental Racism, Industrial Pollution, and Residential Mobility*. New York: New York University Press, 2014.

Temper, Leah. "Blocking Pipelines, Unsettling Environmental Justice: From Rights of Nature to Responsibility to Territory." *Local Environment* 24, no. 2 (2019): 94–112.

Temper, Leah, Daniela Del Bene, and Joan Martínez-Alier. "Mapping the Frontiers and Front Lines of Global Environmental Justice: The EJAtlas." *Journal of Political Ecology* 22, no. 1 (2015): 255–78.

Temper, Leah, Federico Demaria, Arnim Scheidel, Daniela Del Bene, and Joan Martínez-Alier. "The Global Environmental Justice Atlas (EJAtlas): Ecological Distribution Conflicts as Forces for Sustainability." *Sustainability Science* 13, no. 3 (2018): 573–84.

Tesh, Sylvia Noble. *Uncertain Hazards: Environmental Activists and Scientific Proof*. Ithaca, NY: Cornell University Press, 2000.

Tickner, Joel, Ken Geiser, and Stephanie Baima. "Transitioning the Chemical Industry: The Case for Addressing the Climate, Toxics, and Plastics Crises." *Environment: Science and Policy for Sustainable Development* 63, no. 6 (2021): 4–15.

Tilsted, Joachim Peter, Alice Mah, Tobias Dan Nielsen, Guy Finkill, and Fredric Bauer. "Petrochemical Transition Narratives: Selling Fossil Fuel Solutions in a Decarbonizing World." *Energy Research and Social Science* 94 (2022): 102880.

Todd, Zoe. "An Indigenous Feminist's Take on the Ontological Turn: 'Ontology' Is Just Another Word for Colonialism." *Journal of Historical Sociology* 29, no. 1 (2016): 4–22.

Tsing, Anna Lowenhaupt. *The Mushroom at the End of the World*. Princeton, NJ: Princeton University Press, 2015.

Tuck, Eve. "Suspending Damage: A Letter to Communities." *Harvard Educational Review* 79, no. 3 (2009): 409–28.

Tully, John. *The Devil's Milk: A Social History of Rubber*. New York: New York University Press, 2011.

United Church of Christ Commission for Racial Justice (UCC). *Proceedings of the First National People of Color Environmental Leadership Summit*. Report. New York: United Church of Christ, 1992. http://rescarta.ucc.org/jsp/RcWebImageViewer.jsp?doc_id=32092eb9-294e-4f6e-a880-17b8bbe02d88/OhClUCC0/00000001/00000070&pg_seq=1&search_doc=.

United Church of Christ Commission for Racial Justice (UCC). *Toxic Wastes and Race in the United States: A National Report on the Racial and Socio-Economic Characteristics of Communities with Hazardous Waste Sites*. Report. New York: United Church of Christ, 1987. https://www.nrc.gov/docs/ML1310/ML13109A339.pdf.

Unruh, Gregory C. "Understanding Carbon Lock-In." *Energy Policy* 28, no. 12 (2000): 817–30.

Valenzuela Pérez, Leonardo F. "Coppered Lives: The Chilean Sacrifice Zone of Quintero Bay." PhD diss., University of Sydney, 2016.

Verbeek, Thomas. "Explaining Public Risk Acceptance of a Petrochemical Complex: A Delicate Balance of Costs, Benefits, and Trust." *Environment and Planning E: Nature and Space* 4, no. 4 (2021): 1413–40.

Verbeek, Thomas, and Alice Mah. "Integration and Isolation in the Global Petrochemical Industry: A Multiscalar Corporate Network Analysis." *Economic Geography* 96, no. 4 (2020): 363–87.

Von Werlhof, Claudia. "Using, Producing, and Replacing Life? Alchemy as Theory and Practice in Capitalism." In *Modern World-System in the Longue Durée*, edited by Immanuel Wallerstein, 71–84. London: Routledge, 2004.

Voulvouli, Aimilia. "Transenvironmental Protest: The Arnavutköy Anti-bridge Campaign in Istanbul." *Environmental Politics* 20, no. 6 (2011): 861–78.

Walker, Gordon P., and Harriet Bulkeley. "Geographies of Environmental Justice." *Geoforum* 37, no. 5 (2006): 655–59.

Walker, Jeremy, and Melinda Cooper. "Genealogies of Resilience: From Systems Ecology to the Political Economy of Crisis Adaptation." *Security Dialogue* 42, no. 2 (2011): 143–60.

Wang, Xinhong, and Yuanni Wang. "Soft Confrontation: Strategic Actions of an Environmental Organization in China." In *Toxic Truths: Environmental Justice and Citizen Science in a Post-truth Age*, edited by Thom Davies and Alice Mah, 220–36. Manchester: Manchester University Press, 2020.

Wesseling, Joeri H., Stefan Lechtenböhmer, Max Åhman, Lars J. Nilsson, Ernst Worrell, and Lars Coenen. "The Transition of Energy Intensive Processing Industries towards Deep Decarbonization: Characteristics and Implications for Future Research." *Renewable and Sustainable Energy Reviews* 79 (2017): 1303–13.

White, Damian. "Just Transitions/Design for Transitions: Preliminary Notes on a Design Politics for a Green New Deal." *Capitalism, Nature, Socialism* 31, no. 2 (2020): 20–39.

Whyte, Kyle Powys. "Indigenous Climate Change Studies: Indigenizing Futures, Decolonizing the Anthropocene." *English Language Notes* 55, no. 1 (2017): 153–62.

Whyte, Kyle Powys. "Indigenous Experience, Environmental Justice and Settler Colonialism." In *Nature and Experience: Phenomenology and the Environment*, edited by Bryan F. Bannon, 157–74. Lanham, MD: Rowman and Littlefield, 2016.

Whyte, Kyle Powys. "Too Late for Indigenous Climate Justice: Ecological and Relational Tipping Points." *WIREs: Climate Change* 11, no. 1 (2020): e603.

Wiebe, Sara M. *Everyday Exposure: Indigenous Mobilization and Environmental Justice in Canada's Chemical Valley*. Vancouver: UBC Press, 2016.

Wilder, Elisabeth, and Phil Brown. "Environmental Factors in Health." In *Handbook of Environmental Sociology*, edited by Beth Schaefer Caniglia, Andrew Jorgenson, Stephanie A. Malin, Lori Peek, and David N. Pellow, 243–65. Cham, Switzerland: Springer, 2021.

Wright, Beverly. "Race, Politics, and Pollution: Environmental Justice in the Mississippi River Chemical Corridor." In *Just Sustainabilities: Development in an Unequal World*, edited by Julian Agyeman, Robert D. Bullard, and Bob Evans, 125–45. Cambridge, MA: MIT Press, 2003.

Wu, Qiyan, Xiaoling Zhang, Hongbo Li, Hao Chen, Zaijun Li, and Zhenyong Shang. "Pro-growth Giant Business, Lock In, Sustainable Urban Development and Effect on Local Political Economy: The Case of Petrochemical Industry at Nanjing." *Journal of Cleaner Production* 107, no. 16 (2015): 324–32.

Wylie, Sara, Nick Shapiro, and Max Liboiron. "Making and Doing Politics through Grassroots Scientific Research on the Energy and Petrochemical Industries." *Engaging Science, Technology, and Society* 3 (2017): 393–425.

Wylie, Sara Ann. *Fractivism: Corporate Bodies and Chemical Bonds*. Durham, NC: Duke University Press, 2018.

Yergin, Daniel. *The New Map: Energy, Climate, and the Clash of Nations*. London: Penguin, 2020.

Yusoff, Kathryn. *A Billion Black Anthropocenes or None*. Minneapolis: University of Minnesota Press, 2018.

Zavestoski, Stephen. "The Struggle for Justice in Bhopal: A New/Old Breed of Transnational Social Movement." *Global Social Policy* 9, no. 3 (2009): 383–407.

INDEX

Page locators in italics refer to figures.

Aamjiwnaang First Nation (Ontario), 60, 77
adaptability, 3, 16, 21–23, 49, 51–52, 100, 142
Africa, 9, 28, 90, 110
Agyeman, Julian, 15
Alchemists, The (Ratcliffe and Heath), 46
alchemization, 44, 46–48
alliances, 85, 124, 140; labor and environmental, 56, 60, 63, 130; #NoDAPL and, 71–72. *See also* multiscalar activism
Alliance to End Plastic Waste, 110
alternatives to petrochemical planetary politics, 2, 10–16, 24, 29, 141–51; avoidance of damage-centered research, 57–58; pluriverse as, 13–15, 140, 151
Ambros, Dieter, 31
Ambros, Otto, 31
American Chemical Council, 110
ancestral lands, loss of, 69, 71
Anthropocene, 98–99
anti-plastics movement, 71–72, 76, 89, 91–92, 110
anti-PX (paraxylene) protests, in China, xiv, 55, 62, 84–86
Appel, Hannah, 18

articulation, 3, 72–73, 84
Atchafalaya Basin (Louisiana), 78, 82, 88
Attenborough, David, 72
Australia wildfires, 96
authoritarian states, 14, 29, 69, 84–85
Azmeel (Aramco contractor), 65

Baima, Stephanie, 106
Bangladesh, 90
Barca, Stefania, 98
Barry, Andrew, 18
BASF, 28, 31–32, 35, 43, 60, 114
Battle of Grangemouth, The (Lyon), 133–34
Bauer, Fred, 146
Bayer, 31, 32
Bayou Bridge oil pipeline (Cancer Alley), xii, 77–80, *80*
Bear, Laura, 48
Beck, Ulrich, 10
Bell, Daniel, 126
Benanav, Aaron, 126
"Beyond GDP Growth" campaign (OECD and EU), 120
Bhopal gas leak (1984), 34, 58

Biden administration, 76, 81, 105
"bifurcation" approach, 117
biodiversity, loss of, 143–44
bisphenol A (BPA), 8, 10, 104–5
Black Lives Matter, 81, 144
"Black Love Canals," 59
"Blockadia," 73, 93
Blue Planet II (BBC series), 72
Bluestone, Barry, 67
"brand audits," 92, 96
Braskem, *36*, 37
Break Free from Plastic movement, 71–72, 91–92, 96
Brexit, 39, 108
British Petroleum (BP), 35; BP Baku-Tbilisi-Ceyhan oil pipeline, 18; Forties Pipeline, 133; Grangemouth as boomtown and, 121, 131–32; PESTEL analysis of, 51
Brown, David, 67
BTEX group (benzene, toluene, ethylbenzene, and xylene), 8, 104
Buch-Hansen, Hubert, 34
bucket brigades, 60, 79
Bullard, Robert, 15, 59, 81
burial sites, of Black communities, 81
byproducts ("two-for-one principle"), 104

Canada, xi–xiii, 34, 60, 77
cancer, 49, 53–54, 63, 91; blood bags and, 4, 115; BTEX group of volatile organic compounds, 8, 104; Taixi Village (Taiwan), 93
Cancer Alley (Louisiana), x–xii, 12, 53, 55; Bayou Bridge Pipeline project, xii, 77–80, *80*; bucket brigades in, 60; cancer risk assessment in, 61; as Death Alley, 61; as former slave plantation, 59; multiscalar activism in, 76–82; practical local constraints of, 146–47; United Nations report on, 81; "Welcome to Cancer Alley" billboards, 60
capitalism: colonialism entangled with, 96, 116; complexity thinking in operations of, 29–30; critiques of, 127–28; divination, relationship to, 48; edifices of, 6–7; the global related to, 4; military entangled with, 45; politics of climate change and, 73; racial, 6, 11, 13, 15, 53, 93, 98, 141, 151. *See also* colonialism

carbon capture and storage (CCS), 124
carbon democracy, 18
carbon lock-in, 4–5, 142, 146, 147
Carbon Tracker, 123
Carson, Rachel, 12, 33, 49
cartels, 28, 30, 34, 48; IG Farben, 31–32, 42
Center for Biological Diversity, 80
Centre for International Environmental Law, 92, 101
Chakrabarty, Dipesh, 4, 99
Chandler, Alfred, 30, 43
chemical dispersants, ix, 153n2
chemical industry, 30, 35–36, 90, 106, 123
"chemical recycling," 91, 109–10, 124, 149
Chemical Valley (Sarnia, Ontario), 60, 77
Chen, Sibo, 85–86
Chertkovskaya, Ekaterina, 127
Chile, 60–61
China, 73, 168n90; anti-PX (paraxylene) protests in, xiv, 55, 62, 84–86; coal use in, 39, 40, 45, 82; COVID-19 pandemic and, 39, 40, 83; "ecological civilization" and, 84; embedded activism in, 14, 84, 88; *hukou* system of household registration in, 66; LNG trade deal with United States and, 82–83; media suppression in, 85–86; National Sword policy in, 51, 90; "resigned activism" in, 62, 84; "rightful resistance" in, 62, 84, 85; "self-sufficiency" in, 39, 43, 45; smog days in, 84, 86, 87, 114; "soft confrontation" in, 84; "strolls" (*jiti sanbu*) in, xiv, 62, 85; "turnip" saying in, 87–88; as world's largest petrochemical producer and consumer, xiv, 35, 39, 84
China National Offshore Oil Corporation (CNOOC), 82, 84
China National Petroleum Corporation (CNPC), 84
Chisso Chemical Corporation, 58
"chlorine cycle" (Porto Marghera), 129–30
chronic emergency, 100, 119
Ciplet, David, 129
circular economy, 10, 16, 38, 50, 109–10, 124
civil society, 22, 85–86
Clarke, Linda, 129
Clean Air Act of 1970, 63
Clean Water Act of 1972, 63

climate change denial, funding of, 6, 38, 84, 111, 122
climate divestment movement, 75, 112, 122, 136
climate emergency, 3, 39, 92, 96, 100; alarmist accounts of, 119–20; difficult decarbonization and, 122; extreme weather events, 96; IPCC reports on, 72, 75; marine plastics crisis overshadowed by, 110–11; plastics as "evil twin of," 102
Coca-Cola, 96
Cohen, Felix, 142
Colborn, Theo, 101
Collins, Philip, 126
collusion, 23, 28, 29, 34; as foundational practice, 44, 106, 113; IG Farben and Standard Oil, 31–32; legacies of, 48–51
colonialism: capitalism entangled with, 6–7, 28, 96, 116; "ontology" as, 99; toxic, 2, 4, 14, 90. *See also* capitalism
Coming of the Postindustrial Society, The (Bell), 126
commercialization of products, 30, 32–33, 43, 48, 75, 90
Commoner, Barry, 33, 102–4, 128–29
complexity science, 21–22, 49, 51
complex systems, 20–23, 29–30, 128, 142
Concerned Citizens of Norco, 60
Connolly, William, 4, 22, 149–50
Consolidated Contractors International Company, 65
consumer goods, 32–33
Convent (Louisiana), 61
Cooper, Melinda, 22
co-optation, 16, 123–24, 139
corporate events, 25–26, 37, 157n92; as curated performances, 27, 38, 107. *See also* petrochemical industry, global
Cosme, Ines, 127–28
Courtyard, Olivier, 75
COVID-19 pandemic, xiv–xv, 1, 19, 37, 100, 106, 119; bailouts, 123; China and, 39, 40, 83; degrowth and, 126, 140; INEOS hand sanitizer plants, 136, 144; profitability of, 39, 44; single-use plastics and, 50, 74, 83, 112, 113, 143–44; zoonotic spillover and, 96, 143–44
Cowen, Deborah, 9, 45

"cracking," 5
Crazy Horse, 89
Crepelle, Adam, 78
critical environmental justice studies perspective, 11, 13
critical interventions, 3, 27, 51–52, 142, 147–51
Crotty, Tom, 47, 116
crude oil, 8, 39, 83, 138; crash of 2020, 1, 39, 40, 74, 106, 123, 144
crude-oil-to-chemicals (COTC) projects, 39, 73–74

Dakota Access Pipeline (DAPL), 71, 76–77, 93
D'Alisa, Giacomo, 125
damage-centered research, 57–58
D'Andrea, Dimitri, 135
Dauvergne, Peter, 50
DDT (dichlorodiphenyltrichloroethane), 12, 33, 59, 102
decarbonization, 15, 64, 112, 113, 139; contested pathways for, 120–21; "decarbonization divide," 121; difficulty of, 122–24. *See also* degrowth
decolonization, 13, 58, 79
deep time, 3–4, 12
degrowth, 15, 120–22, 150–51; decarbonization linked to, 120, 124; dilemmas of, 126–28; "post-growth" versus, 125; reckoning with, 124–26. *See also* decarbonization; economic growth
deindustrialization, xi, 126; "noxious," 67–68
Delaware, 81
Delgamuukw decision (Canada), 77
demand for petrochemicals, 5–7, 6, 47, 102, 116; China, 43–44, 83; during COVID-19 pandemic, 39–40, 44, 83, 113; manufacturing of, 14, 104, 109, 143; market forecasts, 74–75, 111; reducing, 75, 124; war and, 5, 28, 30, 106
Demaria, Federico, 125
Diamond (Louisiana), 60, 61
DIDOS (drive in and drive out), 68
dirt, as "matter out of place," 147
disasters and accidents: 1970s and 1980s, 58; Australia wildfires (2019), 96; Bhopal gas leak (1984), 34, 58; "Black Love Canals," 59; Deepwater Horizon oil spill

disasters and accidents (continued)
(2010), ix, 153n1; Fujian Province (2013, 2015, and 2017), 85; Jiangsu Province (2019), 86; Love Canal, New York (1978), 12, 49, 58, 59; marine plastics crisis, 39, 43, 51, 72, 74; Minamata, Japan (1956), 58; Quintero and Puchuncaví toxic gases (2018), 61; "unruly" toxic and explosive substances, 58

disembedding from petrochemicals, 148

divestment movement, 75, 112, 122, 136

Douglas, Mary, 147

Dow, 35, 43

DowDuPont, 43, 104

dualistic perspectives, 13, 20, 21, 98

Dumping in Dixie (Bullard), 59

Earth Day (1970), 49

"ecological civilization," 84

ecologically unequal exchange, 14, 62, 90–91

economic growth, 17, 40, 147; critiques of, 120, 125, 140, 147; as dominant priority, 7, 75, 98, 103, 105, 120, 125, 127, 130. *See also* degrowth; green capitalism / growth

Economist, 122

"economy-as-machine," 22

"embedded activism," 14, 84, 88

employment blackmail, 24, 56, 63, 130

Energy Transfer Partners, 78, 79, 83

entanglement, 4, 6, 18, 22, 95, 143; critical interventions and, 148; "new materialist" reflections on, 99

environment, as spaces "where we live, work, and play," 63

environmental crisis, 18, 148; fathoming, 97–101; proactive stances by corporations, 49–50; as threat to petro-capitalism, 5, 11, 44, 95

environmental injustice, xiii–xv, 2; and anti-plastics movement, 89; ecologically unequal exchange, 14, 62, 90–91; five-hundred-year history of, 12–13. *See also* toxic injustice

environmental justice activism, x–xi, 58–62; 1950s through 1980s, 58–60, 113; 1990s and 2000s, 60; achievements of, 69–70; alliances within, 56, 60, 63–64, 71–73; "Blockadia," 73, 93; critical environmental justice studies perspective, 11, 13; double movement, 2; environmentalism of the poor, 62; growth-led decarbonization policies and, 121; murders of activists, 8, 28, 62; protracted struggles, 75–76; resonance of, 11–15; rollbacks of gains, 61, 112, 140; working-class environmentalism, 55

Environmental Justice Atlas (EJAtlas), 157n95

Environmental Protection Act (United States, 1970), 63

Environmental Protection Agency (United States), 61

Equatorial Guinea, 18

Escobar, Arturo, 13–14, 21, 44, 48, 151

"essential" industry and products, 1, 2, 5, 46, 97, 102, 148; and COVID-19 pandemic, 142, 143–45; versus "indispensability," 143–45; in petrochemical flowcharts, 7–8

Esso Engineering, 31

Estes, Nick, 88–89, 93

European Chemical Industry Council (CEFIC), 7, 105

European Chemicals Agency, 105

European Petrochemical Association (EPCA), 33–34, 47, 107

European Petrochemicals Conference (Amsterdam, 2016), 111–12

European Registration, Evaluation, Authorisation and Restriction of Chemicals (REACH), 50, 105, 108

European Union: "Beyond GDP Growth" campaign, 120; roadmap to ban chemicals (2022), 149; Seveso Directive (1982), 58

Evans, Bob, 15

"expendability," 2, 13, 66, 69, 144–45, 168n90; of entire populations, 57, 144

extractive industries, 10–11; environmentalism of the poor and, 62; movement against, 73; opposition to by workers, 133; reliant on global supply chain, 45

Exxon Corporation, 31, 96

ExxonMobil, 35, 37, 39, 43. *See also* Standard Oil Company

Facing the Planetary (Connolly), 149

Falkirk-Grangemouth Investment Zone, 137

feedstocks, 7, 33; "advantaged," 40–42; coal as, 39, 40; oil as, 30, 111–12; "recycled," 45, 109–10; shale gas, 40–41, 45, 73, 103–4, 112, 134; "virgin," 45, 109–10
Felli, Romain, 129
Feltrin, Lorenzo, 67, 129–30
fenceline communities, 2, 153n2; challenge of enduring toxic injustice, 69–70; comments from residents, 53–55; COVID-19 pandemic and, 19; "jobs versus environment" dilemma, 56, 64, 128; labor protests, 56, 63–69; possibilities for resistance, 56–57, 72; separation of workers from, 68; worldviews of, 23. *See also* Grangemouth (Scotland); Nanjing (China); St. James Parish (Louisiana)
Feola, Giuseppe, 127–28
Ferguson, James, 9, 11
Ferguson, Niall, 107
financial crisis of 2008, 40, 68, 125
firefighting foam, 104
First World War. *See* World War I
flowcharts, petrochemical, 7–8, 25
Floyd, George, 81, 144
Fontenit, Germain, 146
"forever chemicals," 104, 114, 115
Formosa Plastics, 80–82
Forties Pipeline, 133
fossil fuels, 12; end of, 122, 134; net zero rhetoric, 123; tar sands, 103; "virgin," 45, 109–10. *See also* crude oil; oil and gas industry; shale gas
Foucault, Michel, 7
Foytlin, Cherri, 78, 79
fracking (hydraulic fracturing), 40, 45, 73, 101; Indigenous opposition to, 77; lethal gas leaks, 134; and LNG trade between China and US, 82–83; opposition to in Scotland, 131
Fridays for Future school climate strikes, 72, 96
Future of Polyolefins Summit (Antwerp, 2019), 43

game, operational logic of, 27–28, 38, 41, 45–46
garbage imperialism, 14
GDP metric, 125

Geiser, Kenneth, 103, 106
genetically modified organisms (GMO), 10
Germany, 28, 31–32
Gilio-Whitaker, Dina, 13, 142
Glasgow construction workers, 129
Global Alliance for Incinerator Alternatives, 110
Global Community Monitor, 60
Global Petrochemical Map, 56, 92, 157n95
Global South, 124, 125, 129
globe, distinguished from planet, 3–4, 99
Goldman Environment Prize, 91
Gómez-Barris, Macarena, 29
Grace, W. R., 31
Gramsci, Antonio, 3, 16, 22
Grangemouth (Scotland), 19, 53–55, 67–68; fossil fuel refusal in, 130–36; Growth Deal, 137; "just transitions" and, 121
Great Game between Russia and Britain, 28
Great Louisiana Toxic March, 60
"Great Texas Freeze," 39
green capitalism / growth, 16, 101, 121, 136; just transitions and, 129, 139–40. *See also* economic growth
greenhouse gasses, 82, 112, 120, 123
green hydrogen, 124
Green New Deal proposals, 121, 129, 137
Grove, Jairus, 28
Growth Deal package (Scotland and UK), 137
"growthism," critiques of, 120
Gulf Coast (United States), 33, 83
Gulf countries, 64–66

Habshan Gas Complex Expansion project, 65
Hall, Stuart, 3, 22, 72
hand sanitizer plants, 136, 144
Hanieh, Adam, 32
Haraway, Donna, 98
"hard-to-abate" industrial sectors, 4, 121, 123–24
Harrison, Bennett, 67
Harrison, Jill Lindsey, 129
Hayek, Friedrich, 22
health problems, 4, 8, 44, 101; acro-osteolysis, 33–34, 49; deceit and denial about, 29, 33–34, 48–49, 57, 103, 113–15; employment blackmail and, 24, 56; pneumoconiosis, 66

Healthy Gulf, 80
Heath, Ursula, 46, 132
Henriksen, Lasse Folke, 34
Hickel, Jason, 121, 127–28
"Highway of Tears" (British Columbia), xiii
Hoffman, Andrew, 49
hope, 93–94, 100, 142
Houston, Texas, freeze (2021), 106
hukou system of household registration (China), 66
human rights violations, 28, 31, 36, 62
hydrogen cyanide, 8, 28

Ialenti, Vincent, 5
IG Farben, 28, 31–32, 42, 159n14
IHS Markit, 83
imagination, technologies of, 48
Imperial Chemical Industries (ICI), 42, 52
imperialist logic, 10–11
incommensurability, ethic of, 14
India, 48, 59, 93
Indigenous Environmental Network, 79
Indigenous peoples, 12–13, 98–99; federal recognition of, 78; Gixtsan, 77; "Highway of Tears" (British Columbia), xiii; history of resistance to oil and gas pipelines, 71, 76–77, 93–94; Houma, 78–79; Keystone Pipeline XL mobilization, 76; Lakota, 89; Ogoni, 62; Sioux, 78; Standing Rock #NoDAPL resistance, 71, 76–77, 93; "water of life" ("being a good relative") concept, 78; Wet'suwet'en, xi, xii, xiii, 77
"indispensability," 13, 142, 143–45
INEOS, *36*, 37, 41, 43, 68, 83, 116; alchemical vision of, 46–48; environmental tour of, 130–31, *131*; hand sanitizer plants, 136, 144; injunction against protestors, 55; outsourced labor, 132; Petroineos, 138; "roadmap to net zero," 136; social contract eroded by, 132–36; "unloved" assets bought by, 43, 132; US shale gas shipped by, 134
Institute of Public and Environmental Affairs (China), 87
insurance industry, 115
interconnected issues, 2; spatial interlocks, 35, *37*; upstream and downstream industries, 21, 37–39

Intergovernmental Panel on Climate Change (IPCC), 72, 75, 96
International Energy Agency (IEA), 5, 74–75, 111, 149
International Labour Organization (ILO), 64
International Petroleum Week (IP Week) (2020), 37
International Renewable Energy Agency (IRENA), 122–23, 124
Italy, 63–64

Jackson, Tim, 125, 146
Jamnagar, India, 93
Japan, 56, 82
Jeffreys, Diarmuid, 32
"jobs versus environment" dilemma, 56, 64, 128
Johnson, Gerry, 44
Jones, Peter J. S., 111
Joseph, Harry, 78
Juneteenth, 81
"just transformations," 138–40
Just Transition Commission (Scotland), 138
just transitions, 15, 56, 63–64, 118, 120, 128–30; designing, 139–40, 148–49; planetary, 128–29; proactivity need for, 121–22, 138–40. *See also* transition; transitions

kafala (visa-sponsorship) system, 64–65
Kallis, Giorgos, 125
Keystone Pipeline XL mobilization, 76
Kimmerer, Robin Wall, 99
Klein, Naomi, 73, 93
Koch Methanol, 83
Kuznets, Simon, 125

labor protests, 56, 63–69; acute differences in conditions for struggle, 68–69; indirect, 65; labor-environmental ("blue-green") coalitions, 56, 68; by outsourced workers, 64, 66–67
Labor Statute (1970, Italy), 63
"Land, plastics as," 4, 147
landfills, 12, 59
Las Ventanas (Chile), 61
Latour, Bruno, 99
Lavigne, Sharon, 80–81

"leakage," 110
L'eau est la vie (Water Is Life): From Standing Rock to the Swamp (film), 79
Legaspi, Efren, 61
Lennon, Myles, 13
Lepawsky, Josh, 17, 73, 147
Li, Yifei, 84, 87–88, 92
Liboiron, Max, 4, 14, 17, 73, 99, 147
Licit Life of Capitalism, The (Appel), 18
Liegey, Vincent, 126
Lipsig-Mummé, Carla, 129
liquified natural gas (LNG), 39–40, 82–83
litigation, 59, 96, 104, 112, 165–66n38; St. James Parish, 78, 80–81; toxic liability crisis, 113–16
lobbying, 34, 49, 107
lock-in: carbon lock-in, 4–5, 142, 146, 147; multiscalar petrochemical, 145–47
logistics, 45
loops, 23, 26
Lora-Wainwright, Anna, 62
Lou, Loretta, xiv–xv
Louisiana, 59–60, 78. *See also* Cancer Alley (Louisiana)
Louisiana Bucket Brigade, 79, 80
Love Canal, New York, disaster (1978), 12, 49, 58, 59
Lyon, Mark, 133–34

MacBride, Samantha, 109
Mack, Oliver, 51
Malm, Andreas, 100
March against Death Alley, 61
marine plastics crisis (2018), 39, 43, 51, 72, 74, 89, 109; "brand audit," 92; overshadowed by climate emergency, 110–11
market forecasts, 74–75, 106–7, 111, 149
Markowitz, Gerald, 29, 49
Marquez, John, 13
Martínez-Alier, Joan, 62
Marx, Karl, 89
mass overconsumption, 14
"master story," 98
Material Politics (Barry), 18
Mazzucato, Mariana, 125, 126
McGoey, Linsey, 115
McKibben, Bill, 74
Meadows, Donella, 117

Middle East, 40
migrant workers, 64–66, 68
militaristic strategies, 2–3, 9, 23; rhetoric of, 27, 29; strategization of society, 44–45; volatility, uncertainty, complexity, and ambiguity (VUCA), 29, 39, 51, 116; wars of position, 3, 16, 28. *See also* strategy
Milkoreit, Manjana, 117
Minamata, Japan, disaster (1956), 58
Mississippi Chemical Corridor. *See* Cancer Alley (Louisiana)
Mitchell, Timothy, 7, 18
mole, figure of, 88–89
Monsanto, 10, 33–34, 49
Montreal Protocol on Substances that Deplete the Ozone Layer (1987), 49
Morales, Joel, 83
Movement for the Survival of the Ogoni People, 62
multiscalar activism, 2–3, 11–12, 52, 122; anti-PX protests as, 84–86; battles of industrial transformation, 15–17; Break Free from Plastic movement, 71–72, 91–92; in Cancer Alley, 76–82; complex systems addressed by, 23; connecting struggles along the plastics value chain, 89–93; as contextual and relational, 73; critical interventions, 148–51; and decarbonization, 130; discreet, in China, 87; by fenceline communities, 16, 24; maintaining hope, 93–94; scaling up resistance, 16, 73, 88; scaling wide and scaling down, 16, 73; between St. James Parish and Indigenous movements, 77–79; swarming, politics of, 149–50; turnip and mole figures, 87–89. *See also* alliances
Mushroom at the End of the World, The (Tsing), 16
mythological figures, role-play with, 45–48

Nanjing (China), xiv, 19, 54–55, 66, 86–89, 147
National Air Toxic Assessment (US EPA), 61
National Environmental Policy Act, 77
National Geographic, 72
National Petroleum Refiners Association (NPRA), 33

National Public Radio, 110
National Sword policy (China), 51, 90
Nazis, 8, 28, 31
Nederland, Texas, 83
Nelson, Anitra, 126
neoliberalism, 21, 22, 100
net zero, 16, 72; contradictions, 136–38; discussed at COP26, 112–13; as endgame for fossil fuels, 122; loopholes in, 112, 149; market-led solutions, 121; "net zero is not zero," 112; trasformismo strategies, 123–24
Newell, Peter, 16, 75, 123
Niger Delta, 62
Nigeria, 62
#NoDAPL resistance movement, 71, 76–77, 93
nonhuman/more-than-human actors, 4, 13, 99, 100
nonstick cookware, 104
North Atlantic corporate elite, 35
North Sea Pipeline, 136
"noxious deindustrialization," 67–68
nuclear industry, 12
"nurdles," 10

Obama administration, 76
Occupational Safety and Health Act of 1970, 63
Oceana International, 60–61
Ocean Conservancy, 91
oceans, 5, 10, 60–61, 91
O'Connor, James, 100
Oil, Chemical, and Atomic Workers (OCAW), 60
oil and gas industry: at COP26, 113; "net zero" pledges, 112; oil crisis (1973), 34; petrochemical companies as part of, 97; "Seven Sisters," 32; transparency in, 50; United States, 30; vertically integrated, 9, 35, 37, 39, 41, 111, 123, 161n68. *See also* fracking (hydraulic fracturing)
"oil itself," 18
ontology, 99
Operation Clean Sweep, 110
outsourced workers, 64, 66–67, 69
overcapacity, 34, 40, 126

paraxylene (PX), xiv, 55, 62, 84–86
Paris Agreement, 26, 39, 111–12

Paulson, Susan, 125
PBS *Frontline*, 110
PCB (polychlorinated biphenyls), 12, 33, 59
Pellow, David, 13, 57, 144
per- and polyfluoroalkyl substances (PFAS), 104–5, 114, 116
personal protective equipment (PPE), 83, 123
PESTEL analysis, 51
pesticides, 10, 12, 33
petrochemical industry, global: attention focused away from, 96–97, 102; "carbon lock-in," 4–5, 142; collusive practices, 23, 28, 29, 31–32, 44, 48–51, 106; as complex system, 20–21; corporate worldviews, 7–11, 18, 47; crises affecting, 1–2, 5; cumulative production, 1950 to 2015, 6; dependence on, 15, 16, 24; as driver of oil demand, 5, 74; ecological crisis as threat to, 5, 11, 44, 95; as "exception" to environmental crisis, 97; expansion of, 8, 10–11, 17, 23, 68, 73–75, 83, 88, 103, 124, 130–36, 145; frontstage versus offstage dynamics, 107–8; as "hard-to-abate" sector, 4, 121, 123; history of, 30–44; imperialist logic of, 10–11; individual companies, 35–36; internal conflicts as productive for, 26; labor protests in, 56, 63–69; market forecasts, 74–75, 106–7, 111; mergers and acquisitions, 34–35; military-strategic worldview, 23, 29, 141; networks within, 19–21, 25, 35, *36*, *37*, 147; number of workers, 64; opportunity and threat, 23, 72; as part of oil companies, 97; as percentage of chemical industry, 4, 106; pressure on, 1–2, 23, 44, 50, 64, 72–75; regional profiles, 39–42; responsibility avoided by, 9–10, 16, 103, 115; rules for success, 41–44; self-regulation strategies, 34, 49, 110, 149; systematic sociological analysis of, 18–19; as threat to planetary life, 101–6; toxicity concealed by, 8, 29, 33–34, 46, 48; upcycle in global chemical markets (2018), 43; upstream and downstream industries, 21, 37–39; World War II collaborations with Nazi Germany, 31–32. *See also* corporate events; demand for petrochemicals; strategy

214

INDEX

Petrochemicals Europe, 7, 74
PetroChina, 138
Petroineos, 138
Philippines, 91
Phillips 66, 78
Piñera, Sebastián, 60–61
pipeline projects, xii, 18, 71, 76–80, 93–94
planet, distinguished from globe, 3–4, 99
planetary boundaries, 5, 96, 117
planetary just transitions, 128–29
planetary life, petrochemical industry as threat to, 101–6
planetary thinking, 3–4, 7
Plastic or Planet campaign (*National Geographic*), 72
plastic packaging, in South Asia, 89–90
plastics: hidden costs of, 101; illusory nature of, 48; "as Land," 4, 147; as stranded assets, 75, 123
plastics crisis, 108–11
Plastics Industry Association, 144
plastics lifecycle approach, 76
Plumwood, Val, 98
pluriverse, 13–15, 140, 151
Polanyi, Karl, 2
pollution: air, 60–61, 80, 91, 144; "critically polluted" areas, 92–93; planetary boundaries exceeded by, 5, 96, 117; smog, 84, 86, 87, 114
Pollution Is Colonialism (Liboiron), 4
Polyolefins Americas, 83
poor, environmentalism of, 62
"populist speculators," 48
Porto Marghera (Venice), 129–30
"post-growth," 125
precautionary approaches, 102, 104–5
Primed for Success (Spitz), 31–32
prior and informed consent, 76, 90
process maps, 7–8
protests, 55–56; anti-PX (paraxylene), xiv, 55, 62, 84–86; Great Louisiana Toxic March, 60; March against Death Alley, 61; "transenvironmental," 85; "Welcome to Cancer Alley" billboards, 60. *See also* environmental justice activism
Public Health System (1970, Italy), 63
Puchuncaví-Quintero bay (Chile), 61
purity, myth of, 147, 150

Race to Zero Campaign (United Nations), 1, 112
racism, xiii, 59; environmental, 57, 80, 81; systemic, xiv, 2, 72, 81
Ratcliffe, Jim, 46–48, 68, 132
Raworth, Kate, 21
REACH regulations (Europe, 2007), 50, 105, 108
recycling: "chemical recycling," 91, 109–10; toxicity and carbon footprint of, 43, 45, 91, 109
Recycling Reconsidered (MacBride), 109
regional profiles, 39–42
"regrettable substitutions," 104–5
regulations, 34, 50–51; REACH regulations (Europe, 2007), 50, 105, 108
relational tipping point, 117, 150
resistance, 15–17; critical interventions, 3, 27, 51–52, 142, 147–51; and proliferation, 73–76; "rightful," 62, 84, 85; "strolls" (*jiti sanbu*), xiv, 62, 85. *See also* multiscalar activism
Responsible Care program, 34, 50
RISE St. James, 80
Robinson, Cedric J., 66
Rodríguez-Labajosa, Beatriz, 125, 128
Rosner, David, 29, 49
Route 9 corridor (Delaware), 81
Rowe, Aimee Carrillo, 14
Russia: petrochemical use, 40; Ukraine, invasion of, 28–29, 39, 40, 75, 149
Ruwais refinery (UAE), 65–66

SABIC (Saudi Basic Industries Corporation), *36*, 37
"sachets," single-use, 90
"sacrifice zone" concept, 57, 60–61
"safe" threshold levels of exposure, 57
Sarnia, Ontario, 60, 77
Saro-Wiwa, Ken, 62
Saudi Arabia, 64–65, 73
Savage Ecology (Grove), 28
scale, 13, 16–17, 45, 73, 110; micro and macro levels, 19, 23–24
science, 30, 42, 57, 98, 103
Scotland, 53–55; climate change policy (2019), 121; green transition, plans for, 137–38

Scott, James, 7–8, 9, 29, 45
Scottish Green Party, 138
Scramble for Africa, 28
Seeing Like a State (Scott), 45
"seeing like a state," 9
"seeing like the petrochemical industry," 27, 44, 52
self-alchemization, 44, 46–48
Sengupta, Somini, 75
settler colonialism, xiv, 13–14, 77
"Seven Sisters" oil companies, 32
Seveso, Italy, disaster (1976), 58
Seveso Directive (1982), 34, 58
shale gas, 40–41, 45, 73, 103–4, 112, 134
Shapiro, Judith, 84
Shared Histories (McCreary), xii
Shaw, Martin, 44–45
Shaw, Susan, 102
Shell, 28, 35, 60, 62; community buy-out from (2002), 60; human rights abuses by, 62
Shi Chenggang, 82
Shove, Elizabeth, 75
Sierra Club, 79
Silent Spring (Carson), 12, 33, 49
simplifications, 11, 21, 29, 52
single-use plastics, 14, 40, 101, 110; and COVID-19 pandemic, 50, 74, 112, 113, 143–44; "sachets," 90
Sinopec, *36*, 37, 43, 84
social contract, industrial, 64, 67, 121; INEOS's erosion of, 132–36
"social license to operate," 109
society, strategization of, 44–45
socio-ecological systems, 21, 22, 117
Soper, Kate, 125
South Africa, 45, 60
Southeast Asia: Break Free from Plastic movement, 71–72, 91–92; plastic packaging crisis, 89–90
Sovacool, Benjamin, 121
Spitz, Peter, 31–32, 47
Spivak, Gayatri Chakravorty, 3–4
Standard Oil Company, 31–32. *See also* ExxonMobil
Standing Rock protests (#NoDAPL), 71, 76–77, 88, 93
state-owned enterprises, 34, *36*, 37, 40, 73, 84

state simplifications, 11, 29
Steinhardt, Christoph, 85
Stemming the Tide (Ocean Conservancy), 91
Stengers, Isabelle, 10, 98
Stevis, Dimitris, 129
St. James Parish (Louisiana), 19, 53–55, 61; Bayou Bridge Pipeline and, xii, 77–80, *80*; Formosa Plastics opposition, 80–81; methanol plants, 78, 83; RISE St. James, 80
stranded assets, 75, 123
strategy, 44–51; commercialization as, 30; co-optation, 16, 123–24, 139; corporate, 41–44; game, operational logic of, 27–28, 38, 41; as military concept, 2, 29; neoliberal systems thinking, 22; self-alchemization, 44, 46–48; self-regulation, 34, 49, 110, 149; shift from defensive to proactive stances, 49–50; sociological analysis of, 44; "strategic ignorance," 49, 115; strategization of society, 44–45; war gaming, 45–46. *See also* militaristic strategies; wars of position
Sunoco Logistics Partners, 78
Superfund Act of 1980, 12, 34, 59, 105
supply chains, global, 9–10, 18, 33; COVID-19 pandemic and, 144; decarbonization and, 121; entanglement of military and trade, 45; green energy, toxic consequences of, 129; waste offloaded by, 9–10, 14–15. *See also* value chains, petrochemical
Supreme Court (United States), 76–77
Supreme Court of Chile, 61
Supreme Court of United Kingdom, 62
survivance, 57
sustainability, 15–16, 24, 72, 93; corporate, 50, 110–12, 124, 126, 149; "just sustainabilities," 15, 139; sustainable growth, 125
swarming, politics of, 149–50
systems thinking, 21–22
Sze, Julie, 11, 69–70

Taiwan, 93
Taixi Village (Taiwan), 93
tar sands, 77, 103–4
technological innovation, discourse of, 10, 43, 98, 106, 124; dubious future possibilities, 123–24; mythologizing of, 47–48; opposition to complex systems, 128

INDEX

technological solutions, 10, 43, 97, 117, 147
Teflon, 104, 114
threats to petrochemical industry: complexity as, 23; ecological crisis as, 5, 11, 44, 95, 106–16; mechanistic approach to, 44; PESTEL analysis of, 51; plastics crisis, 108–11; tipping points, 116–18, 150; toxic liability crisis, 113–16
Thunberg, Greta, 72
Tickner, Joel, 105
tipping points, 116–18, 150
Todd, Zoe, 99
toxic colonialism, 2, 4, 14, 90
toxic expertise, 29, 49, 124
"Toxic Expertise: Environmental Justice and the Global Petrochemical Industry" (2015–20) (Mah), x, xiv, 17–20
Toxic Expertise project: Global Petrochemical Map, 56, 157n95; Grangemouth research, 132–36; St. James Parish research trips, 79
toxic injustice, 17, 56–59, 62, 69–71; decarbonization divide and, 121; enduring, 56, 69–70, 72, 142, 151; systemic, 11. *See also* environmental injustice
toxicity: deceit and denial about, 8, 29, 33–34, 46, 48–49, 57, 103, 113–16; inherent in petrochemicals, 104
toxic liability crisis, 113–16
Toxics Release Inventory Program (United States, 1986), 34, 49, 59
Toxic Tours (Break Free from Plastic), 92
"Toxic Wastes and Race in the United States" (United Church of Christ), 59
trade, 45, 51; ecologically unequal exchange, 14, 90–91; LNG trade between China and US, 82–83; and logistics, 45
traditional ecological knowledge (TEK), 99
"transenvironmental" protests, 85
transitions, 16, 24, 105–6; democratic, imagination of, 127; energy (green) transitions, 5, 13, 16, 39, 73, 75, 82, 101, 106, 112, 120–23; LNG as "transition fuel," 82; oil demand during, 5, 74; slavery and, 13; unjust, 130. *See also* decarbonization; degrowth; just transitions
transportation, 42, 82–83; multi-gas carriers, 83, 134, 136

trasformismo, 16, 123–24
Triana, Alabama, 12, 59
Trump, Donald, 39, 71, 76, 112
Tsing, Anna Lowenhaupt, 16–17
Tuck, Eve, 14, 57–58
Tulane Environmental Law Clinic, 78
Turkey, 85
"turnip" saying (Nanjing), 87–88

Uhruh, Gregory, 146
Ukraine, Russian invasion of, 28–29, 39, 40, 75, 149
uncertainty campaigns, 57, 103
Union Carbide, 34
unions, 63, 65, 129; *See also* Unite (union)
Unist'ot'en Camp, 77
Unite (union), 68, 132–33, 138
United Arab Emirates (UAE), 64–66
United Church of Christ study (1987), 59
United Nations: Cancer Alley report, 81; Race to Zero Campaign, 1, 112
United Nations Climate Change Conferences: COP21 (Paris, 2016), 111; COP24 (Katowice), 129; COP26 (Glasgow), 26, 96, 100, 111, 112–13, 122; COP27 (Sharm el-Sheikh), 100
United Nations Declaration on the Rights of Indigenous Peoples, 76
United Nations Environment Assembly (Nairobi, 2022), 75, 149
United Nations Environment Program, 115
United States: Black communities, disproportionate pollution of, 11–12; Break Free from Plastic Pollution Act introduced in, 92; deindustrialization, 67; LNG trade deal with China, 82–83; oil industry in Equatorial Guinea, 18; shale gas revolution, 40, 45; stagnation of petrochemical industry in 2000s, 40; Superfund Act of 1980, 12, 34, 59, 105; Toxics Release Inventory Program, 34, 49, 59
"unrelated diversification," 41
US Army Corps of Engineers, 78, 80–82
US Department of Health and Human Services, 144
US Military Tribunal (Nuremberg), 31

217

INDEX

value chains, petrochemical, 7, 9, 37–38; connecting struggles along, 89–93. *See also* supply chains, global

value extraction, versus value creation, 125, 126

Venture Global, 82

Verbeek, Thomas, 35

vertical integration, 9, 35, 37, 39, 41, 111, 123, 161n68

vinyl chloride, 33–34, 49, 63, 104

violence: China, 66, 86; in Gulf countries, 65; increase in, 69; petrochemical industry linked with, 8, 28, 62; by police, 65, 81, 86; state-sanctioned racial, 15–16, 144

volatility, uncertainty, complexity, and ambiguity (VUCA), 29, 39, 51, 106, 116

Vollmann, William T., 65

Von Hernandez, 91

Voulvouli, Aimilia, 85

Walker, Jeremy, 22

Wang, Xinhong, 66

war: environmental activism in terms of, 73, 93, 100; as "form of life," 28; against Indigenous peoples, 93; innovation and, 42; profitability of, 28–29, 75; sociology of, 44–45

war gaming, 45–46

Warren County, North Carolina, 12, 59

wars of position, 3, 16, 28, 44; legacies of collusion, 48–51. *See also* strategy

waste: Black communities, dumping in, 11–12; incineration of in Southeast Asia, 14, 72, 90–91; marine plastics crisis (2018), 39, 43, 51, 72, 74, 89; most waste labeled as "hazardous," 90; municipal waste management, 109; national incineration ban (Philippines), 91; nuclear, 5, 6; offloaded by supply chains, 9–10, 14–15; plastic packaging, in South Asia, 89–90

waste colonialism, 14, 90

waste-to-energy, 91

water protectors, 78–79

Werlhof, Claudia von, 48

Westervelt, Rob, 106

White, Damian, 139–40, 148–49

Whyte, Kyle Powys, 97–98, 117, 150

working class, and deindustrialization, xi, 126

working-class environmentalism, 55, 63–64

World Business Council for Sustainable Development (WBCSD), 112

World Petrochemical Conferences, 106, 107, 109; "Navigating Towards Net Zero" (March 2022), 122

worldviews: dominant patriarchal capitalist, 48; of fenceline communities, 23; military-strategic, 23, 141; of petrochemical industry, 7–11, 18, 47

World War I, 8, 28; as "Chemists' War," 28d

World War II, 8, 28, 106; postwar growth of petrochemical industry, 30–32

Wu, Fengshi, 85

Wu, Qiyan, 147

Xi Jinping, xiv, 85, 86

Yates, Eric, 33

YCI Methanol One greenfield investment project, 83

Yergin, Daniel, 74

Yusoff, Kathryn, 13

Zhao Yufen, 85

zoonotic spillover, 96, 143–44

Zyklon B, 31